"A beautiful book and an important one as well. Mi[...] enced Jesuit retreat director and a talented writer, [...] way of praying with St. Ignatius Loyola's Spiritual Exercises. But this is much more than a guide for a fulfilling personal retreat; it is also a compendium of inspiring meditations, useful insights, and practical advice for anyone who seeks a closer relationship with God. In these pages is a wealth of knowledge that I will surely be using in the future—both in counseling others and in my own prayer life."

James Martin, S.J.
Author of *The Jesuit Guide to (Almost) Everything*

"*The First Spiritual Exercises*, written and piloted by Fr. Michael Hansen, S.J., is an important breakthrough in our understanding of the Spiritual Exercises and for potentially extending an experience of the Spiritual Exercises of St. Ignatius to many, many more people of all ages than other more familiar forms of the Exercises. The author's impeccable research briefly opens a window onto Ignatius's earliest practices in giving this first version of the Exercises and invites the reader to experience one or more of these four-week experiences for oneself. His prose is both attractive and enlightening. Each one of the retreats highlights essential aspects of the Ignatian vision of a God who desires to grace each retreatant with a relationship of mutuality and friendship in the service of others and the Gospel. Great care is displayed in the inclusion of texts for and about women as well as grounding every retreat in key Gospel texts that introduce the person making these Exercises to a deeply Gospel spirituality as well as Ignatian approaches to prayer and transformation into discipleship."

Janet K. Ruffing, R.S.M.
Professor in the Practice of Spirituality and Ministerial Leadership
Yale Divinity School

"Michael Hansen, S.J., helps readers meet the living God who wants a personal relationship with them. From years of experience he knows the Spiritual Exercises of St. Ignatius of Loyola very well and leads the reader in a creative and easy-to-follow way through them without jargon and with a deft hand. I am very happy to recommend this book and I sense that St. Ignatius rejoices that his great work has been made so accessible to modern readers."

William A. Barry, S.J.
Author of *A Friendship Like No Other*

"If you are looking for a clear, simple, and practical approach to developing your prayer life in the Ignatian tradition, *The First Spiritual Exercises* is well worth procuring. One of Ignatius's most radical and contentious insights was that the Creator engages directly with the heart of the creature. What I particularly like about the exercises in *The First Spiritual Exercises* is that they invite, stimulate, and give us freedom, if we dare, to dispose ourselves to experience such an encounter."

Brendan Kelly, S.J.
Master of Jesuit Novices, Australia

"These are challenging times for Christians trying to sustain a lively faith. Growing disillusionment with institutional religion and turbulent controversies within mainline denominations pose serious hurdles in our walk of faith. These present conditions parallel to the historical situation in which Ignatius of Loyola introduced his Spiritual Exercises as a practical way of grounding faith in concrete personal experience of God's love, forgiveness, call, and faithfulness in one's life. Jesuit Michael Hansen's *The First Spiritual Exercises* captures in a helpful way Ignatius's process of spiritual renewal and makes it an accessible and useful tool for deepening an intimate connection with God today. I highly recommend it."

Wilkie Au
Author and Professor of Theological Studies
Loyola Marymount University

"Michael Hansen has graced us with a fresh look at Saint Ignatius's *Spiritual Exercises*. Rooted deep in both Ignatius's understanding of the spiritual life and also the realities of Christian discipleship in the contemporary world, Hansen offers us a thorough immersion in the Ignatian school of divine love. I highly recommend Hansen's text for use among religious and lay people, in retreat centers, in schools, in parishes, and in conversations among friends. He extends to us Ignatius's conviction that God deals directly with his beloved creatures and invites us to deepen our response to God's generous love."

Tim Muldoon
Author of *The Ignatian Workout*

"This work is astoundingly clear, faithful to the *Spiritual Exercises*, and beautiful as well."

Marlene Marburg
Campion Centre of Ignatian Spirituality
Melbourne, Australia

"This is one of the great books on Ignatian Spirituality. It takes people from where Ignatius first found them, in their prayers and devotions, and quickly moves them into formal prayer. I have been using it for four years, and those to whom I have given it marvel at its power to move them into an intimate relationship with God. Michael Hansen is a born teacher, who enables people through the use of imagination to experience and reflect on their experience of God's love and discover its dynamic in their own selves."

Des Purcell, S.J.
Canisius Centre of Ignatian Spirituality
Sydney, Australia

the FIRST

Spiritual

EXERCISES

Four

Guided Retreats

As Originally Conceived by St. Ignatius Loyola

Adapted by Michael Hansen, S.J.

ave maria press AmP notre dame, indiana

© 2013 by Michael Hansen

All rights reserved. No part of this book may be used or reproduced in any manner whatsoever, except in the case of reprints in the context of reviews, without written permission from Ave Maria Press®, Inc., P.O. Box 428, Notre Dame, IN 46556, 1-800-282-1865.

Founded in 1865, Ave Maria Press is a ministry of the United States Province of Holy Cross.

www.avemariapress.com

Paperback ISBN-10 1-59471-378-2, ISBN-13 978-1-59471-378-1

E-book ISBN-10 1-59471-379-0, ISBN-13 978-1-59471-379-8

Cover image © CORBIS

Cover and text design by David Scholtes.

Printed and bound in the United States of America.

Library of Congress Cataloging-in-Publication Data

Hansen, Michael (Michael Francis), 1951-

  The first spiritual exercises : four guided retreats / Michael Hansen.

       p. cm.

  Includes bibliographical references and index.

  ISBN 978-1-59471-380-4 (pbk. : alk. paper) -- ISBN 1-59471-380-4 (pbk. : alk. paper)

  1. Ignatius, of Loyola, Saint, 1491-1556. Exercitia spiritualia. 2. Spiritual retreats--Catholic Church. 3. Spiritual exercises. 4. Spiritual life--Catholic Church. I. Title.

  BX2179.L8H275 2013

  269'.6--dc23

                          2012039851

If you walk
in the way of God,
you will live
in peace forever.
Learn where there is wisdom,
where there is strength,
where there is understanding,
so that you may at the same time discern
where there is length of days, and life,
where there is light for the eyes,
and peace.
—Baruch 3:3–14

CONTENTS

INTRODUCTION

In this very moment, as I hold this book, the Trinity holds me, loved and safe. As the prophet Isaiah affirms, I am precious and honored. I am loved unconditionally as I am, yet known fully as the person I can be. Today, and everyday, I am being invited to listen to my sacred desires, to grow in my spiritual life, for the Trinity has so much more to give to me.

St. Ignatius Loyola, himself a man of great desires, published *The Spiritual Exercises* in 1548. It held instructions to give his Exercises in two ways: the Full Spiritual Exercises and the First Spiritual Exercises. The Full Spiritual Exercises are made for thirty days enclosed in a spirituality center or for thirty weeks during daily life. The First Spiritual Exercises are made over four weeks in daily life.

In form, the First Spiritual Exercises are offered to me as one of four retreats. Each retreat is created for the gift of inner peace and a particular desire—these being my desire to experience divine love; to live in the light of mercy, healing, or freedom; to grow in friendship with Jesus; and to be of service to others.

The retreats are presented in the first half of the book, along with some introductory and concluding articles given under the titles of Spiritual Desire and Spiritual Progress. The second half of the book provides "guides and helps" for my retreat and afterwards. The "Spiritual Conversation" guides show me how to move into spiritual conversation after a spiritual exercise or number of exercises.

Each retreat and spiritual exercise is rooted in two fundamental texts—the Christian scriptures and the Ignatian *Spiritual Exercises*. With very few exceptions, to keep this manual focused and clear, the only references in this book will be to those two texts.

Finally, this book does not provide a commentary on the Spiritual Exercises, an exposition of the biblical texts, or even reflections on Ignatian spirituality. The aim of the book is simple and practical—to guide me in my retreat and give me the helps I need to make it well.

THE FIRST
Spiritual
EXERCISES

Spiritual Desire

MY DESIRE FOR INNER PEACE

The LORD bless you and keep you; the LORD make his face to shine upon you, and be gracious to you; the LORD lift up his countenance upon you, and give you peace. (Nm 6:24–26)

Have I ever felt a deep yearning for an inner peace that sets me searching for it? Have I looked for it in a vacation or quietness or financial security, yet sensed the peace I am after is a lot deeper than these? Have I been seeking meaning in the big picture, one that not only makes sense of the universe and humanity but also gives me the energy and inner peace to live graciously within it? When such movements tug at my soul, it is likely I am looking for the inner peace given to those who walk in the way of God.

This inner peace sings in harmony with who I am before my Creator; it delights in what makes me unique. It is a song of profound tranquility flowing beneath my daily life, which is good, for life itself can bring me to times of great need. At such times I may feel the radical need for love, the ache for forgiveness, the attraction of greater service, the want of healing, the desire for freedom, or the longing for divine friendship. Once I truly desire any one of these needs, the lack of it will gradually carve a hole, an emptiness, in my soul. Life is more agitated, driven, or fragmented. I feel an inner disquiet. Yet, these needs can also set my feet on the path to a generous God and a certain, wonderful peace of soul.

The First Spiritual Exercises of St. Ignatius Loyola were created to help a person ask for and receive this inner peace. In them, six great gifts from God are sought in four retreats.

The first great gift is the gift of unconditional love. The inner peace that comes with this is utterly unmistakable for any other experience. I feel the love of God as so overwhelmingly unconditional, so gently intimate, that I am left with a deep-seated peace—a serenity that will survive all sorts of trials, selfishness, and loss. I become aware of the many extraordinary gifts that the Creator has given me through love, and I have the inner peace that tells me I need not turn anywhere else for what I need. Profound gratitude comes with this peace.

The second great gift is the gift of service. The interior peace of service abides in the heart of Christian and social action. I have ceased finding happiness in serving me and mine and feel drawn to serve a greater good. I sense a boundless generosity dwelling in me but realize how little I use it. When I do use it, I feel the inner peace that reveals that service of others is deeply right to who I am—one made in the image of a giving God and called to be a disciple of Jesus. Great energy comes with this peace.

The third great gift is the gift of forgiveness. The inner peace received with forgiveness comes when I realize how totally powerless I am to be free of the disorder and sin in my life. Yet, I find God has not abandoned me. Indeed, I am entangled by this disorder and living in a darkness until my God forgives and embraces me as I am. And God gives me more—unexpected feasts in lean times, consolations, and even the company of his only Son. Pure wonder comes with this peace.

The fourth great gift is the gift of healing. The inner peace of healing is given in times of long illness or suffering. Mysteriously, I may or may not be physically healed, but I feel a serenity and strength regardless. Akin to a night-light, this very personal peace shines within the darkness of illness or suffering. In this light Jesus reveals his own vulnerability, my dignity is not extinguished, anxieties fade, and personal wholeness takes new shapes. Divine intimacy comes with this peace.

The fifth great gift is the gift of freedom. The inner peace of freedom is like a spring of living water bubbling up in the center of my life. Everything looks fresh and is seen in a new light. Suddenly free, I become truly aware of the prison of my attachments, of the disorder in my life. Or, slowly free, I feel myself awaken and inner peace grow as I shed the things that I no longer need. In this retreat, I connect rightly with creation, Creator, and myself. Deep reverence comes with this peace.

The sixth great gift is friendship with Jesus. It is the inner peace one feels with a best friend. My friend accepts me totally. I feel whole, more complete, and I walk with bounce and life. We are there for each other—my friend shapes my identity and calls me out of myself. All else seems right with the world, even with the whole universe. Though trials may come or hard service be chosen, Jesus as a friend for life gives me a certain serenity. Quiet joy comes with this peace.

These six gifts were given to St. Ignatius, though initially his faith journey was rough going. He became lost in dead ends, snared in exhausting and pointless activities, felt the enticements of both the good and bad spirit, and was tugged in opposite directions by each. His life plans were changed again and again by circumstances. But God delighted in him, patiently teaching him, giving him many graces, and gently calling him forward. Over time the holy desires of Ignatius grew within God's desires for him. His service to God matured and his choices ripened until he felt the full measure of God's inner peace in his life. This makes him an experienced guide, one who knows the terrain, and he has given us a map—his book of retreats, *The Spiritual Exercises*.

THE GOD OF INNER PEACE

> For the mountains may depart and the hills be removed, but my steadfast love shall not depart from you, and my covenant of peace shall not be removed, says the LORD, who has compassion on you. (Is 54:10)

If I desire the gift of inner peace and bring my desire to prayer, I can be sure of one thing—I am going to meet the giver of peace. So who is this God of Peace?

Wisdom, in the Bible, is often seen as a person. Ben Sira remembers how his heart was stirred and how much he desired wisdom. He says he grappled with wisdom and directed his soul to her. In this energetic relationship, wisdom is freely given to him and with her the gift of much serenity. In his advice, he implores me to surrender to the wisdom of God, for inner peace cannot be bought by money or work. I can only open myself, heart and soul, to the God of Peace:

> My soul grappled with wisdom, and in my conduct I was strict; I spread out my hands to the heavens, and lamented my ignorance of her. I directed my soul to her, and in purity I found her. With her I gained understanding from the first; therefore I will never be forsaken. My heart was stirred to seek her; therefore I have gained a prize possession. I opened my mouth and said, "Acquire wisdom for yourselves without money. Put your neck under her yoke, and let your souls receive instruction; it is to be found close by. See with your own eyes that I have labored but little and found for myself much serenity." (Sir 51:19–21, 25–27)

Jesus promised to send me the Spirit. Within the same promise, he wants to give me his peace. This peace is not the world's peace. It is not given as the world might try through wealth, workshops, or the accumulation of things. It disperses fears and troubles because it is the presence and promise of Jesus to be with me. Inner peace never stands alone; it is always experienced in divine relationship.

> I have said these things to you while I am still with you. But the Advocate, the Holy Spirit, whom the Father will send in my name, will teach you everything, and remind you of all that I have said to you. Peace I leave with you; my peace I give to you. I do not give to you as the world gives. Do not let your hearts be troubled, and do not let them be afraid. (Jn 14:25–27)

St. Paul also encourages me not to be afraid. He writes that in gentleness and joy I can rely on God because our God is the God of Peace. This peace is so special that it surpasses all human understanding—it is full of the mystery of divine love. It is richer than ordinary peace because it is not a lack of noise or a mood, but it is a relational grace, guarding my heart and near to my heart.

> Rejoice in the Lord always; again I will say, Rejoice. Let your gentleness be known to everyone. The Lord is near. Do not worry about anything, but in everything by prayer and supplication with thanksgiving let your requests be made known to God. And the peace of God, which surpasses all understanding, will guard your hearts and your minds in Christ Jesus. (Phil 4:4–7)

In steadfast love, the Lord makes a covenant of peace with me. The gospels reveal the fullness of this compassion—God becomes human in Jesus and reconciles all creation to himself by making peace through the Cross. This is union of love and peace at their most potent.

> In him all the fullness of God was pleased to dwell, and through him God was pleased to reconcile to himself all things, whether on earth or in heaven, by making peace through the blood of his cross. (Col 1:19–20)

In many ways I experience God's peace through the Son of God himself. When Jesus responds directly to my need, he gives me inner peace as a second gift, a deep resonance of my new life.

Thus he heals the woman with the chronic hemorrhage, saying, "Daughter, your faith has made you well; go in peace, and be healed of your disease" (Mk 5:34). He forgives the woman who was a sinner, saying, "Your faith has saved you; go in peace" (Lk 7:50). He explains his Father's deepest desire: "By the tender mercy of our God, the dawn from on high will break upon us, to give light to those who sit in darkness and in the shadow of death, to guide our feet into the way of peace" (Lk 1:78–79).

And in the presence of fear, when the disciples felt their boat was sinking, he says to the wind and sea, "Peace! Be still!" (Mk 4:39), just as he would for anyone facing the terrors of life. Later, weeping over the city of Jerusalem, before his passion, he says, "If you, even you, had only recognized on this day the things that make for peace!" (Lk 19:42).

Stirred heart, untroubled heart, guarded heart, heart going in peace—whichever I am, from the above I can appreciate the intimacy of God's inner peace. Where desire is born there it is answered—in the heart at peace in its lover and Creator.

THE HEART OF INNER PEACE

After considering the God of Peace in relationships, I may now profitably explore the subtle movements of inner peace in my heart. This is where my heartbeat measures the wing beat of the Spirit—that is, in the world of spiritual consolation and desolation.

Ignatius explains spiritual consolation:

> I use the word "consolation" when any interior movement is produced in the soul which leads her to become inflamed with the love of her Creator and Lord, and when as a consequence, there is no creature on the face of the earth that the person can love in itself, but they love it in the Creator and Lord of all things. . . . I give the name "consolation" to every increase of hope, faith and charity, to all interior happiness which calls and attracts to heavenly things and to the salvation of one's soul, leaving the soul quiet and at peace in her Creator and Lord. (*Spiritual Exercises* 316)

When Ignatius describes the First Spiritual Exercises, he notes the desires people might have in making them. Putting aside adult faith formation and reconciliation, the only desire named by him is the desire for "a certain level of peace of soul" (*Spiritual Exercises* 18). This appears to be very minimal, until the connection is made between the "certain peace of soul" and the consolation that leaves "the soul quiet and at peace in her Creator." Inner peace is really a gift of spiritual consolation, not a little peace of mind that I know some catechetical truths and receive the Catholic sacraments. Once this is known, a great deal is revealed about the aim and purpose of the First Spiritual Exercises.

Ignatius states it is characteristic of the good spirit "to give courage and strength, consolations, tears, inspirations, and quiet, making things easy and removing all obstacles so that the person may move forward in doing good" (*Spiritual Exercises* 315). Here quiet, or inner peace, is linked to clarity of understanding and freedom. If I am feeling confused, blocked, lost, overburdened, or empty, I will naturally seek greater direction in my life. The First Spiritual Exercises provide the structure, resources, and relationships to help me find this direction and move forward in doing good. They help to remove obstacles, stimulate insights, and strengthen me with inner peace.

Another way to understand inner peace as consolation is to consider its contrary. This Ignatius does, speaking from his own hard-won experience.

> "Desolation" is the name I give to everything contrary to what is described in Rule Three [On Spiritual Consolation]; for example, darkness and disturbance in the soul, attraction to what is low and of the earth, disquiet arising from various agitations and temptations. All this leads to a lack of confidence in which one feels oneself to be without hope and without love. One finds oneself thoroughly lazy, lukewarm, sad, and as though cut off from one's Creator and Lord. (*Spiritual Exercises* 317)

It is important to recognize the movements of disturbance, darkness, and disquiet in my spiritual life. I need to know what is happening in my soul if I am to take the contrary path away from the desolating spirit. The First Spiritual Exercises will help me to recognize these movements.

Ignatius is incisive about the soul being led by the bad spirit—it will be "weakened, upset or distressed, losing the peace, tranquility and quiet previously experienced" (*Spiritual Exercises* 333). By its contrary, he reveals the true face of inner peace: it encompasses peace, tranquility, and quiet—a pattern of rightness between my soul and its Creator. Is there a larger pattern to spiritual consolations and desolations? St. Ignatius and St. Paul, among many others, tell me there is.

In his Guide to the Discernment of Spirits, Ignatius describes two spirits, the good spirit and the bad spirit. He depicts two spiritual movements in me—one from good to better and one from bad to worse.[1] Paul speaks of two laws: the law of sin and death versus the law of the Spirit of life in Christ. He pictures two minds, but like Ignatius sees that only one brings life and peace.

> The law of the Spirit of life in Christ Jesus has set you free from the law of sin and of death. . . . Those who live according to the Spirit set their minds on the things of the Spirit. To set the mind on the flesh is death, but to set the mind on the Spirit is life and peace. (Rom 8:2, 5–6)

The place and importance of peace as an interior movement is manifest. Inner peace is a characteristic of the good spirit; indeed it is a fruit of the Holy Spirit. As such, it will be one of my greatest guides. Accordingly, the First Spiritual Exercises offers practical exercises to set my mind on the Spirit, to receive the gifts and fruits of the Spirit, and with them peace.

> The fruit of the Spirit is love, joy, peace, patience, kindness, generosity, faithfulness, gentleness, and self-control. If we live by the Spirit, let us also be guided by the Spirit. (Gal 5:22–23, 25)

For Ignatius, peace is the first of all gifts, for it not only brings all other graces but also draws me into love of God and neighbor. Ignatius saw love of God and neighbor, taught by Jesus, as the summary of all good action for eternal life (see Mt 22:36–40).

Indeed, he wrote the First Spiritual Exercises precisely to help me become a lover of God and neighbor, to open me to the gifts and graces of my Creator. He makes this surprising connection in a letter of spiritual advice.

> The peace of our Lord is something interior, and it brings with it all the other gifts and graces necessary for salvation and eternal life. This peace makes us love our neighbor for the love of our Creator and Lord.[2]

In conclusion, each gift of love, service, forgiveness, healing, freedom, and divine friendship is a path to inner peace. Walking this path, with Ignatius as a guide, I will receive the gift I desire and encounter the God of Peace. This God is the God of all consolations (see 2 Cor 1:3). Thus the ultimate end of the First Spiritual Exercises is spiritual consolation: the gifts of faith, courage, hope, strength, purpose in life, deeper love of God and neighbor, greater freedom from attachments, and a certain peace of soul in the Lord.

INTRODUCING
THE FIRST SPIRITUAL EXERCISES

WHAT IS AN IGNATIAN SPIRITUAL EXERCISE?

In the words of St. Ignatius, a spiritual exercise is "every way of examining one's conscience, meditating, contemplating, praying vocally, praying mentally and other spiritual activities" (*Spiritual Exercises* 1). The "other spiritual activities" include exercises for love, freedom, and decision making. Ignatian Spiritual Exercises employ many forms of prayer to engage me through different ways of knowing and feeling. Some call upon my imagination and memory, others on my wise and keen intellect, others still on my heartfelt understanding. Most will awaken in me deep feelings, such as love, sorrow, joy, generosity, and inner peace. They all value my life experience, gently opening it, just as they open the life of Jesus. They knit both stories together where they belong, in the one weave of the living kingdom of God.

In practice, each spiritual exercise is a holy desire, a sacred seed. The Spirit, working through the exercise, ploughs and turns the earth of my life to make me ready for God. I plant the seed, the Lord grows it in secret, and the Creator brings forth a hundredfold harvest (see Mt 13:24–30, 36–43).

This means a spiritual exercise is a structured way to bring me into relationship with God. Making the Sign of the Cross, bathing a child, using a personal gift for good, helping a vulnerable person, praying the Our Father, or serving in a soup kitchen can all be spiritual exercises; indeed, any exercise of faith, hope, or love that moves me toward God and service of neighbor is a spiritual exercise. Certainly I have been doing, and doing well, a great number of spiritual exercises all of my life.

Ignatian Spiritual Exercises are real "exercises" in the sense that they require work, repetition, trust, patience, and a strong desire to see them through to the end. Although each exercise is different, the underlying purpose of all of them is freedom and openness—freedom from disorder, openness to God's grace. Thus Ignatius describes a spiritual exercise as every way of preparing and making ourselves ready to get rid of all disordered affections so that, once rid of them, one might seek and find the divine will in regard to the disposition of one's life for the salvation of the soul. (*Spiritual Exercises* 1, 21, 63)

Some understanding of ordered and disordered affections will help me to better understand this important description. Disordered affections are fears and desires that entangle or imprison me. Like slavers, they take me captive, bind me, and march me away from life. Disturbing and unsettling, they are deep habitual desires that remove me from God and my humanity.[3] They spawn their own children and make me a "disaffected" person. The end result of all this is a disordered love that can grow through me like a weed in a wheat field (see Lk 8:1–8).

Ordered affections move me in the opposite direction. They are expressions of my true self. They tug me toward wholeness, integrity, and service.[4] It is for this that I was created. Naturally seeking communion, they orientate me toward others. They give me the perspective to see the good in my life—the gifts, the promise, the wheat ready for harvesting.

When I move forward in harmony with my holy desires, I experience peace and energy in my life.[5] In this movement the Spirit has greater room to breathe in me. I discover largeness, depth, and beauty in myself. My life becomes fully alive because I am making decisions about it with greater freedom. I worry less about the things that do not matter. As Jesus keeps telling me, it is the Father's good pleasure to give me his kingdom, to give me everything I need for life (see Lk 12:22–32). This living, generous energy is the heart and soul of an Ignatian spiritual exercise.

WHAT ARE THE SPIRITUAL EXERCISES?

The Spiritual Exercises are a set of structured spiritual exercises woven with a particular dynamic into a retreat by St. Ignatius. They are not a loose collection of prayers. Rather, they are integrated exercises that work powerfully together—each day builds on the next, and each week is crafted as a thematic whole. Similarly, each week builds on the previous so that the whole four-week retreat is a single, progressive, and powerful experience of grace.

The Spiritual Exercises began life as the prayer journal of St. Ignatius. In the beginning this journal charted his reflections, graces, questions, feelings, favorite scripture texts, and prayer notes. Later it took shape as an instruction manual when he discovered that others, with similar desires, could receive similar graces when he led them through similar exercises.

The giving of these exercises by Ignatius to others started with spiritual conversations and simple exercises at Loyola and Manresa in Spain. They continued in Barcelona, Alcalá, and Salamanca. With help from the Spirit, Ignatius began to sense the embrace of God's love and the pattern of the Lord's life in each person he was guiding. He structured these patterns into a retreat of some weeks. To this retreat were added useful teachings on the Christian faith and spiritual life. This took place from 1522 to 1527.

When he clarified the art of discernment and decision making, he added both of these to the book he now named *The Spiritual Exercises*. The Exercises were further shaped when he gave them, for over thirty days in seclusion, to his first companions in Paris and Venice. With significant revisions, they were finally completed in Rome between 1539 and 1541.

After making the Spiritual Exercises retreat, the first companions of Ignatius were profoundly affected and changed by them, both in their lives and in their spirituality. The Exercises ignited and confirmed their vocations. They wanted to share this channel of God's grace with others. So giving the Spiritual Exercises became a core ministry of their fledgling religious order—the Society of Jesus. To give them better they felt the need for an instruction manual. Ignatius published this at Rome in 1548. This manual for giving the Exercises is the text of the Spiritual Exercises in use today.

Yet, the Spiritual Exercises are more than a book text. They are an active relationship between myself, the Spirit, and the text, and, if possible, the one giving the Exercises to me. They are what I make or receive or enter into with God. I cannot do them by reading them. I can only do them by doing them. Because they are made in active relationship with God, their effects last for my life. They are about grace habitually rippling through the ecology of my desires, relationships, and actions.

WHAT ARE THE FIRST SPIRITUAL EXERCISES?

In the book of the Spiritual Exercises three forms of the Exercises are described in the twentieth, nineteenth, and eighteenth annotations or introductory notes. These are, respectively, the Full Spiritual Exercises given for thirty days in seclusion, the Full Spiritual Exercises given for thirty weeks in daily life, and the First Spiritual Exercises given for four weeks in daily life.

What makes the latter, the Eighteenth Annotation Exercises, the "First" Spiritual Exercises? To begin with, they are first in the spiritual journey. They are the first spiritual exercises learned by the pilgrim Ignatius seeking God's will. They are the first spiritual exercises he gave to others. They are the first exercises I might give to anyone who desires to make progress in their spiritual life today.

Second, they are first in content. They contain many "first" exercises: the first principle of Christian freedom, first Christian prayers, first virtues, first morning thoughts, first creation, first sin, first methods of prayer, first fruits of the Spirit, first steps of discernment, and so on.

Third, they are first in the order and dynamic of the Exercises. One of the First Spiritual Exercises retreats includes all of the first week of the Full Spiritual Exercises. These and other first exercises must be made first before all the rest.

Fourth, they are first in use. They are the first form of the Spiritual Exercises retreat ever given. Unlike the Full Exercises, they can be given immediately to everyone. They are a complete form of the Spiritual Exercises in their own right. And in Ignatian spirituality, they are not only an excellent place to begin, they are the only place to begin!

The Full Spiritual Exercises, enclosed or in daily life, are made as one retreat. The First Spiritual Exercises are more flexible; they are made as one of four retreats, selected according to one's need. Each retreat responds to the fundamental desire for inner peace and a particular desire for love, service, forgiveness, healing, freedom, or divine friendship. The four retreats are:

1. Inner Peace in Divine Love.
2. Inner Peace in Darkness and Light.
3. Inner Peace in Friendship with Jesus.
4. Inner Peace in the Service of God.

Each retreat guides me in daily prayer through four weeks, Monday to Thursday, and includes Sunday Eucharist and a weekend exercise. I will also learn up to six methods of prayer, be taught up to four Examen prayers, and be introduced to the basic discernment of spirits. At the end, I will be invited to create a program for life for myself. All this happens in the flow of the retreat.

While the above elements are common to all four retreats, the desires, content, and dynamic of each retreat is different. The first retreat is built around a spiritual exercise in the Exercises called the "Contemplation for Attaining Divine Love."[6] To begin a spiritual journey, it is good for me to feel unconditionally loved by God. At its heart, this retreat brings me into a lover's relationship with God, where each desires to give and receive from the other. Beginning with my own experience of love, I contemplate all the gifts I have received from God. This leads into movements of love, gratitude, and service.

The second retreat is for those living in some form of darkness—a serious disorder in life, a long period of suffering, sinfulness, chronic illness, or a driven lack of freedom. God comes to me in that darkness and gives me life there or leads me into the light. This retreat also awakens me to the God who lives in the light of my life, found in love, reconciliation, healing, and freedom. In content, this retreat begins with love, covers the first week of the Full Spiritual Exercises on mercy, gives parallel exercises for healing, and ends with the freedom exercise from the Exercises known as the "First Principle and Foundation."[7]

The third retreat deepens my friendship with Jesus. Since Ignatius builds the life, death, and resurrection of Jesus into the Full Spiritual Exercises, he does not do so in the First Spiritual Exercises. Yet, he lived in deep friendship with Jesus, as his companion, disciple, and mystic. He often directs that prayer should end formally in conversation with Jesus as "if with a friend." Indeed, he and his early companions named themselves "Friends in the Lord." For these reasons, a modern reading of the First Spiritual Exercises may happily include a retreat to nurture friendship with Jesus.

The fourth retreat is for peace in the service of God.[8] It offers exercises to find meaning and relish in my relationship with God, my faith, the Christian community, and social service. It begins with profoundly beautiful ways of praying using breath and body. Deeper into the retreat, I pray the Beatitudes, the gifts of the Spirit, and the works of mercy, and I conclude by creating a program for active and faithful life.

The First Spiritual Exercises were intended from the beginning to serve three needs: to give me the retreat I desire now, to provide me with spiritual exercises I can use for the rest of my life, and to teach me these exercises so that I may teach others. This is very different from the Full Spiritual Exercises, which are usually made once in a lifetime for one purpose. Indeed, I may make the First Spiritual Exercises as many times as I wish.

How did Ignatius himself give the First Spiritual Exercises? Between 1526 and 1527, he gave them in Alcalá and Salamanca. Trying to live the actual life of an apostle, Ignatius made a strange sight in these sophisticated university cities, begging in bare feet and dressed in sackcloth. With four companions, he taught anyone who would listen about the love and service of God (cf. Lk 10:1–16).

He gave the First Spiritual Exercises to a noble woman and her daughter, to the baker and baker's wife, to a hospital orderly, and to university professors and students among others. Young or old, educated or illiterate, male or female, poor or rich—Ignatius saw the First Spiritual Exercises as being useful for everyone. But his dress and long spiritual conversations with people soon caught the attention of the Spanish Inquisition. He was arrested, jailed, and brought before them.

I can get an idea of how Ignatius was giving the First Spiritual Exercises to these people because the Inquisition transcripts of their interviews still exist. To them he was known as Iñigo or Yñigo. Remarkably, I can still hear their voices:

> She said that what she knew of Yñigo was that she had seen him many times come to the house of Mencia de Benavente, who is aunt of this witness; and they spoke in secret many times, and this witness asked her aunt and her aunt's daughter what he talked to them and other women about; and they told him the afflictions they had and he consoled them.
>
> She told Yñigo that she would like to speak with him, and so she did speak with him and asked him to explain the service of God. And Yñigo told her that he would have to talk with her over the period of a month; and during that month she was to confess weekly and receive Communion; and that at first she would be very happy and would not know where the joy came from, and the next week she would be very sad, but that he hoped in God that she would profit a great deal from it; and that if she felt happy during the month, she should not go back over the past. And he said he would explain the three powers, and he did so, and the merit that was gained in temptation, and how venial sin became mortal, and the Ten Commandments and circumstances, and mortal sins and the

five senses and the circumstances of all this. . . . And he told her
how she should love God.

Maria de la Flor, May 10, 1527[9]

And with all these Yñigo has conversed, teaching them the commandments and mortal sins, and the five senses, and the powers of
the soul; and he declares this very well, and declares it all through
the gospel, and through Saint Paul, and other saints; and tells them
that each day they should examine their conscience twice a day,
bringing to memory what sins they have committed . . . and he advises them to go to confession every eight days, and to receive the
sacrament at this same time.

Mencia de Benavente, March 6, 1527[10]

It was a source of wonder to the early Jesuits, on visiting Alcalá and
Salamanca many years later, to find that many of these people who
made the First Spiritual Exercises were still serving others when Ignatius
was an old man. They remembered him very well because through the
First Spiritual Exercises they had been personally touched by God. They
found their life story treasured and had been given a practical, realistic
way to live and serve with God. All this struck deep roots in the lives of
these first Ignatian exercisers.

In later centuries, the First Spiritual Exercises were cherished as a
great gift for bringing a person into relationship with God for love and
service. This was the form of the Exercises most given to others. The Ignatian Congregations, international meetings called for matters of great
moment, "vigorously support . . . to the greatest extent possible" the
First Spiritual Exercises being given to men and women, ecclesiastics,
workers, and the poor. In more recent times the Spiritual Exercises have
been promoted as a source of inspiration, so that "our deep love of God
and our passion for his world should set us on fire—a fire that starts
other fires."[11]

How did Ignatius himself feel about the Spiritual Exercises? Nine
years after being examined and freed from jail at Alcalá, he writes to a
friend:

Still, let me repeat once and twice and as many more times as I am
able: I implore you, out of a desire to serve God Our Lord, to do
what I have said to you up to now. May His Divine Majesty never

ask me one day why I did not ask you as strongly as I possibly could!

The Spiritual Exercises are all the best that I have been able to think out, experience and understand in this life, both for helping somebody to make the most of themselves, as also for being able to bring advantage, help, and profit to many others. So, even if you don't feel the need for the first, you will see that they are much more helpful than you might have imagined for the second.

Ignatius to Rev. M. Miona, 16, 1536 [12]

EXPECTATIONS

WHAT THE FIRST SPIRITUAL EXERCISES DESIRE OF ME

The Lord desires to free and enliven me in some manner, to gift me with deep inner peace. So the First Spiritual Exercises desire me to be openhearted and liberal toward God, even if my personal experience of God is just beginning or newly desired.

Ignatius once reflected that "many persons whose lives can hardly be called Christian, have not the faintest idea that they could become great saints if they allowed themselves to be formed by God's grace and not resist His actions."[13] So each spiritual exercise hopes for a little surrender to allow the Creator to work in me (see 2 Cor 4:16–5:1, 5).[14]

Rooted in the Christian spiritual tradition, the First Spiritual Exercises assume a belief in God and openness to the tripersonal God, the Trinity. Such a faith charts a divine love that began with God's desire to create the universe, moved through the Son in his Incarnation, and will return, with all creation, through the Spirit to the Father.

Consequently, the First Exercises expects me to have, or desire to have, a largely gracious image of God, the one who calls me through creation itself into intimate union now and forever.

The Exercises also expect personal faith to be expressed in communion and communal action. While I necessarily exercise alone in my retreat, my gifts are for giving. The Christian community, which is the Body of Christ now in the world, finds its full meaning in giving. My retreat expects the same openness to give and to share.

As I exercise myself in prayer, I will be building up my relationship with God, while remembering that God is also at work in the same exercise. This relationship grows naturally in its own time. I just need to be aware that God is prepared to do this for me. In return, I am expected to be faithful to each exercise and to use the whole of my prayer time each day.[15]

Besides working in the world, the Spirit works for change in the churches and Christian communities. These will always need life-giving structures, better leadership, and greater service. Standing firmly in the promise of the Spirit's life-changing energy, the First Spiritual Exercises desire me to be a part of the church or the Christian community's necessary growth and change. Whatever my form of engagement, the Spiritual Exercises inherently assume that I am part of the future of Christian communities and that they will always need my help.[16]

Ultimately, and perhaps strangely, the First Spiritual Exercises are not about me. Since birth or Baptism, I have been a shard of God's life breaking into the world. The kingdom of God, in the process of changing the world, has always needed committed workers like me. This is the big picture behind my retreat. Each spiritual exercise expects to find this kingdom vision alive in me (see Eph 3:16–19). Even the smallest spiritual exercise wants, in some way, to send me out afire into the world.

WHAT CAN I EXPECT FROM THE FIRST SPIRITUAL EXERCISES?

I can expect a deeper relationship with God—in Jesus a true friend, in the Spirit a wise guide, in the Father a welcome home. In some way I will be touched by the unfathomable mystery of the Divine, come face-to-face with my Creator, and feel the full power of that gentle presence. Generosity underpins everything, for between two lovers, St. Ignatius tells me, each desires to give the other "what they have or are able to give" (*Spiritual Exercises* 231).

So I may expect to find a new clarity in my desires, genuine peace and joy, and a growing freedom to order my life for the service of God.[17] To encourage and direct this growth, I will be given a structured retreat with specific desires. Each spiritual exercise will have a clear framework, given in a certain order, for a particular dynamic and grace. My retreat proceeds step by step, day by day, and week by week.

Unlike retreats that are guided by what each day brings, the First Spiritual Exercises have a very clear program. Each retreat has its own map, and it knows where it is going. In this sense, my retreat is "shaped" prayer, shaped to cradle desire and hold me in the active presence of God.

If I were to embark on a program of physical exercise, I would begin with the given of my body and its present condition. In my desire to be fitter, I would apply the exercise program to my current level of fitness. Or, when I meet someone and desire to form a relationship with them, I begin with the given of who I am and who they are. In each case, with honesty, I can do little else. So too, when I make a retreat, I begin with the given of myself and apply the spiritual exercise to my present desire and readiness.[18]

This means my retreat is radically open to my personal history. I pour into it my own desires and life experience. This is a standout feature of the First Exercises—after learning the structure of an exercise, there is no outside or dogmatic content, but the content is always my ordinary, but precious, lived experience. Indeed the First Exercises hold my personal journey, wherever it has taken me, in the most affirming and reverent way.

And I bring something else to my retreat, rarely noticed: the immeasurable mystery of my unique, eternal personhood. So I can truly expect my First Spiritual Exercises retreat to be something no one has ever seen before.

For greater support, I may organize myself to be individually guided or join a group to make my retreat with them. To have a Giver of the First Spiritual Exercises is very highly recommended. The Ignatian guides to Spiritual Conversation, found in the back of this book, will reveal why.

Finally, I should expect some interior movements in my heart, mind, and soul. These will be best noticed in my feelings and affections, but they could also rise in my insights and convictions. The good spirit will encourage and initiate these movements as I move toward God. The bad spirit will pull me in the opposite direction. In these two movements I will discover the rhythms of spiritual consolation and desolation. These arise naturally in any serious retreat or spiritual growth. But I need not fear, for the Lord will give me every means to make good progress.[19]

DO I HAVE THE QUALIFICATIONS TO MAKE A RETREAT?
There is nothing in the First Spiritual Exercises that I cannot do. I need no special education, holiness, or health. I do not need to be churched. I always apply the spiritual exercise to my present understanding, faith, and well-being.[20] Since all four retreats are a living relationship with God, the only thing I need to begin is the desire to open myself to the Divine. I choose one retreat from the four available and just begin. Where I am now is where God is waiting for me.

WILL I HAVE TO MAKE BIG CHANGES IN MY LIFE?
The goal of a First Spiritual Exercises retreat is to help me take a few generous steps in the right direction, not to immediately change the whole

course of my life. Small, desired, slow, planned, savored, realistic, habitual, confirmed, fruitful steps are at the heart of these Exercises. Only in this way, Ignatius tells me, can my progress be real, well maintained, and built upon.

WHAT IS MY COMMITMENT?

My retreat commitment is four weeks, with twenty-five to forty minutes of prayer four days a week, preferably Monday to Thursday. This is followed by the Sunday Eucharist and its weekend exercise. It adds up to about twenty-two days. While this is a serious commitment, with real sacrifices, it is only made once a year, and the graces received can be quite extraordinary.

THE FOUR RETREATS

INNER PEACE IN DIVINE LOVE

[I]
created you. . . .
[I] formed you. . . .
Do not fear,
for I have redeemed you;
I have called you
by name, you are mine.
When you pass through the waters,
I will be with you;
and through the rivers,
they shall not overwhelm you;
when you walk through fire you shall not be burned,
and the flame shall not consume you.
For I am
the LORD your God,
the Holy One of Israel, your Savior. . . .
Because you are precious in my sight,
and honored, and I love you.
—Isaiah 43:1–4a

The culminating exercise of the Full Spiritual Exercises is the "Contemplation for Attaining Divine Love." It begins with the note that love consists in mutual communication. St. Ignatius continues, "The lover gives and communicates to the loved one what they have, or something of what they have, or are able to give; and in turn the one loved does the same for the lover. Each gives to the other" (*Spiritual Exercises* 231).

This giving and receiving relationship of love cradles my retreat. It goes to the very roots of who I am. The Trinity, loving communication personified, shows me that I am created for eternal communion. Jesus means it when he says to his Father, "All mine are yours, and yours are mine" (see Jn 17:10).

On the road to Emmaus, the unrecognized risen Jesus talked to two of his disciples and helped them to remember his loving actions and promises. At the end of the day, Jesus breaks and shares the evening bread with them, and reveals the very roots of who he is. Reflecting later on their conversation with Jesus, the disciples realize he had led them through a contemplation of divine love. No wonder they exclaimed, "Were not our hearts burning within us?" (see Lk 24:13–35).

This retreat, like the journey on the road to Emmaus, is essentially my opportunity for one long conversation with Jesus, to remember the history of loving action between me and the Trinity. In the first week, I pray with my own experience of being loved and bring it into the present. In the second week, I accept the invitations of God the Father, Jesus, and Spirit to abide in their love.

In the third and fourth week, I move slowly and lavishly through each point of the "Contemplation for Attaining Divine Love," the last exercise in the Spiritual Exercises. I will see the traces of divine love burning its way through my life. As I clothe myself in this love, I may seek Christ's inner peace and the burning desire to put our love into action.

> Clothe yourselves with love, which binds everything together in perfect harmony. And let the peace of Christ rule in your hearts, to which indeed you were called in the one body. And be thankful. Let the word of Christ dwell in you richly. . . . And whatever you do, in word or deed, do everything in the name of the Lord Jesus, giving thanks to God the Father through him. (Col 3:14–17)

THE RETREAT STRUCTURE

This retreat is a twenty-two-day retreat in daily life. Prayer is made four days a week, preferably Monday to Thursday, for four weeks. Each prayer day includes a time for prayer and reflection after prayer. Together they add up to a daily commitment of about fifty minutes. There are some weekend exercises, and Sunday Eucharist is recommended.

THE RETREAT DYNAMIC

My retreat is to be experienced as a whole, with a dynamic that moves through all four weeks. The daily prayer texts of each exercise have been carefully chosen, as single texts and as an ecology of texts. As single texts, they are part of the spiritual exercise. They provide the content and context of my exercise and my relationship with God. They also shed light on central elements of my faith.

As an ecology of texts, where there is more than one text, each text illuminates the others, offering a progression of meaning, or a contrast of content, or a balance of masculine and feminine experience.

Furthermore, the daily texts provide a meaningful progression throughout the week. They are balanced as a weekly group and are to be prayed in a weekly dynamic. Certain images, actions of God, or sets of grace and desire are developed throughout a week.

In like manner, the exercises of each week as a whole are chosen to guide me through certain movements that are only experienced when I make the full four-week retreat. They deliberately introduce me to many different images of God, inviting a variety of divine relationships and giving me a taste of the extraordinary richness in knowing and loving God.

SPIRITUAL JOURNALING

Ignatius directs: "After finishing the exercise I will either sit down or walk around for a quarter of an hour while I see how things have gone for me during the contemplation or meditation" (*Spiritual Exercises* 77).

For the First Spiritual Exercises, a special journal called the Listening Book is used. It will be essential for remembering and discerning the graces I receive in prayer. The Ignatian Guide to Spiritual Journaling (page 349) outlines how to do this.

SPIRITUAL CONVERSATION

Spiritual conversation, personal or group, is very highly recommended. See the Ignatian Guide to Spiritual Conversation found at the end of this book.

Retreat Map   Inner Peace in Divine Love

WEEK ONE	REMEMBERING LOVE
Monday	I remember being loved.
Tuesday	I remember being loved and grateful.
Wednesday	I remember being loved and responding.
Thursday	I remember a loving friendship.
Sunday	Action in memory of love

WEEK TWO	DWELLING IN LOVE
Monday	I abide in the love of Jesus.
Tuesday	I dwell in the love of the Father.
Wednesday	I remain in the love of the Spirit.
Thursday	Inseparable from God's love
Sunday	Action in union with love

WEEK THREE	LOVE AT WORK
Monday	I remember the gifts I have received.
Tuesday	I see how God dwells in creation.
Wednesday	I see how God dwells in me.
Thursday	I see how God works in creation and me.
Saturday	Reconciliation Examen
Sunday	Action in gratitude of love

WEEK FOUR	LOVE IN SERVICE
Monday	Every gift descends like the sun's rays.
Tuesday	Every gift flows like water.
Wednesday	Give me only the grace to love you.
Thursday	Awareness Examen
Saturday	Program for Life
Sunday	Action in peace with love

Week One	Remembering Love
Monday	I remember being loved.
Tuesday	I remember being loved and grateful.
Wednesday	I remember being loved and responding.
Thursday	I remember a loving friendship.
Sunday	Action in memory of love
	Eucharist

SPIRITUAL DIRECTION

The first half of my retreat is about love in relationship. It is easy to forget that I have a great gift in the joyful memories of my life. This week I bring them into my day. I remember experiences of being loved that have been lost, forgotten, or simply relegated to the past.

Building on an awareness exercise created by Anthony DeMello, S.J., the exercises of this week have the following movements: I remember being loved, and remembering, I feel loved. Then returning to the present I bring the feeling with me. With the experience of being loved in the present, I feel more alive and grateful.

The prayer method is the same each day, so once learned, I can relax into the week. Each daily spiritual exercise ends with a short conversation with God and closes with the Our Father. I conclude my week with Sunday Eucharist. If I am unable to celebrate the Eucharist, I may fruitfully make the alternative exercise.

The daily prayer texts reveal different expressions of God's love—passionate love, steadfast love, tender love, renewing love, and life-giving love.

Monday	I Remember Being Loved.
Preparation	I take a relaxed position with a straight back, my body poised for prayer. I make a gesture of reverence and humility. I read the prayer text about passionate love.
Opening Prayer	I ask for the grace to direct my whole self toward God.
Desire	I desire to feel the love in my life.
Prayer	Using my imagination, I remember an experience of being really loved.

I go back in time to re-create this experience as best I can with the details of place, weather, conversation, actions, and people. I relive the experience with all my senses—I touch, smell, hear, and feel being so loved.

I remain in this place for a few minutes.

Now, eyes still closed, I come back into the room where I am now. I remember the details of place here. How do I feel? I remain here for a few minutes.

I return again to the place where I was loved. I relive being loved. Do I feel any different than the first time I came here? I remain for a few minutes.

I come back into the room where I am now. How do I feel? Different? Now I move back and forth between both places, spending a minute or so in each.

I note any change of feelings. I do this for five minutes.

| Conversation | I end my prayer in a short conversation with God, talking as to a friend, about what I have just experienced. |

Our Father.[21]

SPIRITUAL DIRECTION

For this exercise, and in the following exercises this week, I may choose the same experience to return to when I remember, or I may choose a different experience.

This exercise reveals that when I remember how I have been loved I reexperience the feeling. I can bring that feeling back into the present, and the feeling is as real now as it was originally.

SUGGESTED PRAYER TIME: 25 MINUTES

Preparation: 5 minutes. Opening Prayer: 1 minute. Desire: 1 minute. Prayer: 15 minutes. Conversation: 3 minutes. Listening Book after prayer: 10 minutes.

PRAYER TEXTS

Set me as a seal upon your heart,
as a seal upon your arm;
for love is strong as death,
passion fierce as the grave.
Its flashes are flashes of fire, a raging flame.

Many waters cannot quench love,
neither can floods drown it.
If one offered for love
all the wealth of his house,
it would be utterly scorned. (Sg 8:6–7)

Tuesday   I Remember Being Loved and Grateful.

Preparation   I take a relaxed position with a straight back, my body poised for prayer. I make a gesture of reverence and humility. I read the prayer text about steadfast love.

Opening Prayer   I ask for the grace to direct my whole self toward God.

Desire   I desire to feel loved and grateful.

Prayer   I remember an experience of being loved and feeling grateful.

I go back in time to re-create this experience as best I can with the details of place, weather, conversation, actions, and people. I relive the experience with all my senses—I touch, smell, hear, and feel being so loved and grateful.

I remain in this place for a few minutes.

Now, eyes still closed, I come back into the room where I am now. I remember the details of place here. How do I feel? I remain here for a few minutes.

I return again to the place where I was loved. I relive being grateful. Do I feel any different than the first time I came here? I remain here for a few minutes.

I come back into the room where I am now. How do I feel? Different? Now I move back and forth between both places, spending a minute or so in each.

I note any change of feelings. I do this for five minutes.

Conversation   I end my prayer in a short conversation with God, talking as to a friend, about what I have just experienced.

Our Father.[22]

SPIRITUAL DIRECTION

It sometimes happens that when I begin remembering a past experience of being loved, the very opposite experience intrudes—an experience of being unloved. Painful relationships are a part of everyone's life, and I will have my own share. But it is important for me not to enter cycles of remembering these hard experiences to bring them into the present. One will simply relive the feelings to no useful purpose now.

If I find myself remembering experiences of not being loved, I need to gently detach myself and remake the exercise, firmly seeking only the joy of being loved. This is what I desire in this particular exercise, and, without denying other past experiences, all else is a real distraction.

SUGGESTED PRAYER TIME: 25 MINUTES

Preparation: 5 minutes. Opening Prayer: 1 minute. Desire: 1 minute. Prayer: 15 minutes. Conversation: 3 minutes. Listening Book after prayer: 10 minutes.

PRAYER TEXTS

Because your steadfast love is better than life,
my lips will praise you.
So I will bless you as long as I live;
I will lift up my hands and call on your name.

My soul is satisfied as with a rich feast,
and my mouth praises you with joyful lips. (Ps 63:3–5)

Wednesday	# I Remember Being Loved and Responding.
Preparation	I take a relaxed position with a straight back, my body poised for prayer. I make a gesture of reverence and humility. I read the prayer text about tender love.
Opening Prayer	I ask for the grace to direct my whole self toward God.
Desire	I desire to feel love and my response.
Prayer	I remember an experience of being loved and my response.

I go back in time to re-create this experience as best I can with the details of place, weather, conversation, actions, and people. I relive the experience with all my senses—I touch, smell, hear, and feel being so loved. I remember my response at the time.

I remain in this place for a few minutes.

Now, eyes still closed, I come back into the room where I am now. I remember the details of place here. How do I feel? I remain here for a few minutes.

I return again to where I was loved. I relive my response. Do I feel any different than the first time I came here? I remain here for a few minutes.

I come back into the room where I am now. How do I feel? Different? Now I move back and forth between both places, spending a minute or so in each.

I note any change of feelings. I do this for five minutes.

Conversation	I end my prayer in a short conversation with God, talking as to a friend, about what I have just experienced.

Our Father.[23]

SPIRITUAL DIRECTION

It is possible to have a past experience that is both my most powerful experience of being loved and my worst experience of being unloved. A family, marriage, or long relationship can contain both, even involve the same person. In this case, for the exercises of this week, I will consciously choose to remember only that part of the relationship or situation where I felt most loved, and I will leave the rest. For the first loved experience is as true now as then.

SUGGESTED PRAYER TIME: 25 MINUTES
Preparation: 5 minutes. Opening Prayer: 1 minute. Desire: 1 minute. Prayer: 15 minutes. Conversation: 3 minutes. Listening Book after prayer: 10 minutes.

PRAYER TEXTS
What does the LORD require of you
but to do justice,
and to love kindness,
and to walk humbly with your God? (Mi 6:8)

Thursday   I Remember a Loving Friendship.

Preparation   I take a relaxed position with a straight back, my body poised for prayer. I make a gesture of reverence and humility. I read the prayer text about renewing love.

Opening Prayer   I ask for the grace to direct my whole self toward God.

Desire   I desire to feel a loving friendship.

Prayer   I remember an experience of loving friendship with a close friend.

I go back in time to re-create this experience as best I can with the details of place, weather, conversation, actions, and people. I relive the experience with all my senses—I touch, smell, hear, and feel being in this loving friendship.

I remain in this place for a few minutes.

Now, eyes still closed, I come back into the room where I am now. I remember the details of place here. How do I feel? I remain here for a few minutes.

I return again to where I am with my friend. I relive our time together. Do I feel any different than the first time I came here? I remain here for a few minutes.

I come back into the room where I am now. How do I feel? Different? Now I move back and forth between both places, spending a minute or so in each.

I note any change of feelings. I do this for five minutes.

Conversation   I end my prayer in a short conversation with God, talking as to a friend, about what I have just experienced.

Our Father.[24]

SPIRITUAL DIRECTION

A deep, committed friendship is a special experience of love because a friendship can only exist when both people desire it. Lovers who become friends, or friends who come to love one another, are doubly blessed. Thus loving friendship is placed at the end of this week's prayer of love.

SUGGESTED PRAYER TIME: 25 MINUTES

Preparation: 5 minutes. Opening Prayer: 1 minute. Desire: 1 minute. Prayer: 15 minutes. Conversation: 3 minutes. Listening Book after prayer: 10 minutes.

PRAYER TEXTS

A friend loves at all times. (Prv 17:17)

The LORD, your God, is in your midst,
a warrior who gives victory;
he will rejoice over you with gladness,
he will renew you in his love;
he will exult over you with loud singing
as on a day of festival. (Zep 3:17–18a)

Sunday   Action in Memory of Love

Desire   I desire to act in memory of love.

Preparation   I read the prayer texts about life-giving love.

In the Eucharist I share a Eucharist meal with Jesus who has loved me.

I remember how he loved me in death and resurrection, and bring that love into the present. I feel his love in the breaking of the bread, in the sharing of his body. With the graces of this week lifting me, I receive the life he offers me.

or

In the World   I share a meal with a person who has loved me.

I open myself to feel the love this person has for me. I break bread and taste the love this person has given to me. I stay in the present moment of love.

With the graces of this week lifting me, I celebrate our relationship in a fresh way. Then I ponder the life Jesus offers me through him or her.

SPIRITUAL DIRECTION

Ignatius encourages me to seek life in four special places. The first two are prayer and Christian action. In them I come face-to-face with God. The second two are Christian community and the world. In the former, I find God through sacramental life and Church action. In the latter, I find God at work in all things—in my world and in all creation.

Each Sunday in this retreat, two spiritual exercises will be offered, reflecting the life of God in the Eucharist and the life of God in the world. Like twins, they reflect the Body of Christ in both communities. During my retreat I am strongly encouraged to celebrate the Sunday Eucharist. If I am unable to do this, then I may fruitfully make the twin exercise "In the World" offered above.

SUGGESTED PRAYER TIME: AS NEEDED

PRAYER TEXTS

[Jesus] took bread and giving thanks, broke it,
and gave it to his disciples, saying:
"Take this, all of you, and eat of it,
for this is my Body, which will be given up for you."
In a similar way, when supper was ended,
he took the chalice.
And, once more giving thanks,
he gave it to his disciples, saying:
"Take this, all of you, and drink from it,
for this is the chalice of my Blood,
the Blood of the new and eternal covenant,
which will be poured out for you and for many,
for the forgiveness of sins.
Do this in memory of me."[25]

As they came near [Emmaus], [Jesus] walked ahead as if he were going on. But [the two disciples] urged him strongly, saying, "Stay with us, because it is almost evening and the day is now nearly over." So he went in to stay with them. When he was at the table with them, he took bread, blessed and broke it, and gave it to them. Then their eyes were opened, and they recognized him; and he vanished from their sight. They said to each other, "Were not our hearts burning within us while he was talking to us on the road, while he was opening the scriptures to us?" That same hour they got up and returned to Jerusalem; and they found the eleven and their companions gathered together. Then they told what had happened on the road, and how he had been made known to them in the breaking of the bread. (Lk 24:28–33, 35)

Very truly, I tell you, unless you eat the flesh of the Son of Man and drink his blood, you have no life in you. Those who eat my flesh and drink my blood have eternal life, and I will raise them up on the last day; for my flesh is true food and my blood is true drink. Those who eat my flesh and drink my blood abide in me, and I in them. Just as the living Father sent me, and I live because of the Father, so whoever eats me will live because of me. (Jn 6:53–57)

Week Two   Dwelling in Love

Monday	I abide in the love of Jesus.
Tuesday	I dwell in the love of the Father.
Wednesday	I remain in the love of the Spirit.
Thursday	Inseparable from God's love
Sunday	Action in union with love
	Eucharist

SPIRITUAL DIRECTION

This is a quiet and contemplative week. I move from awareness of my experiences of love to awareness of God's desire for me. Within the body of each prayer this week, after hearing Jesus's words to me in the upper room of the Last Supper, I am invited into a deeper intimacy with the Trinity.

The verb "to abide" in the New Testament is also translated as "live in" or "dwell in" or "remain in." A strong word in the Gospel of John, it describes a deep union of love, one that is life-giving and fruitful. Jesus imagines this relationship for me when he says, "I am the vine, you are the branches" (Jn 15:5). He does not want to see me cut off from himself or from divine love. Rather he asks me to surrender myself, to abide in the mystery of the Trinity's extravagant love. He puts it simply, "As the Father has loved me, so I have loved you; abide in my love" (Jn 15:9).

The structure of each daily exercise is the same throughout. The Sunday Eucharist and exercise are in the same form as last week. If I am unable to celebrate the Eucharist, I may make the alternative exercise.

Each day the prayer texts reveal more expressions of God's love: abiding love, intimate love, spirit-filled love, inseparable love, and unifying love.

Monday	I Abide in the Love of Jesus.
Preparation	I take a relaxed position with a straight back, my body poised for prayer. I make a gesture of reverence and humility.
Opening Prayer	I ask for the grace to direct my whole self toward Jesus.
Desire	I desire to abide in the love of Jesus.
Prayer	I use my imagination to re-create the scene of the Last Supper with the details of place, conversation, actions, and people. Then I take my place at the table.
	I hear Jesus address me personally. Slowly reading the prayer text, I listen to his joyful words, each singing in my heart.
	In response, I abide in Jesus while saying to him, gently and often, each of the desiring statements below for a few minutes each:
	"I abide in your love."
	"I am enjoyed by you."
	"I feel complete in you."
Conversation	I end my prayer with the Our Father.[26]

SPIRITUAL DIRECTION

In contemplative prayer I can sometimes feel as if nothing is happening. It will be helpful to dismiss all such judgments. I have brought myself into the presence of God and expressed my desire. Whatever follows is prayer, so I have to trust and simply surrender.

There are three steps in the prayer above in which I remain for about three minutes, in quiet presence with each person of the Trinity. If I am distracted during this time, all I need to do is repeat the words I have been saying to that person of the Trinity. So today, if I had been in the presence of Jesus, I would say, "I abide in you," or "I am enjoyed by you," or "I feel complete in you." This will bring me back into my prayer.

SUGGESTED PRAYER TIME: 25 MINUTES

Preparation and Opening Prayer: 2 minutes. Desire: 1 minute. Prayer: 20 minutes. Conversation: 2 minutes. Listening Book after prayer: 10 minutes.

PRAYER TEXTS

As the Father has loved me,
so I have loved you; abide in my love.
If you keep my commandments,
you will abide in my love,
just as I have kept my Father's commandments
and abide in his love.
I have said these things to you
so that my joy may be in you,
and that your joy may be complete.
I do not call you servants any longer,
because the servant does not know what the master is doing;
but I have called you friends,
because I have made known to you everything
that I have heard from my Father. (Jn 15:9–11, 15)

Tuesday | I Dwell in the Love of the Father.

Preparation

I take a relaxed position with a straight back, my body poised for prayer. I make a gesture of reverence and humility.

Opening Prayer

I ask for the grace to direct my whole self toward the Father.

Desire

I desire to dwell in the love of the Father.

Prayer

I use my imagination to re-create the scene of the Last Supper room. Then I take my place at the table. After everyone has eaten, I listen to Jesus address me personally. Slowly reading the prayer text, I consider what he wants for me from his Father. I allow each of his desires to seep into my soul.

In response, I abide in Jesus while saying to him, gently and often, each of the desiring statements below for a few minutes each:

"I dwell in your love."

"I am one in you."

"I am at home in you."

Conversation

I end my prayer with the Our Father.[27]

SPIRITUAL DIRECTION

To disengage from distractions today, all I need to do is gently repeat the words at the end of the appropriate step above. Thus for today, "I dwell in your love," or "I am one in you," or "I am at home in you."

SUGGESTED PRAYER TIME: 25 MINUTES

Preparation and Opening Prayer: 2 minutes. Desire: 1 minute. Prayer: 20 minutes. Conversation: 2 minutes. Listening Book after prayer: 10 minutes.

PRAYER TEXTS

[Father,] I ask not only on behalf of these,
but also on behalf of those who will believe in me through their word,
that they may all be one.

As you, Father, are in me and I am in you,
may they also be in us,
so that the world may believe that you have sent me.

The glory that you have given me I have given them,
so that they may be one, as we are one,
I in them and you in me,
that they may become completely one,
so that the world may know that you have sent me
and have loved them even as you have loved me.

Father, I desire that those also, whom you have given me,
may be with me where I am,
to see my glory, which you have given me because you loved me
before the foundation of the world. (Jn 17:20–24)

Wednesday   I Remain in the Love of the Spirit.

Preparation
I take a relaxed position with a straight back, my body poised for prayer. I make a gesture of reverence and humility.

Opening Prayer
I ask for the grace to direct my whole self toward the Spirit.

Desire
I desire to remain in the love of the Spirit.

Prayer
I use my imagination to return to the upper room where now the disciples are hiding after the crucifixion. Jesus shows me his hands and side. I hear him address me personally. Slowly reading the prayer text, I allow his peace to take root in my being.

In response, I abide in Jesus while saying to him, gently and often, each of the desiring statements below for a few minutes each:

"I remain in your love."

"I am at peace in you."

"I feel alive in you."

Conversation
I end my prayer with the Our Father.[28]

SPIRITUAL DIRECTION
If distracted, and taken out of prayer, I use the words I have been saying to each person to bring me back to prayer. So today, "I remain in your love," or "I am at peace in you," or "I feel alive in you."

SUGGESTED PRAYER TIME: 25 MINUTES
Preparation and Opening Prayer: 2 minutes. Desire: 1 minute. Prayer: 20 minutes. Conversation: 2 minutes. Listening Book after prayer: 10 minutes.

PRAYER TEXTS

When it was evening on that day, the first day of the week,
and the doors of the house where the disciples had met
were locked for fear of the Jews,
Jesus came and stood among them
and said, "Peace be with you."

After he said this, he showed them his hands and his side.
Then the disciples rejoiced when they saw the Lord.

Jesus said to them again, "Peace be with you.
As the Father has sent me, so I send you."

When he had said this, he breathed on them
and said to them, "Receive the Holy Spirit." (Jn 20:19–22)

Thursday — Inseparable from God's Love

Preparation	I take a relaxed position with a straight back, my body poised for prayer. I make a gesture of reverence and humility.
Opening Prayer	I ask for the grace to direct my whole self toward the Trinity.
Desire	I desire the inseparable love of the Trinity.
Prayer	I use my imagination to re-create the upper room again. Soon the Spirit will be here with Pentecost fire, but at present it is just Jesus and I. We stand at a window, looking over domed rooftops, busy streets, and roads from Jerusalem. He tells me how nothing shall ever separate me from his love. Slowly reading the prayer text, I allow his words to grow into the muscles of my heart.
	In response, I abide in Jesus while saying to him, gently and often, each of the desiring statements below for a few minutes each:
	"I am inseparable from your love."
	"I love you."
	"Thank you."
Conversation	I end my prayer with the Our Father.[29]

SPIRITUAL DIRECTION
If distracted, I use the words "I love you," "I am inseparable," or "Thank you," to return myself to prayer.

SUGGESTED PRAYER TIME: 25 MINUTES
Preparation and Opening Prayer: 2 minutes. Desire: 1 minute. Prayer: 20 minutes. Conversation: 2 minutes. Listening Book after prayer: 10 minutes.

PRAYER TEXTS

What then are we to say about these things?
If God is for us, who is against us?
He who did not withhold his own Son,
but gave him up for all of us,
will he not with him also give us everything else?

Who will separate us from the love of Christ?
Will hardship, or distress, or persecution,
or famine, or nakedness, or peril, or sword?
No, in all these things we are more than conquerors
through him who loved us.

For I am convinced that neither death, nor life,
nor angels, nor rulers,
nor things present, nor things to come,
nor powers, nor height, nor depth,
nor anything else in all creation,
will be able to separate us from the love of God
in Christ Jesus our Lord. (Rom 8:31–32, 35, 37–39)

Sunday	Action in Union with Love

Desire I desire to act in union with love.

Preparation First I read the prayer texts about unifying love. Then I choose to seek that unity.

In the Eucharist I focus on the doxology at the end of the Eucharistic prayer. Listening to this ancient prayer, I consider the way divine love flows through Jesus to the Father and Spirit. And if through him, then also through me, with me, and in me.

After communion, I prayerfully watch all the different faces in the Body of Christ as each person walks past me to return to their seat. Through Jesus I am now a part of them and they are a part of me.

I give thanks for the graces of this week and ask myself how I might express my union with him in action.

or

In the World I go to a town center, marketplace, or city square to pray. I sit there, at this gathering place or crossing place of many roads, and watch the flow of people coming into the center, remaining, and then flowing out. Over this scene I imagine the Body of Christ and that all the people flow through him, with him, and in him. I imagine the love they receive doing so, how Jesus feels giving it, and how I feel to be centered in it.

I give thanks for the graces of this week and ask myself how I might express my gratitude in action.

SPIRITUAL DIRECTION

Two spiritual exercises are offered today, reflecting the union with God in the Eucharist and union with God in the world. As twin exercises, they reflect union with Christ in both communities. During my retreat I am strongly encouraged to celebrate the Sunday Eucharist. If I am unable to do this, then I may fruitfully make the twin exercise "In the World" offered above.

SUGGESTED PRAYER TIME: AS NEEDED

PRAYER TEXTS

Through him, and with him, and in him,
O God, Almighty Father,
in the unity of the Holy Spirit,
all glory and honor is yours,
for ever and ever. Amen.[30]

[Jesus] himself is before all things, and in him all things hold together. He is the head of the body, the church; he is the beginning, the firstborn from the dead, so that he might come to have first place in everything. For in him all the fullness of God was pleased to dwell, and through him God was pleased to reconcile to himself all things, whether on earth or in heaven, by making peace through the blood of his cross. (Col 1:17–20)

No one ever hates his own body, but he nourishes and tenderly cares for it, just as Christ does for the church, because we are members of his body. "For this reason a man will leave his father and mother and be joined to his wife, and the two will become one flesh." This is a great mystery, and I am applying it to Christ and the church. (Eph 5:29–32)

I therefore, the prisoner in the Lord, beg you to lead a life worthy of the calling to which you have been called, with all humility and gentleness, with patience, bearing with one another in love, making every effort to maintain the unity of the Spirit in the bond of peace. There is one body and one Spirit, just as you were called to the one hope of your calling, one Lord, one faith, one baptism, one God and Father of all, who is above all and through all and in all. (Eph 4:1–6)

Week Three   Love at Work

Monday	I remember the gifts I have received.
Tuesday	I see how God dwells in creation.
Wednesday	I see how God dwells in me.
Thursday	I see how God works in creation and me.
Saturday	Reconciliation Examen
Sunday	Action in gratitude of love
	Eucharist

SPIRITUAL DIRECTION

The second half of my retreat is about love in action. This week I pray the first half of the "Contemplation for Attaining Divine Love" exercise, and next week the second half. The five-point structure of this prayer is the same for each day, with only the content of points one and three being changed.

Point one, "Be Loved," is a bridge from my spiritual exercises last week. It uses a scriptural image of divine relationship to bring me into union with God.

The Saturday exercise is an invitation to receive the Sacrament of Reconciliation. The grace sought here is to feel God's "constant loving kindness and mercy" as he reconciles me with all creation (*Spiritual Exercises* 71). Ignatius, sharing his own experience, invites me to "exclaim with wonder how the whole of creation lets me live and intercedes for me" even though I may have been destructive of self, community, or creation (*Spiritual Exercises* 60).

If I am unable to receive Reconciliation, I may fruitfully make an act of reconciliation or forgiveness in my own relationships or community.

Further expressions of God's love are revealed in the prayer texts: compassionate love, creative love, unconditional love, active love, and gracious love.

Monday	I Remember the Gifts I Have Received.

Be Loved

After slowly reading the prayer texts, I stand for a few minutes, precious in God's sight and honored. I allow God's compassion to wash through me.

Ask Help

I ask the Spirit for an interior knowledge of all the good I have received.

Remember

I ponder with deep affection how God is loving me:

I remember the benefits I have received: creation, redemption, and personal gifts.

I review how much God has done for me, how much I have been given of what belongs to God.

I reflect on how the Father, Son, and Spirit even wish to give me themselves.

Response

I respond to God as a friend, beautiful creature, or lover.

With the Communion of Saints in support, I express my gratitude.

Offering

I consider what, in all reason and justice, I ought to offer and give God. I conclude saying, as one making a gift with heartfelt love:

Take, Lord, and receive all my liberty,
my memory, my understanding, and my entire will,
all that I have and possess.
You gave it all to me; to you I return it.
All is yours; dispose of it entirely according to your will.
Give me only the grace to love you,
for that is enough for me. (*Spiritual Exercises* 43, 231–35)

SPIRITUAL DIRECTION

Today and through this week, the image of relationship with God used in the "Be Loved" point is always taken from the first prayer text.

SUGGESTED PRAYER TIME: 40 MINUTES

Be Loved: 10 minutes. Ask Help: 1 minute. Remember: 20 minutes. Response: 4 minutes. Offering: 5 minutes. Listening Book after prayer: 10 minutes.

PRAYER TEXTS

Thus says the LORD, he who created you, O Jacob, he who formed you, O Israel: Do not fear, for I have redeemed you; I have called you by name, you are mine. When you pass through the waters, I will be with you; and through the rivers, they shall not overwhelm you; when you walk through fire you shall not be burned, and the flame shall not consume you. For I am the LORD your God, the Holy One of Israel, your Savior . . . . You are precious in my sight, and honored, and I love you. (Is 43:1–4a)

And he said to them, "What are you discussing with each other while you walk along?" They stood still, looking sad. Then one of them, whose name was Cleopas, answered him, "Are you the only stranger in Jerusalem who does not know the things that have taken place there in these days?" He asked them, "What things?" They replied, "The things about Jesus of Nazareth, who was a prophet mighty in deed and word before God and all the people, and how our chief priests and leaders handed him over to be condemned to death and crucified him. But we had hoped that he was the one to redeem Israel." Then he said to them, "Oh, how foolish you are, and how slow of heart to believe all that the prophets have declared! Was it not necessary that the Messiah should suffer these things and then enter into his glory?" Then beginning with Moses and all the prophets, he interpreted to them the things about himself in all the scriptures. (Lk 24:18–21, 25–27)

Your Maker is your husband, the LORD of hosts is his name; the Holy One of Israel is your Redeemer, the God of the whole earth he is called. For the LORD has called you like a wife forsaken and grieved in spirit, like the wife of a man's youth when she is cast off, says your God. For a brief moment I abandoned you, but with great compassion I will gather you. In overflowing wrath for a moment I hid my face from you, but with everlasting love I will have compassion on you, says the LORD, your Redeemer. For the mountains may depart and the hills be removed, but my steadfast love shall not depart from you, and my covenant of peace shall not be removed, says the LORD, who has compassion on you. (Is 54:5–8, 10)

Tuesday   I See How God Dwells in Creation.

Be Loved   After slowly reading the prayer texts, I stand before the
                 Creator as creature, wonderfully made in God's image. I
                 allow God's declaration of my goodness to wash through
                 me.

Ask Help   I ask the Spirit for an interior knowledge of all the good I
                 have received.

Remember   I ponder with deep affection how God is loving me:

                 I see how God dwells in creation,
                 in the elements, giving being,
                 in the plants, giving growth,
                 in the animals, giving sensation,
                 and in humankind, granting the gift of understanding.

Response   I respond to God as a friend, beautiful creature, or lover.

                 With the Communion of Saints in support, I express my
                 gratitude.

Offering   I consider what, in all reason and justice, I ought to offer
                 and give God. I conclude saying, as one making a gift with
                 heartfelt love:

                 Take, Lord, and receive all my liberty,
                 my memory, my understanding, and my entire will,
                 all that I have and possess.
                 You gave it all to me; to you I return it.
                 All is yours; dispose of it entirely according to your will.
                 Give me only the grace to love you,
                 for that is enough for me. (*Spiritual Exercises* 43, 231–35)

SUGGESTED PRAYER TIME: 40 MINUTES

Be Loved: 10 minutes. Ask Help: 1 minute. Remember: 20 minutes. Response: 4 minutes. Offering: 5 minutes. Listening Book after prayer: 10 minutes.

PRAYER TEXTS

O Lord, how manifold are your works!
In wisdom you have made them all; the earth is full of your creatures.
These all look to you to give them their food in due season;
when you give to them, they gather it up;
when you open your hand, they are filled with good things.
When you hide your face, they are dismayed;
when you take away their breath, they die and return to their dust.
When you send forth your spirit, they are created;
and you renew the face of the ground.
May the glory of the Lord endure forever;
may the Lord rejoice in his works—
who looks on the earth and it trembles,
who touches the mountains and they smoke.
I will sing to the Lord as long as I live;
I will sing praise to my God while I have being.
May my meditation be pleasing to him,
for I rejoice in the Lord. (Ps 104:24, 27–34)

Then God said, "Let the earth put forth vegetation: plants yielding seed, and fruit trees of every kind on earth that bear fruit with the seed in it." And it was so. The earth brought forth vegetation: plants yielding seed of every kind, and trees of every kind bearing fruit with the seed in it. And God saw that it was good. God made the two great lights—the greater light to rule the day and the lesser light to rule the night—and the stars. And God saw that it was good. So God created the great sea monsters and every living creature that moves, of every kind, with which the waters swarm, and every winged bird of every kind. And God saw that it was good. God made the wild animals of the earth of every kind, and the cattle of every kind, and everything that creeps upon the ground of every kind. And God saw that it was good.

So God created humankind in his image, in the image of God he created them; male and female he created them. God saw everything that he had made, and indeed, it was very good. (Gn 1:12, 16, 18, 21, 25, 27, 31)

Wednesday   I See How God Dwells in Me.

Be Loved

After slowly reading the prayer texts, I stand for a few minutes and imagine the Spirit living in me, creating a home and sacred place, making me holy. I allow God's unconditional love to wash through me.

Ask Help

I ask the Spirit for an interior knowledge of all the good I have received.

Remember

I ponder with deep affection how God is loving me:

I see how God dwells in me, giving me being, life, and sensation, consciousness, and understanding.
I see how the divine majesty makes a temple of me,
how I have been created in God's likeness and image.

Response

I respond to God as a friend, beautiful creature, or lover.

With the Communion of Saints in support, I express my gratitude.

Offering

I consider what, in all reason and justice, I ought to offer and give God. I conclude saying, as one making a gift with heartfelt love:

Take, Lord, and receive all my liberty,
my memory, my understanding, and my entire will,
all that I have and possess.
You gave it all to me; to you I return it.
All is yours; dispose of it entirely according to your will.
Give me only the grace to love you,
for that is enough for me. (*Spiritual Exercises* 43, 231–35)

SUGGESTED PRAYER TIME: 40 MINUTES
Be Loved: 10 minutes. Ask Help: 1 minute. Remember: 20 minutes. Response: 4 minutes. Offering: 5 minutes. Listening Book after prayer: 10 minutes.

PRAYER TEXTS

Do you not know that you are God's temple
and that God's Spirit dwells in you? . . .
For God's temple is holy, and you are that temple. (1 Cor 3:16–17)

It was you who formed my inward parts;
you knit me together in my mother's womb.
I praise you, for I am fearfully and wonderfully made.
Wonderful are your works; that I know very well.
My frame was not hidden from you,
when I was being made in secret,
intricately woven in the depths of the earth. (Ps 139:13–15)

The Lord fashioned human beings from the earth,
to consign them back to it.
He gave them so many days and so much time,
he gave them authority over everything on earth.
He clothed them in strength, like himself,
and made them in his own image.
He made them a tongue, eyes and ears,
and gave them a heart to think with.
He filled them with knowledge and intelligence,
and showed them what was good and what evil.
He put his own light in their hearts
to show them the magnificence of his works,
so that they would praise his holy name
as they told of his magnificent works. (Sir 17:1–3, 5–10, NJB)

We are the temple of the living God;
as God said, "I will live in them and walk among them,
and I will be their God, and they shall be my people." (2 Cor 6:16)

Thursday   I See How God Works in Creation and Me.

Be Loved   After slowly reading the prayer texts, I stand for a few minutes before the Trinity who each give me life. I imagine them preparing for their work today. I allow their desire for working in the world to wash through me.

Ask Help   I ask the Spirit for an interior knowledge of all the good I have received.

Remember   I ponder with deep affection how God is loving me:

I consider how God works and labors on my behalf in all created things on the face of the earth.

I see how my Lord God acts in the manner of a person at work.

I see how my Creator works in the heavens, elements, plants, fruits, cattle, etc., giving being, conserving life, granting growth and sensation, etc.

Response   I respond to God as a friend, beautiful creature, or lover.

With the Communion of Saints in support, I express my gratitude.

Offering   I consider what, in all reason and justice, I ought to offer and give God. I conclude saying, as one making a gift with heartfelt love:

Take, Lord, and receive all my liberty,
my memory, my understanding, and my entire will,
all that I have and possess.
You gave it all to me; to you I return it.
All is yours; dispose of it entirely according to your will.
Give me only the grace to love you,
for that is enough for me. (*Spiritual Exercises* 43, 231–35)

SUGGESTED PRAYER TIME: 40 MINUTES

Be Loved: 10 minutes. Ask Help: 1 minute. Remember: 20 minutes. Response: 4 minutes. Offering: 5 minutes. Listening Book after prayer: 10 minutes.

PRAYER TEXTS

Jesus answered [the Jews], "My Father is still working, and I also am working. The Father loves the Son and shows him all that he himself is doing; and he will show him greater works than these, so that you will be astonished. Indeed, just as the Father raises the dead and gives them life, so also the Son gives life to whomever he wishes. (Jn 5:17, 20–21)

Sing to the LORD with thanksgiving;
 make melody to our God on the lyre.
He covers the heavens with clouds, prepares rain for the earth,
 makes grass grow on the hills.
He gives to the animals their food,
 and to the young ravens when they cry.
His delight is not in the strength of the horse,
 nor his pleasure in the speed of a runner;
but the LORD takes pleasure in those who fear him,
 in those who hope in his steadfast love. (Ps 147:7–11)

For this reason I bow my knees before the Father, from whom every family in heaven and on earth takes its name. I pray that, according to the riches of his glory, he may grant that you may be strengthened in your inner being with power through his Spirit, and that Christ may dwell in your hearts through faith, as you are being rooted and grounded in love.

I pray that you may have the power to comprehend, with all the saints, what is the breadth and length and height and depth, and to know the love of Christ that surpasses knowledge, so that you may be filled with all the fullness of God. Now to him who by the power at work within us is able to accomplish abundantly far more than all we can ask or imagine, to him be glory in the church and in Christ Jesus to all generations, forever and ever. Amen. (Eph 3:14–21)

Saturday   Reconciliation Examen

I Give Thanks

After reading the prayer texts, I stand for a few minutes before the Father, as son or daughter, and feel his compassion as he puts his arms around me. I sift the month, with gratitude, for times I have received or given forgiveness.

I Ask for Help

I ask the Spirit to intercede for me with sighs too deep for words.

I Review

I move through the last month, day by day:

1. Before the Father of mercies, I recall if I have rejected or withheld love.

2. In the light of the Lord's forgiveness, I sift my thoughts, words, and actions.

3. With the Spirit, I examine the general direction of my life—my true self.

4. I explore one social structure I belong to, discerning good from the unjust.

5. I bring to Jesus any sin or sinful pattern that has real and deadly consequences in my life.

I Respond

I enter the mystery of the Trinity's reconciling and forgiving love. I humbly express my sorrow for what was revealed above, and ask for forgiveness.

I Resolve

I resolve to take one or more of the following paths to reconciliation:

1. To adjust my lifestyle or work, see a counselor or spiritual director, or deepen my personal, family, and church relationships so that the Lord may forgive and reconcile me through them.

2. To bring where I need forgiveness to Jesus, and to call on his merciful love.

3. To take any needed reconciling action, for myself or others I have hurt.

4. To receive the Sacrament of Reconciliation, now and monthly if possible.

5. To make, as envoy for Christ, one small act of reconciliation next month.[31]

SPIRITUAL DIRECTION

Ignatius received a revelation on the road to Rome to begin his lifelong service of God. The Reconciliation Examen above is broadened from the examination of thoughts, words, and deeds suggested by Ignatius. I spend more time on those questions or actions closest to my need.

"Before reaching Rome, I was at prayer in a church and experienced such a change in my soul and saw so clearly that God the Father placed me with Christ his Son that I would not dare doubt it."[32] The Christ before Ignatius is Jesus carrying his Cross. The love that he and Ignatius had for one another, their shared vision of God's kingdom, their desire to feed, liberate, and teach the needy, grew into a profound friendship and an effective, shared mission. Ignatius realized anything that fractured, enticed away, or hid this working relationship leaves one in need of loving reconciliation.

SUGGESTED PRAYER TIME: AS NEEDED

PRAYER TEXTS

[Jesus] said to Simon, "Do you see this woman? I entered your house; you gave me no water for my feet, but she has bathed my feet with her tears and dried them with her hair. You gave me no kiss, but from the time I came in she has not stopped kissing my feet. You did not anoint my head with oil, but she has anointed my feet with ointment. Therefore, I tell you, her sins, which were many, have been forgiven; hence she has shown great love. . . ." Then he said to her, "Your sins are forgiven. . . . Your faith has saved you; go in peace." (Lk 7:44–50)

The tax collector, standing far off, would not even look up to heaven, but was beating his breast and saying, "God, be merciful to me, a sinner!" (Lk 18:13)

If anyone is in Christ, there is a new creation: everything old has passed away; see, everything has become new! All this is from God, who reconciled us to himself through Christ, and has given us the ministry of reconciliation. (2 Cor 5:17–18)

Sunday	Action in Gratitude of Love

Desire

I desire to act in gratitude of love.

Preparation

First I read the prayer texts about grateful love. Then I choose to seek that gratitude.

In the Eucharist

I focus on the Preface at the beginning of the Liturgy of the Eucharist. It is the great memorial prayer of gratitude.

With the graces of the past week fresh within me, I lift up my heart to my Lord. With the naming of the gifts I have received, I give my Lord and God thanks and praise. And in the "Holy, Holy, Holy" I gladly welcome the God of power and might into my life.

or

In the World

I go to a park or shopping center or sports stadium to contemplate a large number of people, varied in age, culture, and life story. I give thanks that the Trinity has loved everyone here. I take the time to consider how the Father created the universe we live in, and how Jesus lived, died, and rose for everyone in front of me. I look up and see how the Spirit hovers protectively over all of us. I look around me and consider, person by person, for some good time, how each one will be raised from death to eternal life.

In gratitude, I slowly pray the Preface prayer to the Father, and say the "Holy, Holy, Holy" over all the people before me.

I give thanks for the graces of this week and ask myself how I might express my gratitude in action.

SPIRITUAL DIRECTION

Many different Prefaces are used throughout the liturgical year, but they all tell the story of salvation history. A Preface is a summary of the gifts I have been grateful for this week.

Two spiritual exercises are offered today, reflecting gratitude in the Eucharist and gratitude in the world. As twin exercises, they reflect the reality of Christ's saving presence in both communities. During my retreat I am strongly encouraged to celebrate the Sunday Eucharist. If I am unable to do this, then I may fruitfully make the twin exercise "In the World" offered above.

SUGGESTED PRAYER TIME: AS NEEDED

PRAYER TEXTS
Priest: Lift up your hearts.
All: We lift them up to the Lord.

Priest: Let us give thanks to the Lord our God.
All: It is right and just.

Priest: It is truly right and just, our duty and our salvation,
always and everywhere to give you thanks,
Father most holy,
through your beloved Son, Jesus Christ,
your Word through whom you made all things,
whom you sent as our Savior and Redeemer,
incarnate by the Holy Spirit and born of the Virgin.
Fulfilling your will and gaining for you a holy people,
he stretched out his hands as he endured his Passion,
so as to break the bonds of death and manifest the resurrection.
And so, with the Angels and all the Saints
we declare your glory,
as with one voice we acclaim:

All: Holy, holy, holy Lord, God of hosts,
heaven and earth are full of your glory.
Hosanna in the highest.
Blessed is he who comes in the name of the Lord.
Hosanna in the highest.[33]

The spirit of the Lord GOD is upon me, because the LORD has anointed me; he has sent me to bring good news to the oppressed, to bind up the brokenhearted, to proclaim liberty to the captives, and release to the prisoners; to proclaim the year of the Lord's favor . . . to provide for those who mourn in Zion—to give them a garland instead of ashes, the oil of gladness instead of mourning, the mantle of praise instead of a faint spirit. (Is 61:1–3a)

Week Four   Love in Service

Monday	Every gift descends like the sun's rays.
Tuesday	Every gift flows like water.
Wednesday	Give me only the grace to love you.
Thursday	Awareness Examen
Saturday	Program for Life
Sunday	Acting in peace with love
	Eucharist

SPIRITUAL DIRECTION

This week the second half of the "Contemplation for Attaining Divine Love" exercise is made with the same five-point structure of prayer used last week. Point one, "Be Loved," continues to use a scriptural image of divine relationship to bring me briefly into union with God.

The Thursday exercise is the Awareness Examen. Its five-part structure has been deliberately used in this retreat to pray the points of the contemplation and to teach me, along the way, the five-point prayer structure of the Awareness Examen. This works well because the Awareness Examen is a daily contemplation on divine love—an exercise to find God's love at work in my daily life. It is taught to me here as an excellent prayer form to use after my retreat.

At the end of the retreat I create a program for life. This will give me a way to order my energies, commitments, and spiritual life. Ignatius saw the Exercises as an opportunity for the "ordering of one's life on the basis of a decision made in freedom from any disordered attachment" (*Spiritual Exercises* 21). At the end of my retreat I will have the opportunity to do just this.

The prayer texts continue to reveal new expressions of God's love: enlightening love, thirst-quenching love, humble love, and peaceful love.

Monday   Every Gift Descends Like the Sun's Rays.

Be Loved   After slowly reading the prayer texts, I stand for a few minutes before the Father of lights, bathed in the brightness of his generosity. I allow his light to wash through me.

Ask Help   I ask the Spirit for an interior knowledge of all the good I have received.

Remember   I ponder with deep affection how God is loving me:

I see how all that is good and every gift descends from on high.

As rays descend from the sun, I see how my limited power descends from the supreme and infinite power above.

Response   I respond to God as a friend, beautiful creature, or lover.

With the Communion of Saints in support, I express my gratitude.

Offering   I consider what, in all reason and justice, I ought to offer and give God. I conclude saying, as one making a gift with heartfelt love:

Take, Lord, and receive all my liberty,
my memory, my understanding, and my entire will,
all that I have and possess.
You gave it all to me; to you I return it.
All is yours; dispose of it entirely according to your will.
Give me only the grace to love you,
for that is enough for me. (*Spiritual Exercises* 43, 231–35)

SPIRITUAL DIRECTION

Again, through this week, the image of relationship with God used in the "Be Loved" point is always taken from the first prayer text.

SUGGESTED PRAYER TIME: 40 MINUTES

Be Loved: 10 minutes. Ask Help: 1 minute. Remember: 20 minutes. Response: 4 minutes. Offering: 5 minutes. Listening Book after prayer: 10 minutes.

PRAYER TEXTS

Every generous act of giving, with every perfect gift, is from above, coming down from the Father of lights, with whom there is no variation or shadow due to change. In fulfillment of his own purpose he gave us birth by the word of truth, so that we would become a kind of first fruits of his creatures. (Jas 1:17–18)

"We must work the works of him who sent me while it is day; night is coming when no one can work. As long as I am in the world, I am the light of the world." When he had said this, he spat on the ground and made mud with the saliva and spread the mud on the man's eyes, saying to him, "Go, and wash in the pool of Siloam" (which means Sent). Then he went and washed and came back able to see. (Jn 9:4–7)

We do not proclaim ourselves; we proclaim Jesus Christ as Lord and ourselves as your slaves for Jesus' sake. For it is the God who said, "Let light shine out of darkness," who has shone in our hearts to give the light of the knowledge of the glory of God in the face of Jesus Christ. (2 Cor 4:5–6)

Tuesday	Every Gift Flows Like Water.
Be Loved	After slowly reading the prayer texts, I stand for a few minutes before the Lord of the spring rains. I allow Jesus, the living water, to wash through me.
Ask Help	I ask the Spirit for an interior knowledge of all the good I have received.
Remember	I ponder with deep affection how God is loving me:
	I see how all that is good and every gift descends from on high.
	As waters flow from a fountain, I see justice, goodness, love, mercy, etc., flowing into all creation and me.
Response	I respond to God as a friend, beautiful creature, or lover.
	With the Communion of Saints in support, I express my gratitude.
Offering	I consider what, in all reason and justice, I ought to offer and give God. I conclude saying, as one making a gift with heartfelt love:
	Take, Lord, and receive all my liberty, my memory, my understanding, and my entire will, all that I have and possess. You gave it all to me; to you I return it. All is yours; dispose of it entirely according to your will. Give me only the grace to love you, for that is enough for me. (*Spiritual Exercises* 43, 231–35)

SUGGESTED PRAYER TIME: 40 MINUTES

Be Loved: 10 minutes. Ask Help: 1 minute. Remember: 20 minutes. Response: 4 minutes. Offering: 5 minutes. Listening Book after prayer: 10 minutes.

PRAYER TEXTS

Let us press on to know the LORD; his appearing is as sure as the dawn; he will come to us like the showers, like the spring rains that water the earth. (Hos 6:3)

A Samaritan woman came to draw water, and Jesus said to her, "Give me a drink." The Samaritan woman said to him, "How is it that you, a Jew, ask a drink of me, a woman of Samaria?" (Jews do not share things in common with Samaritans.) Jesus answered her, "If you knew the gift of God, and who it is that is saying to you, 'Give me a drink,' you would have asked him, and he would have given you living water." The woman said to him, "Sir, you have no bucket, and the well is deep. Where do you get that living water? Are you greater than our ancestor Jacob, who gave us the well, and with his sons and his flocks drank from it?" Jesus said to her, "Everyone who drinks of this water will be thirsty again, but those who drink of the water that I will give them will never be thirsty. The water that I will give will become in them a spring of water gushing up to eternal life." The woman said to him, "Sir, give me this water, so that I may never be thirsty or have to keep coming here to draw water." (Jn 4:7, 9–15)

On the last day of the festival, the great day, while Jesus was standing there, he cried out, "Let anyone who is thirsty come to me, and let the one who believes in me drink. As the scripture has said, 'Out of the believer's heart shall flow rivers of living water.'" Now he said this about the Spirit, which believers in him were to receive; for as yet there was no Spirit, because Jesus was not yet glorified. (Jn 7:37–39)

Wednesday   Give Me Only the Grace to Love You.

Be Loved

After slowly reading the prayer texts, I stand before Jesus and imagine him humbly washing my feet. I allow the utter fullness of God to wash through me.

Ask Help

I ask the Spirit for an interior knowledge of all the good I have received.

Remember

I ponder with deep affection how God is loving me:

I give thanks for all the benefits and gifts I have received.

I recall my retreat, day by day, to see how God has been at work in me.

I look for patterns in my prayer journal: What gives me life?

What is the loving way forward?

Response

I respond to God as a friend, beautiful creature, or lover.

With the Communion of Saints in support, I express my gratitude.

Offering

I consider what, in all reason and justice, I ought to offer and give God. I conclude saying, as one making a gift with heartfelt love:

Take, Lord, and receive all my liberty,
my memory, my understanding, and my entire will,
all that I have and possess.
You gave it all to me; to you I return it.
All is yours; dispose of it entirely according to your will.
Give me only the grace to love you,
for that is enough for me. (*Spiritual Exercises* 43, 231–35)

SUGGESTED PRAYER TIME: 40 MINUTES

Be Loved: 10 minutes. Ask Help: 1 minute. Remember: 20 minutes. Response: 4 minutes. Offering: 5 minutes. Listening Book after prayer: 10 minutes.

PRAYER TEXTS

[During supper] Jesus, knowing that the Father had given all things into his hands, and that he had come from God and was going to God, got up from the table, took off his outer robe, and tied a towel around himself. Then he poured water into a basin and began to wash the disciples' feet and to wipe them with the towel that was tied around him. He came to Simon Peter, who said to him, "Lord, are you going to wash my feet?" Jesus answered, "You do not know now what I am doing, but later you will understand." Peter said to him, "You will never wash my feet." Jesus answered, "Unless I wash you, you have no share with me." Simon Peter said to him, "Lord, not my feet only but also my hands and my head!" Jesus said to him, "One who has bathed does not need to wash, except for the feet, but is entirely clean. And you are clean, though not all of you." For he knew who was to betray him; for this reason he said, "Not all of you are clean."

After he had washed their feet, had put on his robe, and had returned to the table, he said to them, "Do you know what I have done to you? You call me Teacher and Lord—and you are right, for that is what I am. So if I, your Lord and Teacher, have washed your feet, you also ought to wash one another's feet. For I have set you an example, that you also should do as I have done to you. Very truly, I tell you, servants are not greater than their master, nor are messengers greater than the one who sent them. If you know these things, you are blessed if you do them." (Jn 13:3–17)

With what shall I come before the Lord,
    and bow myself before God on high?
Shall I come before him with burnt offerings,
    with calves a year old?
Will the Lord be pleased with thousands of rams,
    with ten thousands of rivers of oil?
Shall I give my firstborn for my transgression,
    the fruit of my body for the sin of my soul?
He has told you, O mortal, what is good;
    and what does the Lord require of you
but to do justice, and to love kindness,
    and to walk humbly with your God? (Mi 6:8)

Thursday   Awareness Examen

I Give Thanks	I give thanks for the graces, benefits, and good things of my day.
I Ask for Help	I ask the Holy Spirit for help to discern my day with openness.
I Review	I review my day, hour by hour, to see how God is working in my life.
I Respond	I respond to what I felt or learned in my review just made.
I Resolve	I resolve with hope and the grace of God to amend my life tomorrow.
	Our Father.[34]

SPIRITUAL DIRECTION

Having learned the five-point structure of the Awareness Examen while praying the Contemplation, I now spend a day learning the general form of the Awareness Examen. In the evening I pray it to review this day.

A daily prayer form, the Awareness Examen sifts my day with gratitude and seeks to discern the traces of God at work in my life. It guides me with consolations, understanding, and inner peace. The best time to pray it is day's end or midday. I can be confident that over time this prayer will root my life in God's life. It is made in five steps:

1. I become aware that I live in the stream of God's love—where all is gift. I review my day, recalling its gifts, large and small, and allow gratitude to well up in me.
2. I make a prayer to the Spirit for discerning light in this examen.
3. I carefully search out how God is working in my life, moving hour by hour, through my day. After some weeks I also look for any pattern of events or relationships that console me or give me inner peace. Conversely, is there a pattern that desolates or deadens me? I begin to see how God works best through me. How may I work best with God tomorrow?
4. I respond to what I experienced in the previous point. I might give thanks or express sorrow. I might feel wonder, sadness, or sheer delight with my Lord. We speak about this.
5. I consider the loving way forward tomorrow. I may desire growth or transformation. I may resolve to develop some virtue or grace or

gift. I might seek to renew. So I act in response to my new awareness. I will do my best and surrender the outcome to God.

The prayer texts below are words of Jesus that speak to each step.

SUGGESTED PRAYER TIME: 15 MINUTES
Thanks: 3 minutes. Help: 1 minute. Review: 7 minutes. Respond: 2 minutes. Resolve: 2 minutes.

PRAYER TEXTS
The Advocate, the Holy Spirit, whom the Father will send in my name, will teach you everything, and remind you of all that I have said to you. (Jn 14:26)

My Father is still working, and I also am working. Indeed, just as the Father raises the dead and gives them life, so also the Son gives life to whomever he wishes. (Jn 5:17, 21)

The tax collector, standing far off, would not even look up to heaven, but was beating his breast and saying, "God, be merciful to me, a sinner!" I tell you, this man went down to his home justified rather than the other; for all who exalt themselves will be humbled, but all who humble themselves will be exalted. (Lk 18:13–14)

You did not choose me but I chose you. And I appointed you to go and bear fruit, fruit that will last, so that the Father will give you whatever you ask him in my name. (Jn 15:16)

Saturday   Program for Life

Preparation Immediately on waking up, I rouse myself to joy by imagining Jesus delighted with my program for life. I will get dressed with thoughts like these.

Opening Prayer I ask for the grace to direct my whole self toward the Trinity.

Desire I desire to create a program for life.[35]

Prayer I read the prayer texts. Then, I draw up an outline of a program for life:

1. What time can I take for enhancing family life? For children? For parents?

2. What time can I take for enhancing work life? For finding God at work in it?

3. What time can I take for enhancing personal life? Recreation? Exercise? Vacation or holiday?

4. What time can I take for prayer life? How often? For personal prayer? Communal prayer?

5. What time can I take for engagement in my church? When? For Eucharist?

6. What time can I take for engagement in my community? What service? When?

7. What time can I take for engagement in my faith life? For a retreat? For a little pilgrimage?

8. Is there a particular spiritual desire, awaiting action, that I have always felt?

9. Is there a particular work of Jesus that I desire to imitate?

10. Is there a particular opportunity I can use in the service of God?

Conclusion After writing my program for life, I examine it as a whole.

I consider my whole self and life in regard to it. Do they enliven each other?

I end by explaining my program for life to Jesus, asking his help.

Our Father.

SPIRITUAL DIRECTION

My program will need to be realistic and sustainable. I want to integrate small actions into my life. I will receive more encouragement and consolation if this does not become a huge, unworkable project.

I can expect some excitement, joy, or sense of rightness with this exercise. I should let these feelings guide me. I can be confident Jesus will supply the strength and fruit of my program.

With life's journey ahead of me, Ignatius proposes I set off in the right direction and, like a pilgrim's ship, "to set ourselves at the arrival port of our pilgrimage, that is in the supreme love of God."[36]

SUGGESTED PRAYER TIME: AS NEEDED

PRAYER TEXTS

I must remind you to frequent the sacraments, to read spiritual books, and to pray with as much recollection as you possibly can. Every day set aside some time so that the soul will not be without its food and, thus, you will not be induced to complain like the one who said "My heart has withered because I have forgotten to eat my bread." (Ps 102:4)[37]

Beloved, whatever is true, whatever is honorable, whatever is just, whatever is pure, whatever is pleasing, whatever is commendable, if there is any excellence and if there is anything worthy of praise, think about these things. Keep on doing the things that you have learned . . . and the God of peace will be with you. (Phil 4:8–9)

In the reform of one's life, one should seek nothing other than the greater praise and glory of God our Lord in and through everything. So it must be borne in mind that a person will make progress in things of the spirit to the degree to which they divest themselves of self-love, self-will, and self-interest. (*Spiritual Exercises* 21)

Like good stewards of the manifold grace of God, serve one another with whatever gift each of you has received. Whoever speaks must do so as one speaking the very words of God; whoever serves must do so with the strength that God supplies, so that God may be glorified in all things through Jesus Christ. (1 Pt 4:7, 10–11)

Sunday   Action in Peace with Love

Desire   I desire to act in peace with love.

Preparation   First I read the prayer texts about peace, compassion, and service.

In the World   I go to a high place overlooking my city, suburb, town, or village. It can be the top of a high building, a scenic lookout, a mountain, an office block, or a tall bridge. I take nothing with me except my program for life.

Once there I invite the presence of God, the Lord of the harvest. I ask to be blessed as I make the Sign of the Cross. Then, casting my eyes over the scene below me, I make all that I see a witness to my desire to act in peace with love.

Then I read my program for life, aloud if possible. I offer it to the Trinity and wait some minutes in silence, imagining the delight of Father, Son, and Spirit as they receive it.

Finally, I look out at all before me and, with love, I see the kingdom of God.

and

In the Eucharist   At the offertory, I use my imagination to place my program for life with the bread and wine as they are taken to the altar. With the prayer of the people, I offer it humbly to God, asking for the strength to carry it out.

At the end of the Eucharist, I imagine God giving me back my program for life, blessing me, and saying with the minister, "Go in peace, glorifying the Lord by your life."

SPIRITUAL DIRECTION

Two spiritual exercises are offered today, reflecting love and service in the world and the Eucharist. In the final days of my retreat I make both exercises. If I am unable to celebrate the Eucharist, then I may fruitfully make just the "In the World" exercise.

St. Ignatius introduced the "Contemplation for Attaining Divine Love" with the note that love is about communication between two lovers, each desiring to give and receive from the other. I began my retreat there. But Ignatius had a second note, appropriate to end my retreat. He said, "It will be good to notice that love ought to find its expression in deeds rather than in words."[38]

SUGGESTED PRAYER TIME: AS NEEDED

PRAYER TEXTS

Priest: May almighty God bless you, the Father, and the Son, and the Holy Spirit.
All: Amen.

Priest: Go in peace, glorifying the Lord by your life.
All: Thanks be to God.[39]

Peace I leave you; my peace I give to you. I do not give to you as the world gives. Do not let your hearts be troubled, and do not let them be afraid. (Jn 14:27)

When [Jesus] saw the crowds, he had compassion for them, because they were harassed and helpless, like sheep without a shepherd. Then he said to his disciples, "The harvest is plentiful, but the laborers are few; therefore ask the Lord of the harvest to send out laborers into his harvest." [He] gave them authority over unclean spirits, to cast them out, and to cure every disease and every sickness. These twelve Jesus sent out with the following instructions: "As you go, proclaim the good news, 'The kingdom of heaven has come near.' Cure the sick, raise the dead, cleanse the lepers, cast out demons. You received without payment; give without payment. Take no gold, or silver, or copper in your belts, no bag for your journey, or two tunics, or sandals, or a staff; for laborers deserve their food. Whatever town or village you enter, find out who in it is worthy, and stay there until you leave. As you enter the house, greet it. If the house is worthy, let your peace come upon it; but if it is not worthy, let your peace return to you. (Mt 9:36–38; 10:1, 5a, 7–13)

Clothe yourselves with love, which binds everything together in perfect harmony. And let the peace of Christ rule in your hearts, to which indeed you were called in the one body. (Col 3:14–15)

INNER PEACE IN
DARKNESS AND LIGHT

By the tender mercy of our God,
the dawn from on high will break upon us,
to give light to those who sit in darkness
and in the shadow of death,
to guide our feet into the way of peace.
—Luke 1:78–79

Thus says the high and lofty one
who inhabits eternity, whose name is Holy:
I dwell in the high and holy place, and also with those
who are contrite and humble in spirit,
to revive the spirit of the humble,
and to revive the heart of the contrite.
I have seen their ways, but I will heal them;
I will lead them and repay them with comfort,
creating for their mourners the fruit of the lips.
Peace, peace, to the far and the near,
says the Lord; and I will heal them.
—Isaiah 57:15, 18–19

The mercy of God, healing, and true freedom are great mysteries. To Ignatius they were part of the mystery of divine love, so he placed surrender to God's tender love at the heart of this retreat.

There are many forms of inner darkness—the pervasive gray of disorder in my life, the unrelenting black of living with evil or the results of sinfulness, the bleak nights of chronic illness or suffering, the dark pit of the unfree where attachments imprison me, and the blinding confusion that the bad spirit can wrap around my eyes.

Some of this darkness is the result of my own actions, some is from the actions of others, and some is no fault of anyone—simply dark places that come with my life's journey. Some may even be spiritual desolation, which Ignatius called "darkness in the soul" (*Spiritual Exercises* 313–16).

If God were only a God of the light, I would be left stranded, blinded, or alienated in the dark, a Lazarus entombed forever. But God is not like this; I am given light when I sit in darkness. God becomes my companion here or leads me into the full light. In either place God the Father offers me his only Son, Jesus, a man who calls himself "light."

Jesus spoke to them, saying, "I am the light of the world. Whoever follows me will never walk in darkness but will have the light of life" (Jn 8:12).

There are many ways into deeper intimacy with God. This retreat is one of them. In the first half, I move through love and sin to mercy and wonder. As I track through the darker side of my humanity, I am given a surer route to wholeness. In powerlessness and vulnerability, I am brought very close to God. Both are powerful places for love to burn bright. After mercy, healing is sought and greater freedom from attachments. Throughout this retreat, God gives light to my eyes and reveals that the great dark is broken forever.

> [God] has rescued us from the power of darkness and transferred us into the kingdom of his beloved Son, in whom we have redemption, the forgiveness of sins. For in him all the fullness of God was pleased to dwell, and through him God was pleased to reconcile to himself all things, whether on earth or in heaven, by making peace through the blood of his cross. (Col 1:13–14, 19–20)

THE RETREAT STRUCTURE

This retreat is a twenty-five-day retreat in daily life. Prayer is made four days a week, preferably Monday to Thursday, for four weeks. Each prayer day includes a time for prayer and reflection after prayer. Together they add up to a daily commitment of about fifty minutes. There are some weekend exercises, and Sunday Eucharist is recommended.

THE RETREAT DYNAMIC

My retreat is to be experienced as a whole, with a dynamic that moves through all four weeks. The daily prayer texts of each exercise have been carefully chosen, as single texts and as an ecology of texts. As single texts, they are part of the spiritual exercise. They provide the content and context of my exercise and my relationship with God. They also shed light on central elements of my faith.

As an ecology of texts, where there is more than one text, each text illuminates the others, offering a progression of meaning, or a contrast of content, or a balance of masculine and feminine experience.

Furthermore, the daily texts provide a meaningful progression throughout the week. They are balanced as a weekly group and are to be prayed in a weekly dynamic. Certain images, actions of God, or sets of grace and desire are developed throughout a week.

In like manner, the exercises of each week as a whole are chosen to guide me through certain movements that are only experienced when I make the full four-week retreat. They deliberately introduce me to many different images of God, inviting a variety of divine relationships and giving me a taste of the extraordinary richness in knowing and loving God.

SPIRITUAL JOURNALING

Ignatius directs: "After finishing the exercise I will either sit down or walk around for a quarter of an hour while I see how things have gone for me during the contemplation or meditation" (*Spiritual Exercises* 77).

For the First Spiritual Exercises, a special journal called the Listening Book is used. It will be essential for remembering and discerning the graces I receive in prayer. The Ignatian Guide to Spiritual Journaling (page 349) outlines how to do this.

SPIRITUAL CONVERSATION

Spiritual conversation, personal or group, is very highly recommended. See the Ignatian Guide to Spiritual Conversation found at the end of this book.

Retreat Map   Inner Peace in Darkness and Light

WEEK ONE   **THE MYSTERY OF LOVE**

Monday   Inner peace

Tuesday   Re-creation

Wednesday   Encouragement

Thursday   Harmony

Saturday   Particular Examen

Sunday   Memory of water

WEEK TWO   **THE MYSTERY OF MERCY**

Monday   Father at work in the world

Tuesday   Spirit at work in my weakness

Wednesday   Light and darkness

Thursday   Jesus at work in tender love

Saturday   Reconciliation Examen

Sunday   Feast for a celebration

WEEK THREE   **THE MYSTERY OF HEALING**

Monday   *Ephphatha*! Be opened!

Tuesday   Stand up and walk!

Wednesday   Tormenting demon, come out!

Thursday   *Talitha cum*, rise!

Saturday   Healing Examen

Sunday   Sabbath for setting free

WEEK FOUR   **THE MYSTERY OF FREEDOM**

Monday   Praise

Tuesday   Reverence

Wednesday   Service

Thursday   Foundation for Life

Friday   Program for Life

Saturday   Awareness Examen

Sunday   Being a light of the world

Week One The Mystery of Love

Monday	Inner peace
Tuesday	Re-creation
Wednesday	Encouragement
Thursday	Harmony
Saturday	Particular Examen
Sunday	Memory of water
	Eucharist

SPIRITUAL DIRECTION

The spiritual exercises of this week are a preparation for the following weeks, for without a heartfelt experience of God's personal love, it is difficult to receive the graces of this retreat. Guilt or disengagement can take the place of a deep openness to God's mercy, healing, and invitation to freedom. Rather, I first need the full embrace of God's love.

So this week I will meet five faces of divine love and pray with two prayer methods. The first method is Imaginative Contemplation; the second, learned at the end, is the Particular Examen. The first sharpens my image of God's action; the second hones my desire.

Ignatius goes into great detail in the first week of the Full Spiritual Exercises, carefully guiding both the method and the content. He assumes everyone is a learner. The same exercises are included in this retreat. So, too, the same content and the same detailed systematic steps of Imaginative Contemplation are deliberately used in every week of this retreat.

For the Thursday exercise on harmony I will need a new article of clothing. Something inexpensive but attractive that I can buy before Thursday.

At the end of the week I learn the Particular Examen for the following weeks.

On Sunday, the Sacrament of Baptism is offered as a source of new life.

Monday   Inner Peace

Preparation	Immediately on waking, I rouse my desire for inner peace by imagining Jesus calming the sea around me. I will get dressed with thoughts like these.
	At my prayer place, I stand, my mind raised up, to consider how God is looking at me with serenity. I make a gesture of reverence and humility.
Opening Prayer	I ask for the grace to direct my whole self toward the Trinity.
Desire	I desire inner peace in the Trinity.
Prayer	I read the prayer texts to understand the power of deep inner peace.
	Using my imagination, I re-create a favorite place where, like Mary, I might sit happily with the Trinity. I imagine the details of place, sounds, smells, etc. Then, as guided below, I hear what each person of the Trinity has to say to me:
	I turn to my Creator. He tells me not to be afraid, that he honors and loves me. I welcome his protection from the fires and floods of my life. I hear his assurance that I will never be abandoned or overwhelmed.
	I turn to Jesus, who takes my fears and troubles in his hands and gives me his peace.
	I turn to the Spirit, the comforter, who invites me to surrender myself to her.
	I rest against the heart of God my Mother. Calm and quiet begin to flow through me.
Conversation	I end in a short conversation with the Trinity, giving thanks.[40]
	Our Father.

SPIRITUAL DIRECTION

This exercise matches Imaginative Contemplation with prayer texts to seek serenity, inner peace, and flowing quiet.

SUGGESTED PRAYER TIME: 30 MINUTES

Preparation: 5 minutes. Opening Prayer: 1 minute. Desire: 1 minute. Prayer: 20 minutes. Conversation: 3 minutes. Listening Book after prayer: 10 minutes.

PRAYER TEXTS

[Martha] had a sister named Mary, who sat at the Lord's feet and listened to what he was saying. But Martha was distracted by her many tasks; so she came to him and asked, "Lord, do you not care that my sister has left me to do all the work by myself? Tell her then to help me." But the Lord answered her, "Martha, Martha, you are worried and distracted by many things; there is need of only one thing. Mary has chosen the better part, which will not be taken away from her." (Lk 10:39–42)

Thus says the LORD, he who created you, O Jacob, he who formed you, O Israel: Do not fear, for I have redeemed you; I have called you by name, you are mine. When you pass through the waters, I will be with you; and through the rivers, they shall not overwhelm you; when you walk through fire you shall not be burned, and the flame shall not consume you. For I am the LORD your God, the Holy One of Israel, your Savior. I give Egypt as your ransom, Ethiopia and Seba in exchange for you. Because you are precious in my sight, and honored, and I love you. (Is 43:1–4a)

Peace I leave with you; my peace I give to you. I do not give to you as the world gives. Do not let your hearts be troubled, and do not let them be afraid. (Jn 14:27)

O LORD, my heart is not lifted up, my eyes are not raised too high; I do not occupy myself with things too great and too marvelous for me. But I have calmed and quieted my soul, like a weaned child with its mother; my soul is like the weaned child that is with me. (Ps 131:1–2)

Tuesday   Re-creation

Preparation   Immediately on waking, I rouse myself to joy by imagining that the new life I need is coming today. I get dressed with thoughts like these. At my prayer place, I stand, my mind raised up, to consider how God is looking at me with creativity. I make a gesture of reverence and humility.

Opening Prayer   I ask for the grace to direct my whole self toward the Creator.

Desire   I desire re-creation in my life.

Prayer   I read the prayer texts to consider the Lord's creative action.

Using my imagination, I re-create the valley of dry bones. In some detail, I add the bones, colors, sounds, smells, etc. At my feet I place the dry bones of my own life: perhaps the bones of a lost dream, a barren relationship, a past hurt, a crippling injustice, or a heart-space of brittle fragility. Then, guided by the points below, I take part in the action of Ezekiel's story:

I enter the scene. The Lord commands me to prophesy. I imagine and experience, step by step, what happens when I say what he commands:

"I lay sinews on you, and cause flesh to come upon you, and you shall live."

"I cause breath to enter you, and you shall live."

"I open your graves, and bring you up from your graves."

"I put my spirit within you, and you shall live."

After imagining God's people come to life, I hear the bones of my own life move. I see them being covered in sinews and flesh. I watch them stand up and enter me. I feel the Spirit of the Lord knit this lost life back into me. I am filled with her breath of life.

Conversation   I end in a short conversation with the Creator, giving thanks.

Our Father. [41]

SPIRITUAL DIRECTION

This exercise is an Imaginative Contemplation in the valley of dry bones, the first prayer text.

SUGGESTED PRAYER TIME: 30 MINUTES

Preparation: 5 minutes. Opening Prayer: 1 minute. Desire: 1 minute. Prayer: 20 minutes. Conversation: 3 minutes. Listening Book after prayer: 10 minutes.

PRAYER TEXTS

The hand of the LORD came upon me, and he brought me out by the spirit of the LORD and set me down in the middle of a valley; it was full of bones. He led me all around them; there were very many lying in the valley, and they were very dry. He said to me, "Mortal, can these bones live?" I answered, "O Lord GOD, you know." Then he said to me, "Prophesy to these bones, and say to them: O dry bones, hear the word of the LORD. Thus says the Lord God to these bones: I will cause breath to enter you, and you shall live. I will lay sinews on you, and will cause flesh to come upon you, and cover you with skin, and put breath in you, and you shall live; and you shall know that I am the LORD." So I prophesied as I had been commanded; and as I prophesied, suddenly there was a noise, a rattling, and the bones came together, bone to its bone. I looked, and there were sinews on them, and flesh had come upon them, and skin had covered them; but there was no breath in them. Then he said to me, "Prophesy to the breath, prophesy, mortal, and say to the breath: Thus says the Lord God: Come from the four winds. . . ." I prophesied as he commanded me, and the breath came into them, and they lived, and stood on their feet, a vast multitude. Thus says the Lord God, I am going to open your graves, and bring you up from your graves, O my people . . . . I will put my spirit within you, and you shall live." (Ez 37:1–10, 12, 14a)

We have this treasure in clay jars, so that it may be made clear that this extraordinary power belongs to God and does not come from us. We are afflicted in every way, but not crushed; perplexed, but not driven to despair. . . . We do not lose heart. Even though our outer nature is wasting away, our inner nature is being renewed day by day. (2 Cor 4:7–8, 16)

Wednesday   Encouragement

Preparation   Immediately on waking, I rouse myself to hope by imagining Jesus encouraging me everywhere today. I get dressed with thoughts like these. At my prayer place, I stand, my mind raised up, to consider how God is looking at me with encouragement. I make a gesture of reverence and humility.

Opening Prayer   I ask for the grace to direct my whole self toward Jesus.

Desire   I desire encouragement.

Prayer   I read the prayer texts of how Jesus always encourages people.

Using my imagination, I re-create the scene of the woman who anointed the feet of Jesus. In detail, I add the people, colors, sounds, smells, etc. Then, guided by the points below, I focus on the people as the scene unfolds:

I become the woman and experience what she desires and experiences. I feel the truth of her relationship with herself. I sense the reactions of Simon and the Pharisees. I become aware of how radically Jesus changes those relationships.

Jesus encourages me to take heart. I consider how he stands up for me and does not condemn. This gives me courage. His profound acceptance opens my heart, and I tell him what I need.

Conversation   I end in a short conversation with Jesus, giving thanks.

Our Father. [42]

SUGGESTED PRAYER TIME: 30 MINUTES

Preparation: 5 minutes. Opening Prayer: 1 minute. Desire: 1 minute. Prayer: 20 minutes. Conversation: 3 minutes. Listening Book after prayer: 10 minutes.

PRAYER TEXTS

May the God of steadfastness and encouragement grant you to live in harmony with one another, in accordance with Christ Jesus, so that together you may with one voice glorify the God and Father of our Lord Jesus Christ. (Rom 15:5–6)

A woman in the city, who was a sinner, having learned that [Jesus] was eating in the Pharisee's house, brought an alabaster jar of ointment. She stood behind him at his feet, weeping, and began to bathe his feet with her tears and to dry them with her hair. Then she continued kissing his feet and anointing them with the ointment. Now when the Pharisee who had invited him saw it, he said to himself, "If this man were a prophet, he would have known who and what kind of woman this is who is touching him—that she is a sinner." Turning toward the woman, [Jesus] said to Simon, "Do you see this woman? I entered your house; you gave me no water for my feet, but she has bathed my feet with her tears and dried them with her hair. You gave me no kiss, but from the time I came in she has not stopped kissing my feet. You did not anoint my head with oil, but she has anointed my feet with ointment. Therefore, I tell you, her sins, which were many, have been forgiven; hence she has shown great love. But the one to whom little is forgiven, loves little." Then he said to her, "Your sins are forgiven. . . . Your faith has saved you; go in peace." (Lk 7:37–39, 44–48, 50)

[Jesus] said to Simon, "Put out into the deep water and let down your nets for a catch." Simon answered, "Master, we have worked all night long but have caught nothing. Yet if you say so, I will let down the nets." When they had done this, they caught so many fish that their nets were beginning to break. So they signaled their partners in the other boat to come and help them. And they came and filled both boats, so that they began to sink. But when Simon Peter saw it, he fell down at Jesus' knees, saying, "Go away from me, Lord, for I am a sinful man!". . . Then Jesus said to Simon, "Do not be afraid; from now on you will be catching people." (Lk 5:4–10)

May our Lord Jesus Christ himself and God our Father, who loved us and by his grace gave us eternal encouragement and good hope, encourage your hearts and strengthen you in every good deed and word. (2 Thes 2:16–17, NIV)

Thursday   Harmony

Preparation	I take a new article of clothing, simple and inexpensive.
Opening Prayer	I ask for the grace to direct my whole self toward Jesus.
Desire	I desire to be clothed in the harmony of love.
Prayer	I take the new article of clothing and place it on my lap. I slowly read the prayer texts to consider how love might clothe me. I bless the clothing, asking God to clothe me in a new self.

I imagine compassion, kindness, humility, meekness, and patience being woven into the thread of my new clothing. Then I see the whole piece, its color, cut, and feel, as one garment of love.

I put it on and feel myself clothed in divine love. After remaining like this for a while, I feel the harmony of love binding me with family, friends, fellow Christians in turn, and even all of humanity and creation.

So held, I imagine the peace of Christ ruling in my heart.

Conversation	I end in a short conversation with the Holy Spirit, giving thanks.

Our Father. [43]

SPIRITUAL DIRECTION

To prepare for my Particular Examen on Saturday, I resolve tomorrow to express my gratitude more often to those who love me.

SUGGESTED PRAYER TIME: 30 MINUTES

Preparation: 5 minutes. Opening Prayer: 2 minutes. Desire: 1 minute. Prayer: 20 minutes. Conversation: 2 minutes. Listening Book after prayer: 10 minutes.

PRAYER TEXTS

You have stripped off the old self with its practices and have clothed yourselves with the new self, which is being renewed in knowledge according to the image of its creator. In that renewal there is no longer Greek and Jew, circumcised and uncircumcised, barbarian, Scythian, slave and free; but Christ is all and in all!

As God's chosen ones, holy and beloved, clothe yourselves with compassion, kindness, humility, meekness, and patience. Bear with one another and, if anyone has a complaint against another, forgive each other; just as the Lord has forgiven you, so you also must forgive.

Above all, clothe yourselves with love, which binds everything together in perfect harmony. And let the peace of Christ rule in your hearts, to which indeed you were called in the one body. And be thankful. Let the word of Christ dwell in you richly; teach and admonish one another in all wisdom; and with gratitude in your hearts sing psalms, hymns, and spiritual songs to God. And whatever you do, in word or deed, do everything in the name of the Lord Jesus, giving thanks to God the Father through him. (Col 3:9–17)

When the soldiers had crucified Jesus, they took his clothes and divided them into four parts, one for each soldier. They also took his tunic; now the tunic was seamless, woven in one piece from the top. So they said to one another, "Let us not tear it, but cast lots for it to see who will get it." This was to fulfill what the scripture says, "They divided my clothes among themselves, and for my clothing they cast lots." (Jn 19:23–24)

As many of you as were baptized into Christ have clothed yourselves with Christ. There is no longer Jew or Greek, there is no longer slave or free, there is no longer male and female; for all of you are one in Christ Jesus. (Gal 3:27–28)

Saturday   Particular Examen

Start of day

I Resolve   Upon rising, I firmly resolve to carefully practice my
                          particular desire today.

During the day

I Mark   I mark each experience of my desire with a simple, sym-
                          bolic action.

End of day

I Ask for Help   I ask God to help me see clearly in my review.

I Review   I review the day to see how God has been working in
                          my particular desire.

I Compare   I compare hour by hour, day by day, week by week, my
                          progress in my desire.

I Resolve   I firmly resolve to act with my desire tomorrow.

                          Our Father.[44]

SPIRITUAL DIRECTION

The Particular Examen focuses on a particular desire. Following Ignatius, "I ask for what I desire more earnestly in connection with particular
things" (*Spiritual Exercises* 199). It may be any holy desire directed to my
good or the service of others. So I might choose to pray this examen if
I have a particular desire but have never known a way to nourish it or
bring it into action.

Or, I might have a particular desire that is revealed through its opposite; for instance, I may notice a destructive pattern of selfishness in a
certain relationship, and now I desire to practice generosity in it.

While I strive to embody my particular desire, I may also ask God to
act through it. This way, God's generosity acts through my generosity.
I allow God to complete all I have been doing through faith (see 2 Thes
1:11–12). With such a wonderful possibility, my day begins and ends
with firm resolve.

To progress more quickly, whenever I realize my particular desire in
the day, I make a small, symbolic body gesture of gratitude. This need
not be public or long, just a symbol that expresses that I have received or
practiced my particular desire.

For my Particular Examen today, I review how I have expressed gratitude to those who love me. Next Monday, I pray the Particular Examen to see what I am doing for Christ in my daily life. I shall need to practice that desire from my rising in the morning until the evening.

SUGGESTED PRAYER TIME: 15 MINUTES

Desire: 1 minute. Review: 10 minutes. Compare: 2 minutes. Resolve: 2 minutes.

PRAYER TEXTS

Pursue love and strive for the spiritual gifts. (1 Cor 14:1a)

We always pray for you, asking that our God will make you worthy of his call and will fulfill by his power every good resolve and work of faith. (2 Thes 1:11)

SPIRITUAL DIRECTION

It is worth considering the "particular" in life. If I want to dance with another person, I need to learn particular steps. If I need to be healed, I go to a particular doctor, look at particular symptoms, and have a particular treatment. If I find a particular thing utterly desirable, I might sell or abandon all I have to get it. If I am lost, I use a particular map to find my way home. When I grieve, it is because I have lost someone I particularly love. Indeed, if I desire to progress in any activity, be it intellectual, musical, sporting, artistic, or spiritual, I need to do particular exercises.

"Particular" is the way I live in depth, the way I search with focus, the way I heal, the way I find, the way I enjoy, the way I choose, and the way I act in union with Christ and others. All these shapes of "particular" are held in the Particular Examen.

Sunday	Memory of Water
Desire	I desire newness of life.
Preparation	I read the prayer texts to penetrate the meaning of Baptism.
In Church/Home	In this exercise I take a little pilgrimage to the baptismal font of my local church. Following the steps below, I bring my Baptism back to life:
	With my hand upon the font, I close my eyes and imagine my Baptism. I see who was there, hear what was said, and consider the actions done. I see myself, a small child held by my parents, or an adult presented by my sponsors.
	After remembering the waters of my Baptism and the life in it, I read the baptismal liturgy from the prayer texts. To better prepare myself for the rest of my retreat, I ask God to bless me now as I renew my baptismal vows.
	Finally, I put on the new article of clothing from my Thursday prayer, remembering I was dressed in a baptismal gown. Then as now, I am putting on Christ. I give thanks for the graces of this week and ask myself how I might express this new life in action.
In the Eucharist	I receive Communion, especially aware that I am a new creation in Christ.

SPIRITUAL DIRECTION

To have more time and quiet, I may make my visit to the font on Saturday rather than Sunday. Depending on the new article of new clothing, I may put it on before I go to church or dress there.

If I am unable to go to a church, I use a large bowl of water at home to symbolize the font. If I am unbaptized, I ask God to bless this bowl of water as a symbol of life. Then, holding it, I share with God what newness of life I desire in my retreat. For greater strength ahead, I may even make some or all of the vows of Baptism if I so desire.

Or going further, if I am unbaptized, I might consider being baptized as a part of my present journey into new life. During or after my retreat, I could enroll for adult Baptism in my local church.

SUGGESTED PRAYER TIME: AS NEEDED

PRAYER TEXTS

Do you not know that all of us who have been baptized into Christ Jesus were baptized into his death? Therefore we have been buried with him by baptism into death, so that, just as Christ was raised from the dead by the glory of the Father, so we too might walk in newness of life. (Rom 6:3–4)

Blessing of the Water

Let us ask God to give new life in abundance through water and the Holy Spirit. We ask you, Father, with your Son to send the Holy Spirit upon the water of this font. May all who are buried with Christ in the death of Baptism rise also with him to newness of life.

Renewal of My Vows

Do you reject sin so as to live in the freedom of God's children? (I do.)

Do you reject the glamour of evil, and refuse to be mastered by sin? (I do.)

Do you reject Satan, father of sin and prince of darkness? (I do.)

Do you believe in God, the Father Almighty, Creator of heaven and earth? (I do.)

Do you believe in Jesus Christ our Lord who was crucified, died, and was buried, rose from the dead, and is now seated at the right hand of the Father? (I do.)

Do you believe in the Holy Spirit, the catholic Church, the Communion of Saints, the forgiveness of sins, the resurrection of the body, and life everlasting? (I do.)

This is our faith. This is the faith of the Church. We are proud to profess it, in Christ Jesus our Lord. Amen. Is this the faith you wish to be baptized in? (I do.)

Baptism

I baptize you in the name of the Father, the Son, and the Holy Spirit. Amen.[45]

So if anyone is in Christ, there is a new creation: everything old has passed away; see, everything has become new! (2 Cor 5:17)

Week Two   The Mystery of Mercy

Monday	Father at work in the world	Particular Examen
Tuesday	Spirit at work in my weakness	Particular Examen
Wednesday	Light and darkness	Particular Examen
Thursday	Jesus at work in tender love	Particular Examen
Saturday	Reconciliation Examen	
Sunday	Feast for a celebration	
	Eucharist	

SPIRITUAL DIRECTION

The exercises of this week will bring me face-to-face with the God of mercy. The Hebrew word *hesed* is more nuanced than "mercy" in English. It can be translated as tender love, loving kindness, steadfast love, loving compassion, even loyalty. It involves a prior commitment and is an action made only in personal relationships. It may be divine forgiveness. The plural form of "womb," *rahamîm*, is also translated as mercy. Here God's mercy is beautifully imaged as a nurturing womb.

Using the prayer forms of Imaginative Contemplation and Meditation this week covers the big stories of my faith—love and sin, resistance and acceptance, sorrow and wonder. The exercises are from the first week of the Full Spiritual Exercises. To move down this path is challenging because I am asked to drop my defenses, to own the patterns of sin and disorder in my life, so that I might experience in depth the mercy of God. Then, seeing my true nature and the nature of God, I come home to the Trinity in vulnerability, sorrow, and utter humility.

This retreat is titled "Inner Peace in Darkness and Light." Ignatius gave these exercises to heighten the dark reality of sin so that the Father's love, through Jesus on the Cross, might be experienced all the more powerfully as a light in the darkness. Ignatius wanted me to contrast the darkness and the light by pointing to the reality of sin outside me and inside me, and to its real consequences.

But in modernity I am deluged with scenes of "hell on earth" in every newscast. I am saturated with the effects of war, greed, conflict, abuse, selfishness, and death. So, in this retreat, while keeping the same content and dynamic, I will consider love at work as the first reality. In this way, the Father's love at work throws the shadows of sin into sharper relief.

His tender mercy puts the sinner, and the effects of sin, literally into a new light. I consider love outside me and inside me, and its real consequences. Saturated in love, I abhor sin and choose life. I become a light in the world.

> If you had walked in the way of God, you would be living in peace forever. Learn where there is wisdom, where there is strength, where there is understanding, so that you may at the same time discern where there is length of days, and life, where there is light for the eyes, and peace. (Bar 3:13–14)

I pray the Particular Examen tomorrow, seeking to do some small action for Christ in the day. The weekend offers the Reconciliation Examen and the Sacrament of Reconciliation as sources of life.

Monday   Father at Work in the World

Preparation

Immediately on waking, I rouse myself to sorrow by standing in the shoes of one who has seriously offended their partner, friend, or superior who has in the past given them many favors. I get dressed with thoughts like these.

At my prayer place, I stand to consider how the Father is gazing at me with mercy. I make a gesture of reverence and humility.

Opening Prayer

I ask for the grace to direct my whole self to the service of the Father.

Desire

I desire the tender mercy of the Father, even while feeling embarrassment and confusion at how little I merit this mercy.

Prayer

I read the prayer texts to consider how the Father works.

Then I consider one person who has become ensnared in a lifestyle of sinful choices or trapped because of one deadly sin. I imagine such a person or, knowing someone like this, I stand back to look objectively at his or her life.

I see how this person's choices created a darkness that moved through his or her life, at home and work, how he or she became unfree, cut off from life. I consider how the person's actions move against his or her lifelong fundamental goodness. I watch how destructive these choices and actions are to others, how they hurt children and families, how corrosive of even past good. I understand this person might be justly condemned. Perhaps I have even grieved to see it.

Now I imagine the effects of the Father's infinite mercy in this person. I watch forgiveness flow through his or her fundamental goodness and see it reawaken. I catch love mending self-worth and watch generosity bud on half-dead relationships. Slowly, a life turns around. All undeserved, sustaining kindness is given in the face of its opposite. I go over this movement of mercy in more detail with my understanding, arousing my feelings as well.

Conversation	I conclude by imagining Christ before me on the Cross. I ask him why he, Lord of all creation, became human, and why he loved me and why he was killed.
	Then I ask myself, "What have I done for Christ? What am I doing for Christ? What ought I to do for Christ?"
	Still seeing him on the Cross, I go over whatever comes to mind.
	Our Father.[46]

SPIRITUAL DIRECTION

I pray the Particular Examen this evening to review what I did for Christ today. Tomorrow my Particular Examen is to feel sorrow for my sins and identify, with wonder, God's mercy in my day.

SUGGESTED PRAYER TIME: 35 MINUTES

Preparation: 3 minutes. Opening Prayer: 1 minute. Desire: 1 minute. Prayer: 20 minutes. Conversation: 10 minutes. Listening Book after prayer: 10 minutes.

PRAYER TEXTS

[I, the LORD,] took [my people] up in my arms. . . . I led them with cords of human kindness, with bands of love. I was to them like those who lift infants to their cheeks. I bent down to them and fed them. (Hos 11:3–4)

My Father is still working, and I also am working. The Father loves the Son and shows him all that he himself is doing; and he will show him greater works than these, so that you will be astonished. Indeed, just as the Father raises the dead and gives them life, so also the Son gives life to whomever he wishes. (Jn 5:17, 20–21)

Jesus said to [the Pharisees], "If God were your Father, you would love me, for I came from God and now I am here. . . . Why do you not understand what I say? It is because you cannot accept my word. You are from your father the devil, and you choose to do your father's desires. He was a murderer from the beginning and does not stand in the truth, because there is no truth in him. When he lies, he speaks according to his own nature, for he is a liar and the father of lies." (Jn 8:42–44)

Tuesday   Spirit at Work in My Weakness

Preparation

Immediately on waking, I rouse myself to sorrow by seeing myself chained, immobilized, and dying by my own choices, before the very Spirit who gave me life and freedom. I get dressed with thoughts like these.

At my prayer place, I stand to consider how the Spirit is gazing at me with mercy. I make a gesture of reverence and humility.

Opening Prayer

I ask for the grace to direct my whole self to the service of the Spirit.

Desire

I desire a mounting and intense sorrow for my sins.

Prayer

I read the prayer texts to understand the wrestle between grace and sin.

I take an overview of my own history of this struggle. Year by year, I recall where I lived, my relationships, and my work. I identify the weeds in my wheat, the reality of my powerlessness, the dark songs in my life.

I consider who I am, lovingly made, an intimate part of all creation, gifted with life, freedom, and responsibility. I am made in the image of God, rich in culture, brimming with unique gifts and life-giving relationships, yet I have diminished myself by the patterns of my personal and social sinfulness.

I consider who God is, the one whose nature, care, and life shine through every gift I have, through the ground of my being and every loving relationship. I trace the Spirit, full of wisdom and power, leading me to a greater good: service of others and deeper humanity. Against this undeniable light, I see the sharp shadows of my disordered desires and bad choices.

In wonder, with surging emotion, I reflect on the Communion of Saints. How have they kept praying for me? The stars, the galaxy, and the elements, the plants and animals, even earth itself—how have they kept me alive until now in the face of my destructive actions? Even my own body, born of stardust, so beautiful in every way, has let me survive in the face of my deadlier choices. More wondrous yet, through all this, the Holy Spirit chose to remain in me.

Conversation	I ask the Spirit for mercy. I thank her for giving me life up till now, proposing to amend my life with her grace.
	Our Father.[47]

SPIRITUAL DIRECTION

I pray the Particular Examen this evening, reviewing moments of sorrow for my sin and times of wonder at God's mercy. For tomorrow's Particular Examen, I want to respond in some small action to the needs of the hungry, thirsty, naked, sick, unwelcomed, or imprisoned.

SUGGESTED PRAYER TIME: 35 MINUTES

Preparation: 5 minutes. Opening Prayer: 1 minute. Desire: 1 minute. Prayer: 25 minutes. Conversation: 3 minutes. Listening Book after prayer: 10 minutes.

PRAYER TEXTS

The Spirit helps us in our weakness; for we do not know how to pray as we ought, but that very Spirit intercedes with sighs too deep for words. And God, who searches the heart, knows what is the mind of the Spirit, because the Spirit intercedes for the saints according to the will of God. (Rom 8:26–27)

Have mercy on me, O God, according to your steadfast love;
according to your abundant mercy blot out my transgressions.
Wash me thoroughly from my iniquity, and cleanse me from my sin.
You desire truth in the inward being;
therefore teach me wisdom in my secret heart.
Create in me a clean heart, O God,
and put a new and right spirit within me.
Do not cast me away from your presence,
and do not take your holy spirit from me.
Restore to me the joy of your salvation, and sustain in me a willing spirit.
A broken and contrite heart,
O God, you will not despise. (Ps 51:1–2, 6, 10, 17b)

Wednesday   Light and Darkness

Preparation

Immediately on waking, I rouse myself to urgency, seeing Jesus ready to show me the real effects of both love and sin. I get dressed with thoughts like these.

At my prayer place, I stand to consider how Jesus is gazing at me with mercy. I make a gesture of reverence and humility.

Opening Prayer

I ask for the grace to direct my whole self to the service of Jesus.

Desire

I ask for an interior sense of the joy felt by those in heaven so that, if lost, powerless, or tempted, I will always remember the love of my eternal Lord.

Prayer

I read the prayer texts to see how actions of love and sin have very real effects.

The first step is to see with the eyes of the imagination the length, breadth, height, and depth of heaven—what is it like? What might I experience?

1. I look with the eyes of my imagination at the great heart of God, at the dance of the risen receiving and giving love. What else do I see?

2. I hear with my ears laughter, bird song, praises, waterfalls, music, and conversations between Jesus and my family and friends. What else do I hear?

3. I smell with my sense of smell new cut grass, the sea, home-cooked food, spring breezes, fragrant oils, and the newborn. What else do I smell?

4. I taste with my sense of taste the sweet things, like homecoming, a stolen kiss, a birthday, a child's wonder, harmony in conscience. What else do I taste?

5. I feel with my sense of touch the caress of intimacy in the Trinity. I feel whole and healed in my body. I embrace those I love. What else touches me?

The second step is to imagine, with the same five senses, the opposite of the above, what I might experience through the effects of sinfulness. So, the image of hell, eternal aloneness, the endless bray of the selfish, the stink of evil, etc.

Conversation	I talk to Jesus, grateful that death has not taken my life. I thank him for his constant, loving kindness, right up to the present moment.
	Our Father.[48]

SPIRITUAL DIRECTION

In my Particular Examen this evening I review how I responded to the needs of the hungry, thirsty, naked, sick, or imprisoned today. In tomorrow's Particular Examen, I desire to see more clearly examples of order and disorder in my city, of love and sinfulness in myself, and of the Trinity in my day.

SUGGESTED PRAYER TIME: 35 MINUTES

Preparation: 5 minutes. Opening Prayer: 1 minute. Desire: 1 minute. Prayer: 25 minutes. Conversation: 3 minutes. Listening Book after prayer: 10 minutes.

PRAYER TEXTS

If your heart turns away and you do not hear, but are led astray to bow down to other gods and serve them, I declare to you today that you shall perish. . . . I have set before you life and death, blessings and curses. Choose life so that you and your descendants may live, loving the LORD your God, obeying him, and holding fast to him. (Dt 30:17–20a)

Now the works of the flesh are obvious: fornication, impurity, licentiousness, idolatry, sorcery, enmities, strife, jealousy, anger, quarrels, dissensions, factions, envy, drunkenness, carousing, and things like these. I am warning you, as I warned you before: those who do such things will not inherit the kingdom of God. By contrast, the fruit of the Spirit is love, joy, peace, patience, kindness, generosity, faithfulness, gentleness, and self-control. (Gal 5:19–23a)

So what advantage did you then get from the things of which you now are ashamed? The end of those things is death. But now that you have been freed from sin and enslaved to God, the advantage you get is sanctification. The end is eternal life. For the wages of sin is death, but the free gift of God is eternal life in Christ Jesus our Lord. (Rom 6:21–23)

Thursday   Jesus at Work in Tender Love

Preparation   Immediately on waking, I rouse myself to hope by recalling that, from my birth, Jesus has never stopped loving me. I get dressed with thoughts like these.

At my prayer place, I stand to consider how Jesus is gazing at me with loving kindness. I make a gesture of reverence and humility.

Opening Prayer   I ask for the grace to direct my whole self to the service of the Trinity.

Desire   I seek to feel the tender love of Jesus.

Prayer   I read the prayer texts to understand the extraordinary depth of God's mercy.

I use my imagination to stand in two vital places. The first place is the foot of the Cross. I enter this scene, imagining the people, actions, and feelings as they unfold. I seek to feel the deep compassion Jesus has for me.

The second place is the door of the empty tomb. Here I seek to feel as Mary Magdalene did when she saw Jesus alive. I take her place, hear Jesus call my name, and go to him. Then I imagine Mary, the Mother of Jesus, joining us. Having earlier met her risen Son, she has joy and tears still shining on her face.

Conversation   The first conversation is with Mary, his Mother, asking her to obtain for me three things from her Son:

1. A felt inner knowledge of the ways I am loved by Jesus and an attraction for them; and a felt inner knowledge for the patterns of my sinfulness and an abhorrence of them.

2. A felt inner knowledge of the order the Spirit brings in my life that I may love it; and a felt inner knowledge for the disorder of my actions, so that finding them abhorrent, I may amend my life. Hail Mary.

3. A felt inner knowledge of the wonders of the world and the universe, that I may rejoice in it; and a felt inner knowledge of the way the world is at its worst, that I may reject its vanities and consumerism.

The second conversation is with the Son, that he may obtain these for me from the Father. Anima Christi.

The third conversation is the same, but to the Father.

Our Father. [49]

SPIRITUAL DIRECTION

I pray the Particular Examen this evening to see how my felt inner knowledge of order and disorder has deepened, how the loving work of the Trinity is more evident, and how I have acted since my prayer.

SUGGESTED PRAYER TIME: 30 MINUTES

Preparation: 3 minutes. Opening Prayer: 1 minute. Desire: 1 minute. Prayer: 15 minutes. Conversation: 10 minutes. Listening Book after prayer: 10 minutes.

PRAYER TEXTS

When they came to the place that is called The Skull, they crucified Jesus there with the criminals, one on his right and one on his left. It was now about noon, and darkness came over the whole land until three in the afternoon, while the sun's light failed; and the curtain of the temple was torn in two. Then Jesus, crying with a loud voice, said, "Father, into your hands I commend my spirit." Having said this, he breathed his last. When the centurion saw what had taken place, he praised God and said, "Certainly this man was innocent." (Lk 23:33, 44–47)

Mary [Magdalene] stood weeping outside the tomb. She turned around and saw Jesus standing there, but she did not know that it was Jesus. Jesus said to her, "Woman, why are you weeping? Whom are you looking for?" Supposing him to be the gardener, she said to him, "Sir, if you have carried him away, tell me where you have laid him, and I will take him away." Jesus said to her, "Mary!" She turned and said to him in Hebrew, "Rabbouni!" (Jn 20:11a, 14–16)

We ourselves were once foolish, disobedient, led astray, slaves to various passions and pleasures, passing our days in malice and envy, despicable, hating one another. But when the goodness and loving-kindness of God our Savior appeared, he saved us, not because of any works of righteousness that we had done, but according to his mercy, through the water of rebirth and renewal by the Holy Spirit. (Ti 3:3–5)

Saturday	# Reconciliation Examen
I Give Thanks	After reading the prayer texts, I stand for a few minutes before the Father, as son or daughter, and feel his compassion as he puts his arms around me.
	I sift the month, with gratitude, for times I have received or given forgiveness.
I Ask for Help	I ask the Spirit to intercede for me with sighs too deep for words.
I Review	I move through the last month, day by day:

1. Before the Father of mercies, I recall if I have rejected or withheld love.

2. In the light of the Lord's forgiveness, I sift my thoughts, words, and actions.

3. With the Spirit, I examine the general direction of my life—my true self.

4. I explore one social structure I belong to, discerning good from the unjust.

5. I bring to Jesus any sin or sinful pattern that has real and deadly consequences in my life.

I Respond	I enter the mystery of the Trinity's reconciling and forgiving love. I humbly express my sorrow for what was revealed above, and ask for forgiveness.
I Resolve	I resolve to take one or more of the following paths to reconciliation:

1. To adjust my lifestyle or work, see a counselor or spiritual director, or deepen my personal, family, and church relationships, so that the Lord may forgive and reconcile me through them.

2. To bring where I need forgiveness to Jesus, and to call on his merciful love.

3. To take any needed reconciling action, for myself or others I have hurt.

4. To receive the Sacrament of Reconciliation, now and monthly if possible.

5. To make, as envoy for Christ, one small act of reconciliation next month.[50]

SPIRITUAL DIRECTION

The Reconciliation Examen above is broadened from the examination of thoughts, words, and deeds suggested by Ignatius. I spend more time on those questions or actions closest to my need.

Ignatius received a revelation on the road to Rome to begin his lifelong service of God. "Before reaching Rome, I was at prayer in a church and experienced such a change in my soul and saw so clearly that God the Father placed me with Christ his Son that I would not dare doubt it."[51] The Christ before Ignatius is Jesus carrying his Cross. The love that he and Ignatius had for one another, their shared vision of God's kingdom, their desire to feed, liberate, and teach the needy, grew into a profound friendship and an effective, shared mission. Ignatius realized anything that fractured, enticed away, or hid this working relationship leaves one in need of loving reconciliation.

SUGGESTED PRAYER TIME: AS NEEDED

PRAYER TEXTS

[Jesus] said to Simon, "Do you see this woman? I entered your house; you gave me no water for my feet, but she has bathed my feet with her tears and dried them with her hair. You gave me no kiss, but from the time I came in she has not stopped kissing my feet. You did not anoint my head with oil, but she has anointed my feet with ointment. Therefore, I tell you, her sins, which were many, have been forgiven; hence she has shown great love . . ." Then he said to her, "Your sins are forgiven . . . . Your faith has saved you; go in peace." (Lk 7:44–50)

The tax collector, standing far off, would not even look up to heaven, but was beating his breast and saying, "God, be merciful to me, a sinner!" (Lk 18:13)

If anyone is in Christ, there is a new creation: everything old has passed away; see, everything has become new! All this is from God, who reconciled us to himself through Christ, and has given us the ministry of reconciliation. (2 Cor 5:17–18)

Sunday   Feast for a Celebration

Desire	I desire to celebrate the mercy of God.
Preparation	I read the prayer texts to marvel at the quality of God's mercy.
In My Home	I celebrate God's wonderful mercy with a special family meal today.
	I wonder, as prodigal son or daughter, how I have "come home" this past week.
In the Eucharist	I imagine myself as the prodigal daughter or son at this Eucharist.
	I become alert, with the confidence and joy of a truly forgiven sinner, to whatever moves me in this Eucharist.
	I celebrate Communion as a feast that the Father desires to give me.

SPIRITUAL DIRECTION

If I am unable to celebrate the Eucharist, I may find a church nearby, or a sacred space, and with a little creativity adapt the Sunday exercise for the same graces.

For my Particular Examen next Monday, I desire a clearer seeing or more attentive listening in my relationships.

SUGGESTED PRAYER TIME: AS NEEDED

PRAYER TEXTS

There was a man who had two sons. The younger of them said to his father, "Father, give me the share of the property that will belong to me." So he divided his property between them. A few days later the younger son gathered all he had and traveled to a distant country, and there he squandered his property in dissolute living. When he had spent everything, a severe famine took place throughout that country, and he began to be in need. So he went and hired himself out to one of the citizens of that country, who sent him to his fields to feed the pigs. He would gladly have filled himself with the pods that the pigs were eating; and no one gave him anything. But when he came to himself he said, "How many of my father's hired hands have bread enough and to spare, but here I am dying of hunger! I will get up and go to my father, and I will say to him, 'Father, I have sinned against heaven and before you; I am no longer worthy to be called your son; treat me like one of your hired hands.'" So he set off and went to his father. But while he was still far off, his father saw him and was filled with compassion; he ran and put his arms around him and kissed him. Then the son said to him, "Father, I have sinned against heaven and before you; I am no longer worthy to be called your son." But the father said to his slaves, "Quickly, bring out a robe—the best one—and put it on him; put a ring on his finger and sandals on his feet. And get the fatted calf and kill it, and let us eat and celebrate; for this son of mine was dead and is alive again; he was lost and is found!" And they began to celebrate. (Lk 15:11–24)

His divine power has given us everything needed for life and godliness . . . so that through them you . . . may become participants of the divine nature. For this very reason, you must make every effort to support your faith with goodness, and goodness with knowledge, and knowledge with self-control, and self-control with endurance, and endurance with godliness, and godliness with mutual affection, and mutual affection with love. Anyone who lacks these things is nearsighted and blind, and is forgetful of the cleansing of past sins. Therefore, brothers and sisters, be all the more eager to confirm your call and election, for if you do this, you will never stumble. For in this way, entry into the eternal kingdom of our Lord and Savior Jesus Christ will be richly provided for you. (2 Pt 1:3–7, 9–11)

Bless the God of all, who everywhere works great wonders, who fosters our growth from birth, and deals with us according to his mercy. (Sir 50:22)

Week Three   The Mystery of Healing

Monday	*Ephphatha*! Be opened!
Tuesday	Stand up and walk!
Wednesday	Tormenting demon, come out!
Thursday	*Talitha cum*, rise!
Saturday	Healing Examen
Sunday	Sabbath for setting free
	Eucharist

SPIRITUAL DIRECTION

There is a profound connection between love, forgiveness, healing, and peace. The exercises of the last two weeks will illuminate the healing exercises this week and vice versa. Our Lord affirms:

> Thus says the high and lofty one who inhabits eternity, whose name is Holy: I dwell in the high and holy place, and also with those who are contrite and humble in spirit, to revive the spirit of the humble, and to revive the heart of the contrite. I have seen their ways, but I will heal them; I will lead them and repay them with comfort, creating for their mourners the fruit of the lips. Peace, peace, to the far and the near, says the LORD; and I will heal them. (Is 57:15, 18–19)

When I pray for healing, my prayers are often for someone in danger of dying. There are only five healing events like this in the gospels. The greater number is for healing the blind, deaf, dumb, paralyzed, or those possessed by demonic spirits. While I may pray to be healed of these disabilities, the cures of the same illnesses also hold great power as metaphors for healing. So I might ask to be healed of a "blindness" in my life, an injustice that keeps me "dumb," a relationship that "paralyzes" me, or a "deadness" that keeps me entombed, and so on. The healing events prayed this week include virtually every healing in the gospels. They have been arranged in groups, of which I pray one event, to take me progressively deeper into the mystery of healing.

One important caution—I will need to be careful if my prayer takes me to a past event that still holds a lot of suffering or strong feelings. I must take Jesus with me. I do not submerge myself in the event, or I will simply be trapped and replay it with all its feelings. I need to stand outside the scene with Jesus, deliberately detach myself, and gently talk to him about my feelings, then and now. He cannot change the past event, but he can heal the meaning of that event for me.

Daily prayer will use the prayer form of Imaginative Contemplation. Also hidden in the prayer texts are many wonderful short prayers, such as, "Lord, Jesus Christ, have mercy on me," and "My Lord and my God." These have enjoyed great use in Christian communities as the Prayer of Desire or Aspiration, short prayers that catch the breath and speed toward God's heart like an arrow.

The weekend introduces the Healing Examen and the Sacrament of the Anointing of the Sick as sources for life.

Monday

Ephphatha! Be Opened!

Preparation

Immediately on waking, I rouse myself to hope by seeing myself as a deaf person, getting ready to go with friends to the roadside, knowing that Jesus will be passing by. I will get dressed with thoughts like these.

At my prayer place, I stand to consider how Jesus is gazing at me with gentle compassion. I make a gesture of reverence and humility.

Opening Prayer

I ask for the grace to direct my whole self to the service of Jesus the healer.

Desire

I desire to see, hear, and speak clearly.

Prayer

I read each of the prayer texts to know how Jesus healed the blind and deaf.

Then I choose *one* of the three healing stories for my prayer. I enter the scene, imagining in some detail the place, weather, people, conversations, and sounds. I experience the actions and feelings as they unfold.

1. If I feel deaf and dumb in a relationship or work situation, I take the place of the deaf and dumb man brought to Jesus. I enter the gospel scene. I sense my friends begging Jesus to lay hands on me. I hear him say, "*Ephphatha*!" that is, "Be opened!" as he opens my ears and tongue. I allow the story to unfold. I hear my first sounds; I speak in wonder.

2. If I feel blind, in some way, wrapped in a cloak, and reduced to sitting on the side of life's road, I take the place of Bartimaeus. I enter the gospel scene. I yell to get the attention of Jesus, "Jesus, Son of David, have mercy on me!" I allow the story to unfold. Now I see.

3. If I have a chronic illness, a draining relationship, or prolonged suffering, I take the place of the blind man guided to Jesus. I enter the gospel scene. I hear Jesus asking, "Can you see anything?" I relive the experience of being half healed, in a halfway place, half alive. I allow the story to unfold. I see clearly.

Then, I surrender my vulnerabilities and healing to the Lord, so that he may better work through me. I offer, if he wills, to help heal and encourage others.

| Conversation | I give thanks to God for my faith, the gift that Jesus declares "makes me well." |

We share our feelings and thoughts.

Our Father.[52]

SPIRITUAL DIRECTION

I pray the Particular Examen this evening, to review moments of clarity in my relationships. For tomorrow's Particular Examen, I desire to be healed of paralysis in my relationships.

SUGGESTED PRAYER TIME: 40 MINUTES

Preparation: 5 minutes. Opening Prayer: 1 minute. Desire: 1 minute. Prayer: 30 minutes. Conversation: 3 minutes. Listening Book after prayer: 10 minutes.

PRAYER TEXTS

They brought to [Jesus] a deaf man who had an impediment in his speech; and they begged him to lay his hand on him. He took him aside in private, away from the crowd, and put his fingers into his ears, and he spat and touched his tongue. Then looking up to heaven, he sighed and said to him, "Ephphatha," that is, "Be opened." And immediately his ears were opened, his tongue was released, and he spoke plainly. They were astounded beyond measure, saying, "He has done everything well; he even makes the deaf to hear and the mute to speak." (Mk 7:32–35, 37)

As [Jesus] and his disciples and a large crowd were leaving Jericho, Bartimaeus son of Timeous, a blind beggar, was sitting by the roadside. When he heard that it was Jesus of Nazareth, he began to shout out and say, "Jesus, Son of David, have mercy on me!" Many sternly ordered him to be quiet, but he cried out even more loudly, "Son of David, have mercy on me!" Jesus stood still and said, "Call him here." And they called the blind man, saying to him, "Take heart; get up, he is calling you." So throwing off his cloak, he sprang up and came to Jesus. Then Jesus said to him, "What do you want me to do for you?" The blind man said, "My teacher, let me see again." Jesus said to him, "Go; your faith has made you well." Immediately he regained his sight and followed him on the way. (Mk 10:46–52)

Some people brought a blind man to [Jesus] and begged him to touch him. He took the blind man by the hand and led him out of the village; and when he had put saliva on his eyes and laid his hands on him, he asked him, "Can you see anything?" And the man looked up and said, "I can see people, but they look like trees, walking."

Then Jesus laid his hands on his eyes again; and he looked intently and his sight was restored, and he saw everything clearly. (Mk 8:22–26)

Tuesday   Stand Up and Walk!

Preparation   Immediately on waking, I rouse myself to hope by imagining Jesus asking me, "Do you want to be made well?" I will get dressed with thoughts like these.

At my prayer place, my mind raised up, I consider how Jesus is looking at me with gentle compassion. I make a gesture of reverence and humility.

Opening Prayer   I ask for the grace to direct my whole self to the service of Jesus the healer.

Desire   I desire to stand up, move, and walk.

Prayer   I read the prayer texts to see how Jesus heals the paralyzed or chronically ill.

Then I choose *one* of the three healing stories for my prayer. I enter the scene, imagining in some detail the place, weather, people, conversations, and sounds. I experience the actions and feelings as they unfold.

1. If I am paralyzed by anger, powerlessness, or despair, I take the place of the sick man found by Jesus at the pool of Beth-zatha. I enter the gospel scene. I hear Jesus ask me, "Do you want to be made well?" I express my feelings about being stuck for so long. I allow the story to unfold. I stand and walk.

2. If I am paralyzed by a life experience, I take the place of the paralyzed man carried to Jesus on a stretcher. I enter the gospel scene. My friends lower me to Jesus, and he says, "Friend, your sins are forgiven." I allow the story to unfold. I hear Jesus say to me, "Stand up, take your mat, and walk." I walk home.

3. If I am paralyzed by an illness or distress, I take the place of the centurion's servant. I enter the gospel scene. I am alone. I hear Jesus say, "Let healing be done for you according to the faith of those who love you." I allow the story to unfold. Paralysis unlocks; I can move.

Then, I surrender my vulnerabilities and healing to the Lord, so that he may better work through me. I offer, if he wills, to help heal and encourage others.

Conversation   I give thanks to God for my faith, the gift that Jesus declares "makes me well."

We share our feelings and thoughts.

SPIRITUAL DIRECTION

I pray the Particular Examen this evening; I review moments of freedom
from paralysis in my relationships. For tomorrow's Particular Examen, I
desire freedom from all that chains me up.

SUGGESTED PRAYER TIME: 40 MINUTES

Preparation: 5 minutes. Opening Prayer: 1 minute. Desire: 1 minute.
Prayer: 30 minutes. Conversation: 3 minutes. Listening Book after
prayer: 10 minutes.

PRAYER TEXTS

In Jerusalem by the Sheep Gate there is a pool, called in Hebrew Beth-
zatha, which has five porticoes. In these lay many invalids—blind, lame,
and paralyzed. One man was there who had been ill for thirty-eight
years. When Jesus saw him lying there and knew that he had been there
a long time, he said to him, "Do you want to be made well?" The sick
man answered him, "Sir, I have no one to put me into the pool when
the water is stirred up; and while I am making my way, someone else
steps down ahead of me." Jesus said to him, "Stand up, take your mat
and walk." At once the man was made well, and he took up his mat and
began to walk. (Jn 5:2–9)

One day, while [Jesus] was teaching . . . the power of the Lord was with
him to heal. Just then some men came, carrying a paralyzed man on a
bed. They were trying to bring him in and lay him before Jesus; but finding no way to bring him in because of the crowd, they went up on the
roof and let him down with his bed through the tiles into the middle of
the crowd in front of Jesus. When he saw their faith, he said, "Friend,
your sins are forgiven you." Then the scribes and the Pharisees began to
question, "Who is this who is speaking blasphemies? Who can forgive
sins but God alone?" When Jesus perceived their questionings, he answered them, "Why do you raise such questions in your hearts? Which
is easier, to say, 'Your sins are forgiven you,' or to say, 'Stand up and
walk'? But so that you may know that the Son of Man has authority on

earth to forgive sins"—he said to the one who was paralyzed—"I say to you, stand up and take your bed and go to your home."

Immediately he stood up before them, took what he had been lying on, and went to his home, glorifying God. Amazement seized all of them, and they glorified God and were filled with awe, saying, "We have seen strange things today." (Lk 5:17–26)

A centurion came to [Jesus], appealing to him and saying, "Lord, my servant is lying at home paralyzed, in terrible distress." And [Jesus] said to him, "I will come and cure him." The centurion answered, "Lord, I am not worthy to have you come under my roof; but only speak the word, and my servant will be healed. For I also am a man under authority, with soldiers under me; and I say to one, 'Go,' and he goes, and to another, 'Come,' and he comes, and to my slave, 'Do this,' and the slave does it."

When Jesus heard him, he was amazed and said to those who followed him, "Truly I tell you, in no one in Israel have I found such faith." And to the centurion Jesus said, "Go; let it be done for you according to your faith." And the servant was healed in that hour. (Mt 8:5–10, 13b)

Wednesday   Tormenting Demon, Come Out!

Preparation

Immediately on waking, I rouse myself to hope by imagining I am trapped and tormented, yet realize that Jesus desires to free me today. I will get dressed with thoughts like these.

At my prayer place, my mind raised up, I consider how Jesus is looking at me with gentle compassion. I make a gesture of reverence and humility.

Opening Prayer

I ask for the grace to direct my whole self to the service of Jesus the healer.

Desire

I desire to be free of inner tormenting demons.

Prayer

I read each of the prayer texts to know how Jesus healed the possessed.

Then I choose *one* of the three healing stories for my prayer. I enter the scene, imagining in some detail the place, weather, people, conversations, and sounds. I experience the actions and feelings as they unfold.

1. If I am desperate, tormented, and unrestrained, always hurting myself or living among the tombs of dead dreams, I take the place of the demoniac. I enter the gospel scene. I hear Jesus say, "Come out of the man, you unclean spirit!" I allow the story to unfold. I am set free.

2. If I am distressed and the child in me is tormented by the past, I take the place of the woman who insisted Jesus heal her daughter. I enter the gospel scene, crying, "Have mercy on me, Lord, Son of David; my daughter is tormented by a demon." I allow the story to unfold. My child is set free.

3. If I am at wits end, tried everything, and the child in me is seized with hurt, I take the place of the father who brings his boy to Jesus. I enter the gospel scene. I cry, "Teacher, I brought you my son. If you are able to do anything, have pity on us and help us." Jesus answers, "All things can be done for the one who believes." Immediately I cry out, "I believe; help my unbelief!" I allow the story to unfold. My child is released.

Then, I surrender my vulnerabilities and healing to the Lord, so that he may better work through me. I offer, if he wills, to help heal and encourage others.

Conversation I give thanks to God for my faith, the gift that Jesus declares "makes me well."

We share our feelings and thoughts.

Our Father.[53]

SPIRITUAL DIRECTION

This evening I pray the Particular Examen, reviewing moments of freedom from the "demons" in my life. For tomorrow's Particular Examen, I desire to seek new life in dead relationships.

SUGGESTED PRAYER TIME: 40 MINUTES

Preparation: 5 minutes. Opening Prayer: 1 minute. Desire: 1 minute. Prayer: 30 minutes. Conversation: 3 minutes. Listening Book after prayer: 10 minutes.

PRAYER TEXTS

[A man with an unclean spirit] lived among the tombs; and no one could restrain him any more, even with a chain; for he had often been restrained with shackles and chains, but the chains he wrenched apart, and the shackles he broke in pieces; and no one had the strength to subdue him. Night and day among the tombs and on the mountains he was always howling and bruising himself with stones. When he saw Jesus from a distance, he ran and bowed down before him; and he shouted at the top of his voice, "What have you to do with me, Jesus, Son of the Most High God? . . . Do not torment me." For he had said to him, "Come out of the man, you unclean spirit!"

Then Jesus asked him, "What is your name?" He replied, "My name is Legion; for we are many." Now there on the hillside a great herd of swine was feeding; and the unclean spirits begged him, "Send us into the swine; let us enter them." So he gave them permission . . . and the herd, about two thousand, rushed down the steep bank into the sea, and were drowned in the sea. . . . Then people came to see what it was that had happened. They came to Jesus and saw the demoniac sitting there, clothed and in his right mind, the very man who had had the legion; and they were afraid.

The man who had been possessed by demons begged him that he might be with him. But Jesus refused, and said to him, "Go home to your friends, and tell them how much the Lord has done for you, and what mercy he has shown you." (Mk 5:3–9, 11–15, 18–19)

A Canaanite woman . . . started shouting, "Have mercy on me, Lord, Son of David; my daughter is tormented by a demon." But [Jesus] did not answer her at all. And his disciples came and urged him, saying, "Send her away, for she keeps shouting after us." He answered, "I was sent only to the lost sheep of the house of Israel." But she came and knelt before him, saying, "Lord, help me." He answered, "It is not fair to take the children's food and throw it to the dogs." She said, "Yes, Lord, yet even the dogs eat the crumbs that fall from their masters' table." Then Jesus answered her, "Woman, great is your faith! Let it be done for you as you wish." And her daughter was healed instantly. (Mt 15:22–28)

"Teacher, I brought you my son; he has a spirit that makes him unable to speak; and whenever it seizes him, it dashes him down; and he foams and grinds his teeth and becomes rigid; and I asked your disciples to cast it out, but they could not do so." [Jesus] answered . . . "Bring him to me." And they brought the boy to him. When the spirit saw him, immediately it convulsed the boy, and he fell on the ground and rolled about, foaming at the mouth.

Jesus asked the father, "How long has this been happening to him?" And he said, "From childhood. It has often cast him into the fire and into the water, to destroy him; but if you are able to do anything, have pity on us and help us." Jesus said to him, "If you are able!—All things can be done for the one who believes." Immediately the father of the child cried out, "I believe; help my unbelief!" . . . [Jesus] rebuked the unclean spirit, saying to it, "You spirit that keeps this boy from speaking and hearing, I command you, come out of him, and never enter him again!" After crying out and convulsing him terribly, it came out, and the boy was like a corpse, so that most of them said, "He is dead."

But Jesus took him by the hand and lifted him up, and he was able to stand. . . . His disciples asked him privately, "Why could we not cast it out?" He said to them, "This kind can come out only through prayer." (Mk 9:17–29)

Thursday   *Talitha Cum*, Rise!

Preparation

Immediately on waking, I rouse myself to hope by seeing myself as one dead, hearing the Lord calling me by name, saying, "Take heart! I will raise you to life." I will get dressed with thoughts like these.

At my prayer place, my mind raised up, I consider how Jesus is looking at me with gentle compassion. I make a gesture of reverence and humility.

Opening Prayer

I ask for the grace to direct my whole self to the service of Jesus the healer.

Desire

I desire to be raised to life.

Prayer

I read each of the prayer texts to know why and how Jesus raised the dead.

Then I choose *one* of the three healing stories for my prayer. I enter the scene, imagining in some detail the place, weather, people, conversations, and sounds. I experience the actions and feelings as they unfold.

1. If I am facing the death of someone I love or of some true part of myself, I take the place of Jairus who repeatedly begs Jesus to heal his dying daughter. I enter the gospel scene, falling at the feet of Jesus, crying, "My little daughter is at the point of death. Come and lay your hands on her, so that she may be made well, and live." I allow the story to unfold. My child awakes to life.

2. If, in some way, I have lost the most important person in my life, I take the place of the widow of Nain. I enter the gospel scene. I see Jesus approach the one I love, touch the coffin, and command, "I say to you, rise!" I allow the story to unfold. He heals me in grief or gives me back the one I love.

3. If a part of me is dead or entombed, I take the place of Lazarus. I enter the gospel scene and hear the prayer of Jesus. I see the stone rolled back. I hear my name with the command, "Come out!" I allow the story to unfold. I am unbound, death lets me go, and I live.

Then, I surrender my vulnerabilities and healing to the Lord, so that he may better work through me. I offer, if he wills, to help heal and encourage others.

Conversation   I give thanks to God for my faith, the gift that Jesus de-
                      clares "makes me well."

                      We share our feelings and thoughts.

                      Our Father.[54]

SPIRITUAL DIRECTION

This evening I pray the Particular Examen, reviewing moments of fresh
life in my relationships.

SUGGESTED PRAYER TIME: 40 MINUTES

Preparation: 5 minutes. Opening Prayer: 1 minute. Desire: 1 minute.
Prayer: 30 minutes. Conversation: 3 minutes. Listening Book after
prayer: 10 minutes.

PRAYER TEXTS

Jairus came and, when he saw Jesus, fell at his feet and begged him repeatedly, "My little daughter is at the point of death. Come and lay your
hands on her, so that she may be made well, and live." So [Jesus] went
with him. [On the way] some people came from the leader's house to
say, "Your daughter is dead. Why trouble the teacher any further?" But
overhearing what they said, Jesus said to the leader of the synagogue,
"Do not fear, only believe." When they came to the house . . . [Jesus] said
to them, "Why do you make a commotion and weep? The child is not
dead but sleeping." And they laughed at him. . . .

He took [the girl] by the hand and said to her, "Talitha cum," which
means, "Little girl, get up!" And immediately the girl got up and began
to walk about. . . . They were overcome with amazement. (Mk 5:22–24a,
35–36, 38–42)

As [Jesus] approached [Nain], a man who had died was being carried
out. He was his mother's only son, and she was a widow. . . . When the
Lord saw her, he had compassion for her and said to her, "Do not weep."
. . . [He] touched the bier . . . and he said, "Young man, I say to you, rise!"
The dead man sat up and began to speak, and Jesus gave him to his
mother. (Lk 7:12–15)

Jesus said to [Martha], "Your brother [Lazarus] will rise again." Martha
said to him, "I know that he will rise again in the resurrection on the
last day." Jesus said to her, "I am the resurrection and the life. Those

who believe in me, even though they die, will live, and everyone who
lives and believes in me will never die. Do you believe this?" She said to
him, "Yes, Lord, I believe that you are the Messiah, the Son of God, the
one coming into the world." When she had said this, she went back and
called her sister Mary, and told her privately, "The Teacher is here and is
calling for you."

When Mary came where Jesus was and saw him, she knelt at his feet
and said to him, "Lord, if you had been here, my brother would not have
died." When Jesus saw her weeping, and the Jews who came with her
also weeping, he was greatly disturbed in spirit and deeply moved. He
said, "Where have you laid him?" They said to him, "Lord, come and
see."

Jesus began to weep. So the Jews said, "See how he loved him!" But
some of them said, "Could not he who opened the eyes of the blind man
have kept this man from dying?" Then Jesus, again greatly disturbed,
came to the tomb. It was a cave, and a stone was lying against it.

Jesus said, "Take away the stone." Martha, the sister of the dead man,
said to him, "Lord, already there is a stench because he has been dead
four days." Jesus said to her, "Did I not tell you that if you believed, you
would see the glory of God?" So they took away the stone.

And Jesus looked upward and said, "Father, I thank you for having
heard me. I knew that you always hear me, but I have said this for the
sake of the crowd standing here, so that they may believe that you sent
me." When he had said this, he cried with a loud voice, "Lazarus, come
out!" The dead man came out, his hands and feet bound with strips of
cloth, and his face wrapped in a cloth. Jesus said to them, "Unbind him,
and let him go." (Jn 11:23–28, 32–44)

Saturday

Healing Examen

I Give Thanks

After reading the prayer texts, I stand before Jesus. He lays his hands on me. I sift the month with gratitude for times I have received or given healing.

I Ask for Help

I ask the Spirit to refresh, anoint, and heal me.

I Review

I move through the last month, day by day:

1. Where am I blind, deaf, dumb, or living a half life?

   Have I blinded or stolen the voice of another?

2. Where am I paralyzed by illness, a life situation, sinfulness, or fear?

   Have I paralyzed another?

3. Where am I tormented by demons, hurting myself?

   Have I demonized another?

4. Where am I dead, drained, grieving, or entombed?

   Have I taken life from another?

I Respond

In God's healing love, I humbly express my particular need, as revealed above.

I Resolve

I resolve to seek healing through one or more of the following paths:

1. To adjust my lifestyle, see a counselor or spiritual director, or deepen my personal, family, and church relationships, so that the Lord may heal me through them.

2. To bring my wounds to Jesus in prayer, that he may clean, heal, and give them new meaning.

3. To take any needed healing action, for myself or others I have hurt.

4. To receive the sacrament of healing now, and monthly if possible.

5. To make, working with the Spirit, one small act of healing next month.

SPIRITUAL DIRECTION

Ignatius wrote no Healing Examen, but this new examen does mirror the Reconciliation Examen. Each of these examens reveals something about the other.

The two last prayer texts are from the Sacrament of the Anointing the Sick. They remember the whole Christian story and make the connection between reconciliation and healing.

I am invited to receive the Sacrament of the Anointing the Sick this week. If possible, pray directly for healing or take a healing action. The Healing Examen can help prepare me for all these. In the "I Review" and "I Resolve" steps above, I spend more time on those questions or actions closest to my need.

SUGGESTED PRAYER TIME: AS NEEDED

PRAYER TEXTS

Is not this the fast that I choose: to loose the bonds of injustice, to undo the thongs of the yoke, to let the oppressed go free, and to break every yoke? Is it not to share your bread with the hungry, and bring the homeless poor into your house; when you see the naked, to cover them, and not to hide yourself from your own kin? Then your light shall break forth like the dawn, and your healing shall spring up quickly; your vindicator shall go before you, the glory of the LORD shall be your rear guard. Then you shall call, and the LORD will answer; you shall cry for help, and he will say, Here I am. (Is 58:6–9a)

The priest will lay hands on your head and anoint your forehead, saying: Through this holy anointing may the Lord in his love and mercy help you with the grace of the Holy Spirit. *Response*: Amen.

He anoints your hands, saying: May the Lord who frees you from sin, save you and raise you up. *Response*: Amen.

Concluding Prayer

Father in heaven, through this anointing grant us comfort in our suffering. When we are afraid, give us courage, when afflicted, give us patience, when dejected, afford us hope, and when alone, assure us of the support of your holy people. *Response*: Amen.[55]

Sunday   Sabbath for Setting Free

Desire   I desire life on the Sabbath.

Preparation   I slowly read the prayer texts to consider being healed in a church.

In My Home   With vividness and detail, I imagine myself in a full church being healed. Then I ask, spending some time on each, the following questions of myself:

1. How do I feel being healed in a church?

2. What healing do I desire? What freedom? Who for?

3. How do I heal the church? What is withered? How can I help?

I conclude with thanksgiving for the graces of this week.

In the Eucharist I imagine myself to be the crippled woman or man attending this Eucharist.

In the "Lamb of God" prayer before Communion, I pray with all my heart, "Lord, I am not worthy that you should enter under my roof, but only say the word and my soul shall be healed."

In Communion, I receive the body and blood of Jesus, confident that he will tenderly and mysteriously heal me.

SPIRITUAL DIRECTION

Prayer this week reveals that faith, union, and healing are inseparable. Indeed, the union between Christ and Church is said to be as deep as sexual intimacy. Life in the Body of Christ, in the Christian community, is always a growth toward wholeness and a sign of our resurrection to come. Ultimately, this is what every healing is really about.

If I am unable to celebrate the Eucharist, I may find a church nearby, or a sacred space, to pray the "Lamb of God" prayer. This prayer comes from the centurion who wanted Jesus to heal his friend (see Mt 8:5–10, 13).

SUGGESTED PRAYER TIME: AS NEEDED

PRAYER TEXTS

[Jesus] was teaching in one of the synagogues on the sabbath. And just then there appeared a woman with a spirit that had crippled her for eighteen years. She was bent over and was quite unable to stand up straight. When Jesus saw her, he called her over and said, "Woman, you are set free from your ailment." When he laid his hands on her, immediately she stood up straight and began praising God. But the leader of the synagogue [was] indignant because Jesus had cured on the Sabbath. . . . The Lord answered him and said, "You hypocrites! Does not each of you on the sabbath untie his ox or his donkey from the manger, and lead it away to give it water? And ought not this woman, a daughter of Abraham whom Satan bound for eighteen long years, be set free from this bondage on the sabbath day?" (Lk 13:10–16)

[Jesus] entered the synagogue, and a man was there who had a withered hand. [The Pharisees] watched him to see whether he would cure him on the sabbath, so that they might accuse him. And he said to the man who had the withered hand, "Come forward." Then he said to them, "Is it lawful to do good or to do harm on the sabbath, to save life or to kill?" But they were silent. He looked around at them with anger; he was grieved at their hardness of heart and said to the man, "Stretch out your hand." He stretched it out, and his hand was restored. (Mk 3:1–5)

No one ever hates his own body, but he nourishes and tenderly cares for it, just as Christ does for the church, because we are members of his body. "For this reason a man will leave his father and mother and be joined to his wife, and the two will become one flesh." This is a great mystery, and I am applying it to Christ and the church. (Eph 5:29–32)

Week Four   The Mystery of Freedom

Monday	Praise
Tuesday	Reverence
Wednesday	Service
Thursday	Foundation for Life
Friday	Program for Life
Saturday	Awareness Examen
Sunday	Being a light of the world
	Eucharist

SPIRITUAL DIRECTION

The meditation called the "First Principle" or "Foundation" is the very first exercise of the Spiritual Exercises. This week I will pray its vision of creation, faith, and freedom. On Thursday, I make two small, sustainable choices that give my life greater freedom and purpose.

The Particular Examen for Monday is for greater acts of praise in my relationships.

In the final days of my retreat I create a program for life and learn the Awareness Examen. Both are sources of new life, and both will carry the graces of my retreat into life after it.

The Awareness Examen has the same structure as the Particular, Reconciliation, and Healing Examens, but it is a "general-purpose" examen unlike the other three "special-purpose" examens. The first four exercises of this week deliberately use the examen structure so that by the end of the week I will have learned the Awareness Examen with unconscious ease.

Monday   Praise

I Enter into the Gift of Praise

I read the prayer texts to contemplate the reality of praise.

I imagine myself in the relationships, becoming the lame man, Elizabeth, or Jesus.

I awaken my praised and praising heart.

I Ask the Holy Spirit for Help

I ask for guidance in this spiritual exercise.

I Journal My Experience of Praise

How, when, and for what do others praise me?

How, when, and for what do I praise myself?

How, when, and for what does the Lord praise me?

I Respond to What Has Emerged

I express to Jesus how I feel when I am praised or praising.

I seek to understand how praise will enhance life.

I praise him.

I Choose for the Future

I contemplate my Listening Book to see what patterns have emerged in point three above:

1. Are there similar gifts? Revealing differences?

2. What consoles me or enlivens me? What desolates or deadens me?

3. Which gifts, revealed in praise, are the most important to me? Which can I do without?

I note these patterns and priorities in my Listening Book.

Our Father.[56]

SPIRITUAL DIRECTION

It is very important that I use my Listening Book for my responses to the questions asked in the third point. Essentially I am moving back through my life experiences, even back to when I was young, to recall and taste my experience of praise. So I give myself significant time to note down my experiences of each question.

In point five, I use the notes I made in my Listening Book for point three. Again, I take the time to find patterns and priorities as outlined above. I circle, underline, and draw connections.

In my Particular Examen tonight, I review moments of praise in my relationships today. In tomorrow's Particular Examen, I desire to act with greater reverence in my relationships.

SUGGESTED PRAYER TIME: 40 MINUTES

Enter the gift of praise: 10 minutes. Ask the Holy Spirit for help: 2 minutes. Listening Book: 13 minutes. Respond: 5 minutes. Choose: 10 minutes.

PRAYER TEXTS

Peter looked intently at [the lame man], as did John, and said, "Look at us." And he fixed his attention on them, expecting to receive something from them. But Peter said, "I have no silver or gold, but what I have I give you; in the name of Jesus Christ of Nazareth, stand up and walk." And he took him by the right hand and raised him up; and immediately his feet and ankles were made strong. Jumping up, he stood and began to walk, and he entered the temple with them, walking and leaping and praising God. (Acts 3:4–8)

When Elizabeth heard Mary's greeting, the child leaped in her womb. And Elizabeth was filled with the Holy Spirit and exclaimed with a loud cry, "Blessed are you among women, and blessed is the fruit of your womb. And why has this happened to me, that the mother of my Lord comes to me? For as soon as I heard the sound of your greeting, the child in my womb leaped for joy." (Lk 1:41–44)

When Jesus had been baptized, just as he came up from the water, suddenly the heavens were opened to him and he saw the Spirit of God descending like a dove and alighting on him. And a voice from heaven said, "This is my Son, the Beloved, with whom I am well pleased." (Mt 3:16–17)

Tuesday   Reverence

I Enter into the Gift of Reverence

I read the prayer texts to contemplate the reality of reverence.

I imagine myself in the relationships, feeling as the wounded man or Jesus felt.

I awaken my reverenced and reverencing heart.

I Ask the Holy Spirit for Help

I ask for guidance in this spiritual exercise.

I Journal My Experience of Reverence

How, when, and for what do others reverence me?

How, when, and for what do I reverence myself?

How, when, and for what does the Lord reverence me?

I Respond to What Has Emerged

I express to Jesus how I feel when I am reverenced or reverencing.

I seek to understand how reverence enhances life.

I reverence him.

I Choose for the Future

I contemplate my Listening Book to see what patterns have emerged in answering point three above:

1. Are there similar gifts? Revealing differences?

2. What consoles me or enlivens me? What desolates or deadens me?

3. Which gifts, revealed in reverence, are the most important? Which can I do without?

I note these patterns and priorities in my Listening Book.

I end with the Our Father.[57]

SPIRITUAL DIRECTION

Reverence means to be in awe of, to show profound respect or veneration of a person. It is to see the Divine in another. It could be for a newborn, a person of great humanity, someone dearly loved, or God. Reverence can be regard, consideration, courtesy, attention, deference, honor, esteem, admiration, homage, or devotion. It implies a special tender care, even for myself.

Again, I give myself significant time with each question in point three. In point five, I use the notes I made in my Listening Book for point three. Again, I take the time to find patterns. There is no rush. I just make connections.

In my Particular Examen tonight, I review moments of reverence in my relationships. In tomorrow's Particular Examen, I desire to act with greater service in my relationships.

SUGGESTED PRAYER TIME: 40 MINUTES

Enter the gift of reverence: 10 minutes. Ask the Holy Spirit for help: 2 minutes. Listening Book: 13 minutes. Respond: 5 minutes. Choose: 10 minutes.

PRAYER TEXTS

Wanting to justify himself, [a lawyer] asked Jesus, "And who is my neighbor?" Jesus replied, "A man was going down from Jerusalem to Jericho, and fell into the hands of robbers, who stripped him, beat him, and went away, leaving him half dead. Now by chance a priest was going down that road; and when he saw him, he passed by on the other side. So likewise a Levite, when he came to the place and saw him, passed by on the other side.

But a Samaritan while traveling came near him; and when he saw him, he was moved with pity. He went to him and bandaged his wounds, having poured oil and wine on them. Then he put him on his own animal, brought him to an inn, and took care of him. The next day he took out two denarii, gave them to the innkeeper, and said, 'Take care of him; and when I come back, I will repay you whatever more you spend.'" (Lk 10:29–35)

Six days before the Passover Jesus came to Bethany, the home of Lazarus, whom he had raised from the dead. There they gave a dinner for him. Martha served, and Lazarus was one of those at the table with him. Mary took a pound of costly perfume made of pure nard, anointed Jesus' feet, and wiped them with her hair. The house was filled with the fragrance of the perfume. (Jn 12:1–3)

Wednesday   Service

I Enter into the Gift of Service

>I read to contemplate the reality of service.
>I imagine myself in the relationships, feeling as a disciple or as Peter felt.
>I awaken my served and serving heart.

I Ask the Holy Spirit for Help

>I ask for guidance in this spiritual exercise.

I Journal My Experience of Service

>How, when, and for what do others serve me?
>How, when, and for what do I serve myself?
>How, when, and for what does the Lord serve me?

I Respond to What Has Emerged

>I express to Jesus how I feel when I am served, when I am serving.
>I seek to understand how service enhances life.
>I offer to serve him.

I Choose for the Future

>I contemplate my Listening Book to see what patterns have emerged in point three above:
>
>1. Are there similar gifts? Revealing differences?
>
>2. What consoles me or enlivens me? What desolates or deadens me?
>
>3. Which gifts, revealed in service, are the most important? Which can I do without?
>
>I note these patterns and priorities in my Listening Book.
>
>I end with the Our Father.[58]

SPIRITUAL DIRECTION

Once again, I give myself significant time with each question in point three. In point five, I use the notes I made in my Listening Book for point three. Again, I take the time to note priorities as outlined above. There is no need to make any decisions.

In my Particular Examen tonight, I review moments of service in my relationships. In tomorrow's Particular Examen, I desire to act with greater freedom in my relationships.

SUGGESTED PRAYER TIME: 40 MINUTES

Enter the gift of service: 10 minutes. Ask the Holy Spirit for help: 2 minutes. Listening Book: 13 minutes. Respond: 5 minutes. Choose: 10 minutes.

PRAYER TEXTS

Let love be genuine; hate what is evil, hold fast to what is good; love one another with mutual affection; outdo one another in showing honor. Do not lag in zeal, be ardent in spirit, serve the Lord. (Rom 12:9–11)

After [Jesus] had washed [his disciples'] feet, had put on his robe, and had returned to the table, he said to them, "Do you know what I have done to you? You call me Teacher and Lord—and you are right, for that is what I am. So if I, your Lord and Teacher, have washed your feet, you also ought to wash one another's feet. For I have set you an example that you also should do as I have done to you." (Jn 13:12–15)

Be strong and of good courage, and act. Do not be afraid or dismayed; for the LORD God, my God, is with you. He will not fail you or forsake you, until all the work for the service of the house of the LORD is finished. (1 Chr 28:20)

Serve one another with whatever gift each of you has received. Whoever speaks must do so as one speaking the very words of God; whoever serves must do so with the strength that God supplies. (1 Pt 4:8-11)

Thursday   Foundation for Life

I Meditate on the Ignatian Foundation Statement

I read the four versions of the Foundation found in the prayer texts. I compare and ponder the four parts in each statement.

Then I consider the Foundation as a whole, to see how each part relates to one great vision.

Finally, I choose a Foundation text that I like.

I Ask the Holy Spirit for Help

I ask for guidance in this spiritual exercise.

I Review My Prayer Experiences of Praise, Reverence, and Service

I read my Listening Book to see what has emerged from the exercises of the last three days:

1. Which gifts are the most important to me? Less important? Which can I do without?

2. Are there similar gifts revealed each day?

3. What consoles me or enlivens me? What desolates or deadens me?

I Respond to What Has Emerged

I respond to my Creator and Lord.

I Resolve to Live with Greater Freedom

With regard to what I have learned in point three, I choose two small, sustainable actions that will give me greater freedom to live as God created me to be:

1. The first is to take one action that frees me for greater praise, reverence, or service.

2. The second is to rid myself of one experience that does the contrary.

Our Father.

SPIRITUAL DIRECTION

The Ignatian "Foundation" statement is a faith vision of all reality. It has been the hidden road map of this week. It is divided into four parts. In part one, I consider how I am created for praise, reverence, and service.

In part two, I consider true freedom. In part three, I consider the balance of indifference. And in part four, I consider my foundational desires and choices.

In point one above, after reading each of the four Foundation statements, I choose the one that best speaks to me.

In point three above, I gather the fruit of the past three exercises. I use my Listening Book to review the insights of the previous three exercises. I underline and draw connections from point five of those days. But this time, I do need to make a decision. This I do in point five.

In point five above, I create a practical list of actions from my review. Then, I read the Foundation text I like. After this, I choose the two practical actions described above. Finally, it is important to check that my choices are realistic, that they fit with my life commitments, and that they confirm who I am.

In my Particular Examen tonight, I review moments of freedom in my relationships.

SUGGESTED PRAYER TIME: 40 MINUTES

Meditate: 10 minutes or as needed. Ask the Holy Spirit for help: 2 minutes. Review: 10 minutes or as needed. Respond: 3 minutes. Resolve: 15 minutes.

PRAYER TEXT 1

The human person is created
to praise,
reverence
and serve God our Lord,
and by so doing save his or her soul;
and it is for the human person that
the other things on the face of the earth are created,
as helps to the pursuit of this end.

It follows from this that the person has to use these things
in so far as they help toward this end,
and to be free of them
in so far as they stand in the way of it.

To attain this, we need to make ourselves indifferent
toward all created things,
provided the matter is subject to our free choice
and there is no prohibition.

Thus for our part we should not want health more than sickness,
wealth more than poverty, fame more than disgrace,
a long life more than a short one—
and so with everything else;
desiring
and choosing
only what leads more to the end for which we are created.[59]

PRAYER TEXT 2

Before the world was made
we were chosen to live in love in God's presence
by praising, reverencing and serving him
in and through his creation.

As everything on the face of the earth exists to help us to do this,
we must appreciate and make use of everything that helps,
and rid ourselves of everything that is destructive
to our living in love in his presence.

Therefore we must be so poised
that we do not cling to any created thing
as though it were our ultimate good,
but remain open to the possibility that love may demand of us
poverty rather than riches, sickness rather than health,
dishonor rather than honor, a short life rather than a long one,
because God alone is our security, refuge and strength.

We can be so detached from any created thing
only if we have a stronger attachment;
therefore our one dominating desire
and fundamental choice
must be to live in love in his presence.[60]

PRAYER TEXT 3

Lord my God,
when your love spilled over into creation
you thought of me.
I am from love, of love, for love.
Let my heart, O God,
always recognize,
cherish,
and enjoy your goodness in all of creation.

Direct all that is me toward your praise.
Teach me reverence for every person, all things.
Energize me in your service.

Lord God,
may nothing ever distract me from your love,
neither health nor sickness, wealth nor poverty,
honor nor dishonor, long life nor short life.

May I never seek
nor choose
to be other than you intend or wish. Amen.[61]

PRAYER TEXT 4

[My name],
the goal of your life is to live with me forever.
I gave you life because I love you.
Your response of love
allows my life to flow into you without limit.
All the things in this world are my gifts,
presented to you so that you can know me more easily
and return your love to me more readily.

I want you to appreciate and use all my gifts
insofar as they help you to develop as a loving person.
But if any of my gifts become the center of your life,
they displace me and so hinder your growth toward your goal.
In everyday life, then, you must hold yourself in balance
before all of my created gifts
insofar as you have a choice and are not bound by some obligation.
You should not fix your desire on health or sickness,
wealth or poverty,
success or failure,
and a long life or a short one.
For everything has the potential of calling forth in you
a deeper response to your life in me.

Your only desire
and one choice should be this:
to want and to choose what better leads
to my deepening my life in you.[62]

Friday	## Program for Life
Preparation	Immediately on waking up, I rouse myself to joy by imagining Jesus delighted with my program for life. I will get dressed with thoughts like these.
Opening Prayer	I ask for the grace to direct my whole self toward the Trinity.
Desire	I desire to create a program for life.
Prayer	I read the prayer texts. Then, I draw up an outline of a program for life:

1. What time can I take for enhancing family life? For children? For parents?

2. What time can I take for enhancing work life? For finding God at work in it?

3. What time can I take for enhancing personal life? Recreation? Exercise? Vacation or holiday?

4. What time can I take for prayer life? How often? Personal prayer? Communal prayer?

5. What time can I take for engagement in my church? When? For Eucharist?

6. What time can I take for engagement in my community? What service? When?

7. What time can I take for engagement in my faith life? A retreat? A little pilgrimage?

8. Is there a particular spiritual desire, awaiting action, that I have always felt?

9. Is there a particular work of Jesus that I desire to imitate?

10. Is there a particular opportunity I can use in the service of God?

Conclusion	After writing my program for life, I examine it as a whole.
	I consider my whole self and life in regard to it. Do they enliven each other?
	I end by explaining my program for life to Jesus, asking his help.
	Our Father.[63]

SPIRITUAL DIRECTION

My program will need to be realistic and sustainable. I want to integrate small actions into my life. I will receive more encouragement and consolation in this than in a huge, unworkable project.

I can expect some excitement, joy, or sense of rightness as I do this exercise. I should let these feelings guide me. I can be confident Jesus will supply the strength and fruit of my program.

With life's journey ahead of me, Ignatius proposes I set off in the right direction, like a pilgrim's ship, "to set ourselves at the arrival port of our pilgrimage, that is in the supreme love of God."[64]

SUGGESTED PRAYER TIME: AS NEEDED

PRAYER TEXTS

I must remind you to frequent the sacraments, to read spiritual books, and to pray with as much recollection as you possibly can. Every day set aside some time so that the soul will not be without its food and, thus, you will not be induced to complain like the one who said "My heart has withered because I have forgotten to eat my bread" (Ps 102:4).[65]

Beloved, whatever is true, whatever is honorable, whatever is just, whatever is pure, whatever is pleasing, whatever is commendable, if there is any excellence and if there is anything worthy of praise, think about these things. Keep on doing the things that you have learned . . . and the God of peace will be with you. (Phil 4:8–9)

In the reform of one's life, one should seek nothing other than the greater praise and glory of God our Lord in and through everything. So it must be borne in mind that a person will make progress in things of the spirit to the degree to which they divest themselves of self-love, self-will, and self-interest. (*Spiritual Exercises* 21)

Be serious and discipline yourselves for the sake of your prayers. Like good stewards of the manifold grace of God, serve one another with whatever gift each of you has received. Whoever speaks must do so as one speaking the very words of God; whoever serves must do so with the strength that God supplies, so that God may be glorified in all things through Jesus Christ. (1 Pt 4:7, 10–11)

Saturday   Awareness Examen

I Give Thanks	I give thanks for the graces, benefits, and good things of my day.
I Ask for Help	I ask the Holy Spirit for help to discern my day with openness.
I Review	I review my day, hour by hour, to see how God is working in my life.
I Respond	I respond to what I felt or learned in my review just made.
I Resolve	I resolve with hope and the grace of God to amend my life tomorrow.
	Our Father.[66]

SPIRITUAL DIRECTION

The Awareness Examen is given at this point of my retreat as a way of prayer after my retreat. It is a wonderful and effective way to keep to my program for life because it sifts my day with gratitude and seeks to discern the traces of God at work in my life. It will guide me with consolations, understanding, and inner peace, and it is made in five steps:

1. I become aware that I live in the stream of God's love—where all is gift. I review my day, recalling its gifts, large and small, and allow gratitude to well up in me.
2. I make a prayer to the Spirit for her discerning light in this examen.
3. I carefully search out how God is working in my life, moving hour by hour, through my day. After some weeks I also look for any pattern of events or relationships that console me or give me inner peace. Conversely, is there a pattern that desolates or deadens me? I begin to see how God works best through me. How may I work best with God?
4. I respond to what I experienced in the previous step. I might give thanks or express sorrow. I might feel wonder, sadness, or sheer delight with my Lord. We speak about this.
5. I consider the loving way forward tomorrow. I may desire growth or transformation. I may resolve to develop some virtue, grace, or gift. I might seek to renew. So I act in response to my new awareness. I will do my best and surrender the outcome to God.

The prayer texts are words of Jesus that speak to each step.

SUGGESTED PRAYER TIME: 15 MINUTES

Thanks: 3 minutes. Help: 1 minute. Review: 7 minutes. Respond: 2 minutes. Resolve: 2 minutes.

PRAYER TEXTS

The Advocate, the Holy Spirit, whom the Father will send in my name, will teach you everything, and remind you of all that I have said to you. (Jn 14:26)

My Father is still working, and I also am working. Indeed, just as the Father raises the dead and gives them life, so also the Son gives life to whomever he wishes. (Jn 5:17, 21)

The tax collector, standing far off, would not even look up to heaven, but was beating his breast and saying, "God, be merciful to me, a sinner!" I tell you, this man went down to his home justified rather than the other; for all who exalt themselves will be humbled, but all who humble themselves will be exalted. (Lk 18:13–14)

You did not choose me but I chose you. And I appointed you to go and bear fruit, fruit that will last, so that the Father will give you whatever you ask him in my name. (Jn 15:16)

Sunday	Being a Light of the World

Desire I desire to be a light of the world.

Preparation I read the prayer texts to see how the light in Christians is at work.

In My Home I take a large candle and light it. I bless it and take it in my hands.

With imagination and desire, I see this light as Jesus, the Light of the World.

I watch its life and its dance, its power to illuminate the truth, its power to dispel darkness.

After five minutes, I see this light as me, called "light of the world" by Jesus.

I watch the flame, my life, and its dance, my power to illuminate truth, and my power to dispel the darkness.

After five minutes, I go over my retreat and bring to mind one gift I have received of love, mercy, healing, or freedom. It may be small. After giving thanks, I imagine this gift is a light, kindled from the very flame in my hands, and see it move out into my relationships and world. Then I bring to mind another gift and do the same, gift after gift, until a river of light moves out into the world.

At the end, after extinguishing the candle, I place it in a special place in my home and conclude with the Our Father.

In the Eucharist I stand at the offertory table in the church and, using my imagination, place upon it a flower, symbol of my retreat graces, and my program for life.

At the offertory procession, I imagine them going up to the altar and I pray:

Take, Lord, and receive all my liberty, my memory, my understanding and my entire will, all that I have and possess. You gave it all to me; to you I return it. All is yours, dispose of it entirely according to your will. Give me only the grace to love you, for that is enough for me. (*Spiritual Exercises* 234)

At the consecration, I see my gifts become a part of the Body of Christ.

> At Communion, I see my gifts shared with the community. At the end of the Eucharist, I imagine God giving me back my program for life, blessing me, and saying with the minister, "Go in peace, glorifying the Lord by your life."

SPIRITUAL DIRECTION

If I am unable to celebrate the Eucharist, I may find a church nearby, or a sacred space, or a symbolic place in the city, to light a candle and make my offering of graces and program for life.

SUGGESTED PRAYER TIME: AS NEEDED

PRAYER TEXTS

I am the light of the world. Whoever follows me will never walk in darkness but will have the light of life. (Jn 8:12)

The people who walked in darkness have seen a great light;
those who lived in a land of deep darkness—on them light has shined.
For the yoke of their burden, and the bar across their shoulders,
the rod of their oppressor, you have broken as on the day of Midian.
(Is 9:2, 4)

[Our Lord Jesus Christ] received honor and glory from God the Father when that voice was conveyed to him by the Majestic Glory, saying, "This is my Son, my Beloved, with whom I am well pleased." You will do well to be attentive to this as to a lamp shining in a dark place, until the day dawns and the morning star rises in your hearts. (2 Pt 1:17, 19b)

You are the light of the world. A city built on a hill cannot be hid. No one after lighting a lamp puts it under the bushel basket, but on the lampstand, and it gives light to all in the house. In the same way, let your light shine before others, so that they may see your good works and give glory to your Father in heaven. (Mt 5:14–16)

INNER PEACE
IN FRIENDSHIP WITH JESUS

The
mountain
may depart and the hills be removed,
but my steadfast love shall not depart from you,
and my covenant of peace shall not be removed,
says the LORD, who has compassion on you.
Seek the LORD while he may be found,
call upon him while he is near.
—Isaiah 54:10; 55:6

Some friends play at friendship but a true friend
sticks closer than one's nearest kin.
—Proverbs 18:24

How often, when asked why I know something or how I got through a particular situation, do I say, "I have a friend who. . . ." This retreat draws on the very ordinary but life-changing experiences of friendship. During it I will experience how Jesus befriends me and others, and how we can both change our lives. Indeed, this retreat is about not just the imitation of Christ but also a friendship born of two people having the same desires and working together.

Jesus is all a best friend can be, yet there is more: this friendship has consequences both human and divine. Friendship between the Father, Jesus, the Spirit, and me is a profound part of creation, the Incarnation, life, love, death, resurrection, salvation, and eternal life itself. It underpins the big story of the universe. I will enter this story in the first and last week of my retreat. The middle weeks are more intimate; they are for deepening my friendship with Jesus.

When Jesus called men and women to be his disciples, several were already friends. Later, solid friendships grew on the road—while working, relaxing, learning, eating, praying, and helping others. But, it was not until the greatest test of friendship, in the garden of Gethsemane and on Golgotha, that he explicitly calls his disciples friends and reveals what it means. There he braids love, sacrifice, shared knowledge, and lasting fruitfulness into friendship. This too will be a part of my friendship with him.

> This is my commandment, that you love one another as I have loved you. No one has greater love than this, to lay down one's life for one's friends. You are my friends if you do what I command you. . . . I have called you friends, because I have made known to you everything that I have heard from my Father. You did not choose me but I chose you. And I appointed you to go and bear fruit, fruit that will last, so that the Father will give you whatever you ask him in my name. (Jn 15:12–16)

After his resurrection, Jesus weaves new cords of love into my friendship with him: vulnerability when he shows me his wounds, gladness when he promises never to leave me, and divine intimacy when he breathes the Spirit into me. I need no longer be afraid. Indeed, this is the goal of my retreat—a friendship with Jesus that gives me meaning, deep inner peace, and real joy in life.

THE RETREAT STRUCTURE

This retreat is a twenty-four-day retreat in daily life. Prayer is made four days a week, preferably Monday to Thursday, for four weeks. Each prayer day includes a time for prayer and reflection after prayer. Together they add up to a daily commitment of about fifty minutes. There are some weekend exercises, and Sunday Eucharist is recommended.

THE RETREAT DYNAMIC

My retreat is to be experienced as a whole, with a dynamic that moves through all four weeks. The daily prayer texts of each exercise have been carefully chosen, as single texts and as an ecology of texts. As single texts, they are part of the spiritual exercise. They provide the content and context of my exercise and my relationship with God. They also shed light on central elements of my faith.

As an ecology of texts, where there is more than one text, each text illuminates the others, offering a progression of meaning, or a contrast of content, or a balance of masculine and feminine experience.

Furthermore, the daily texts provide a meaningful progression throughout the week. They are balanced as a weekly group and are to be prayed in a weekly dynamic. Certain images, actions of God, or sets of grace and desire are developed throughout a week.

In like manner, the exercises of each week as a whole are chosen to guide me through certain movements that are only experienced when I make the full four-week retreat. They deliberately introduce me to many different images of God, inviting a variety of divine relationships and giving me a taste of the extraordinary richness in knowing and loving God.

SPIRITUAL JOURNALING

Ignatius directs: "After finishing the exercise I will either sit down or walk around for a quarter of an hour while I see how things have gone for me during the contemplation or meditation" (*Spiritual Exercises* 77).

For the First Spiritual Exercises, a special journal called the Listening Book is used for remembering and discerning the graces I receive in prayer. The Ignatian Guide to Spiritual Journaling (page 349) outlines how to do this.

SPIRITUAL CONVERSATION

Spiritual conversation, personal or group, is very highly recommended. See the Ignatian Guide to Spiritual Conversation found at the end of this book.

Retreat Map   Inner Peace in Friendship with Jesus

WEEK ONE   JESUS, A FRIEND FOR CREATION

Monday   The Spirit hovers over creation.

Tuesday   The Father raises life in the universe.

Wednesday   The Son is born *Homo sapiens*.

Thursday   I am born in the image of God.

Saturday   Awareness Examen

Sunday   I desire divine relationship.

WEEK TWO   JESUS, A FRIEND FOR EVERY DAY

Monday   Jesus shows me how friends accept.

Tuesday   Jesus shows me how friends receive.

Wednesday   Jesus shows me how friends share.

Thursday   Jesus shows me how friends heal.

Saturday   Healing Examen

Sunday   I desire divine life.

WEEK THREE   JESUS, A FRIEND FOR EVERY TIME

Monday   Jesus shows me how friends listen.

Tuesday   Jesus shows me how friends forgive.

Wednesday   Jesus shows me how friends work.

Thursday   Jesus shows me how friends love.

Saturday   Reconciliation Examen

Sunday   I desire divine intimacy.

WEEK FOUR   JESUS, A FRIEND FOR LIFE

Monday   The Father raises my friend to life.

Tuesday   The Spirit hovers over the friends of Jesus.

Wednesday   The Son calls his friends home.

Thursday   Program for Life

Saturday   Particular Examen

Sunday   I desire divine friendship.

Week One   Jesus, a Friend for Creation

Monday	The Spirit hovers over creation.
Tuesday	The Father raises life in the universe.
Wednesday	The Son is born *Homo sapiens*.
Thursday	I am born in the image of God.
Saturday	Awareness Examen
Sunday	I desire divine relationship.
	Eucharist

SPIRITUAL DIRECTION

The structure of each spiritual exercise this week is the same. Each begins with preparation, including a reading of the scripture texts. In the body of the exercise, there are three steps.

Step 1. The Vision. In this step I use the prayer form of Imaginative Contemplation to see the vision described in the exercise. I set the scene, imagining the place, time, sounds, people, and life. I see the action as the scene unfolds. I need no scientific knowledge or "right way" to imagine each vision. I imagine it in my own way, as I will, with freedom. The four great visions this week are of creation, evolution, the Incarnation, and my birth— each one flowing into the other.

Step 2. The Relationships. In this step I pray with the Prayer of Consideration. Ignatius uses this prayer form to contemplate meanings, comparisons, relish, and consolation prayer (*Spiritual Exercises* 252). Here, I consider the relationships that follow from the vision. I mull over and examine the connections I have with the vision, to see what part I have of it, what difference it makes to me.

Step 3. The Colloquy of the Senses. Ignatius ends a spiritual exercise with a "colloquy" or "conversation" between God and myself. Colloquy means "conversation" in Latin. He suggests we talk as friends. The exercises in this retreat have these friendly conversations, but with a difference—here I will be asked to take a symbol from the heart of my prayer to bless and hold as I converse with Jesus. So this step may be called a "Colloquy of the Senses." This week I will need the following four symbols at hand:

1. Bowl of water
2. Bowl of earth (from my garden)
3. An object owned by my grandparents
4. Hand mirror

The Examen Prayer. Each week I will be given a short Ignatian prayer called the examen. There are four forms of the examen to help me during and after my retreat. This week I will be given the Awareness Examen. As directed, I pray it at the end of the day for the rest of my retreat.

Sunday Spiritual Exercise and Eucharist. After the first week, the Colloquy of the Senses is the only form of Sunday prayer. So that I can experience the progressive graces of the week, each Sunday brings together all the week's prayer symbols. Then, as directed, I take one of them to Sunday Eucharist. This week the symbol will be the "water of creation."

Monday   The Spirit Hovers Over Creation.

Preparation   At my prayer place, I consider how the Spirit hovers over me in her work of continuing creation. I make a gesture of reverence and humility.

I read the prayer texts to anchor myself in the power of divine creativity.

Opening Prayer   With simple words, I offer my whole self to the Spirit.

Desire   I desire to know the creative God.

Prayer   With my imagination, I contemplate the creation of the universe.

First, the vision—I imagine the creation of the universe, 13.7 billion years ago. I see the big bang and the creation of particles and antiparticles, the fundamental forces of gravity, electromagnetism, strong and weak nuclear forces, and the prodigious expansion of everything.

I see, in my own way, protons and neutrons binding in the cooling universe to form hydrogen and helium nuclei, until, at 300,000 years, the first atoms form, and photons of light are released in a sea of radiation. I see the Spirit above and in everything, even in direction itself. I hear, "Let there be light!"

Then, over eons, I see all the elements being progressively created in stars, evermore complex in the burning hearts and explosive deaths.

Second, the relationship—I consider my profound relationship to the beginning of creation. I drink a glass of water. In it I am drinking the hydrogen created in the first moment of creation—for all hydrogen around and within me was created then and none since. I can say, in a very real way, that part of me was there in the beginning.

Every other element in my body was created in generations of stars. Physically, I carry the story of creation within me.

What difference does this make to the way I relate to the universe?

Colloquy of the Senses	In reverence, I take a bowl of water, symbol of the waters of creation. I bless it.

I gently blow over the face of the water, asking myself how I might join in the Spirit's work of loving creation.

I conclude in conversation, as with a friend, by sharing my thoughts and feelings with the Holy Spirit.

Our Father.[67]

SUGGESTED PRAYER TIME: 40 MINUTES

Preparation, Opening Prayer, Desire: 10 minutes. Prayer: 20 minutes. Colloquy of the Senses: 10 minutes. Listening Book after prayer: 10 minutes.

PRAYER TEXTS

In the beginning God created the heavens and the earth. Now the earth was formless and empty, darkness was over the surface of the deep, and the Spirit of God was hovering over the waters. And God said, "Let there be light," and there was light. God saw that the light was good, and he separated the light from the darkness. (Gn 1:1–4, NIV)

Lord, you love all things that exist, and detest none of the things that you have made, for you would not have made anything if you had hated it. How would anything have endured if you had not willed it? Or how would anything not called forth by you have been preserved? You spare all things, for they are yours, O Lord, who love the living. For your immortal spirit is in all things. (Wis 11:24–12:1)

Who has measured the waters in the hollow of his hand and marked off the heavens with a span, enclosed the dust of the earth in a measure, and weighed the mountains in scales and the hills in a balance? Who has directed the Spirit of the LORD, or as his counselor has instructed him? (Is 40:12–13)

At the very dawn of creation your Spirit breathed on the waters, making them the wellspring of all holiness. We ask you, Father, with your Son to send the Holy Spirit upon the water of this font.[68]

Tuesday	**The Father Raises Life in the Universe.**

Tuesday — **The Father Raises Life in the Universe.**

Preparation

At my prayer place, I consider how the Father grew me out of stars, the earth, through evolution, and in my mother's womb. I make a gesture of reverence and humility.

I read the prayer texts to anchor myself in the power of divine generosity.

Opening Prayer With simple words, I offer my whole self to the Father.

Desire I desire to know the life-giving God.

Prayer

With my imagination, I contemplate the creation of sun, earth, and life.

First, the vision—I imagine the first stars grow into galaxies, then spread in filaments and sheets of galaxies. I see 100 billion galaxies expand through time. I contemplate our galaxy as it spins into a spiral and 4.6 billion years ago ignites our sun, which forms the planets. From above I see the earth spinning with violent seas of lava, meteor bombardments, foundling waters, and slowly cooling ecosystems. Life begins in deep, dark, extreme places.

Second, the relationships—I consider my relationship to the unfolding of creation. Static hiss on my radio is the sound of radiation created in the big bang. It surrounds me still in unsuspected intimacy.

I carry within myself the gift of life from the first cells, from tiny bacteria, giving energy and oxygen for the first flourishing. Now, after 3.7 billion years of life on earth, I owe my body's architecture to the sponge and the worm, my sight and spine to the first fish, my hearing and hot blood to early animals. I owe this deep ancestral line to the catastrophic death of species and the wondrous children of sexuality. I owe my body, senses, the primal brain stem, even consciousness, to such emergence in creation.

What difference does this make to the way I relate to all living organisms?

Colloquy of the Senses	In reverence, I take a bowl of earth from my garden, symbol of life. I bless it.

Holding it in my hands, I ponder the trillions of bacteria, millions of protozoa and microbes, thousands of tiny arthropods, and hundreds of larger organisms in it. I roll some of this living earth in my fingers, asking myself how I might join in God's work of nurturing life.

I conclude in conversation, as with a friend, by sharing my thoughts and feelings with the God who is Father and Mother to me.

Our Father. [69]

SUGGESTED PRAYER TIME: 40 MINUTES

Preparation, Opening Prayer, Desire: 10 minutes. Prayer: 20 minutes. Colloquy of the Senses: 10 minutes. Listening Book after prayer: 10 minutes.

PRAYER TEXTS

God said, "Let the waters under the sky be gathered together into one place, and let the dry land appear." And it was so. God called the dry land Earth, and the waters that were gathered together he called Seas. . . . God said, "Let the earth put forth vegetation: plants yielding seed, and fruit trees of every kind on earth that bear fruit with the seed in it." And it was so. . . . And God saw that it was good. And God said, "Let the waters bring forth swarms of living creatures, and let birds fly above the earth across the dome of the sky." So God created the great sea monsters and every living creature that moves, of every kind, with which the waters swarm, and every winged bird of every kind. And God saw that it was good. And God said, "Let the earth bring forth living creatures of every kind: cattle and creeping things and wild animals of the earth of every kind." And it was so. And God saw that it was good. (Gn 1:9–10, 20–24, 25b)

Who commands the sun, and it does not rise; who seals up the stars; who alone stretched out the heavens and trampled the waves of the Sea; who made the Bear and Orion, the Pleiades and the chambers of the south; who does great things beyond understanding, and marvelous things without number[?] (Jb 9:7–10)

Wednesday   The Son Is Born *Homo sapiens.*

Preparation   At my prayer place, I consider how Jesus, as *Homo sapiens*, a human being, shares in my humanity. I make a gesture of reverence and humility.

I read the prayer texts to anchor myself in the power of divine humanity.

Opening Prayer   With simple words, I offer my whole self to Jesus.

Desire   I desire to know the human God.

Prayer   With my imagination, I contemplate the evolution of humanity and Jesus.

First, the vision—I imagine the African forests, 8 to 6 million years ago, and visualize the first hominids, our short, ape-like ancestors, beginning to stand and walk. Various other species appear 3.5 million years ago until two new species arrive, *Homo habilis* and *Homo erectus*, making tools near 2.5 to 2 million years ago. Peking man lives in Asia. And in Europe, 600,000 to 28,000 years ago, Heidelberg man and Neanderthals create art and spirituality.

The first modern humans evolve 195,000 years ago, with larger brains and a talent for exploration. They walk from Africa to Australia 70,000 years ago. From 30,000 to 12,000 years ago, they migrate to Asia, Europe, and the Americas.

Then, 2,000 years ago, in the Middle East—the crossroads of the human species into the rest of the world, the crossroads of civilizations, Asian, Chinese, European, and African, and of empires, Hittite, Babylonian, Egyptian, Persian, Greek, and Roman—in the small village of Bethlehem, Jesus is born.

Second, the relationships—I consider how I share the same ancestors as Jesus; we are directly related. DNA research shows that everyone living today came out of Africa in the last 70,000 years, and had as an ancestor the same woman living 200,000 years ago—including Jesus. Beyond color and culture, we are all profoundly interconnected. Moreover, Jesus entered the seven-million-year-old flow of evolved humanity to be a part of my human story.

What difference does this make to the way I relate to humanity?

Colloquy of the Senses	In reverence, I take an object that belonged to my grandparents, a symbol of my deep humanity. I bless it.

I hold this object to sense and remember all my ancestors in turn, including Jesus. I ask myself how I might join in God's work of evolving humanity.

I conclude in conversation, as with a friend, by sharing my thoughts and feelings with Jesus.

Our Father. [70]

SUGGESTED PRAYER TIME: 40 MINUTES

Preparation, Opening Prayer, Desire: 10 minutes. Prayer: 20 minutes. Colloquy of the Senses: 10 minutes. Listening Book after prayer: 10 minutes.

PRAYER TEXTS

Mary said to the angel, "How can this be, since I am a virgin?" The angel said to her, "The Holy Spirit will come upon you, and the power of the Most High will overshadow you; therefore the child to be born will be holy; he will be called Son of God. And now, your relative Elizabeth in her old age has also conceived a son; and this is the sixth month for her who was said to be barren. For nothing will be impossible with God." (Lk 1:34–37)

Jesus was about thirty years old when he began his work. He was the son (as was thought) of Joseph son of Heli, son of Matthat, son of Levi, son of Melchi, son of Jannai, son of Joseph, son of Mattathias, son of Amos, son of Nahum . . . son of Noah, son of Lamech, son of Methuselah, son of Enoch, son of Jared, son of Mahalaleel, son of Cainan, son of Enos, son of Seth, son of Adam, son of God. (Lk 3:23–38)

In the beginning was the Word, and the Word was with God, and the Word was God. He was in the beginning with God. All things came into being through him, and without him not one thing came into being. What has come into being in him was life, and the life was the light of all people. The light shines in the darkness, and the darkness did not overcome it. And the Word became flesh and lived among us, and we have seen his glory, the glory as of a father's only son, full of grace and truth. From his fullness we have all received, grace upon grace. (Jn 1:1–5, 14, 16)

Thursday   I Am Born in the Image of God.

Preparation

At my prayer place, I consider how my Creator calls me as very good. I make a gesture of reverence and humility.

I read the prayer texts to anchor myself in the power of divine goodness.

Opening Prayer   With simple words, I offer my whole self to the Creator.

Desire   I desire to know the personal God.

Prayer   With my imagination, I contemplate my creation and birth.

First, the vision—I imagine my own birth. I see the city or town where my mother gave birth to me. I watch my family gather around. I imagine the time of day or night, the sound of breathing, of voices of encouragement, the pain as I am born. I hear myself cry out. I am cleaned, wrapped, and placed in my mother's arms, my father beside me. How do I feel?

Now I imagine a new presence. I see the Spirit hovering over me with tender love. In this precious moment I am twice loved—by my parents and my God.

Second, the relationships—I consider how Jesus reveals the Trinity, relating to Father as Son and to the Spirit as God given. He reveals the mystery of three divine persons, Father, Son, and Spirit, living in communion as one God. In the same dance, each gives and receives love, each desires to share life. I consider the creation of the universe as an act of love, and myself as a sign of that love. Astonishingly, I am created in the image of God.

As the self-expression of my Creator, I am like all creation. But unlike all other life, I am an interpersonal being called into relationship with God and free to respond. Jesus becomes human to show me how radically true all this is—that I am born in the image of my parents and my Creator.

What difference does this make to the way I relate to myself?

Colloquy of the Senses

In reverence, I take a hand mirror, the symbol that reveals the face of God. I bless it.

Looking at my own reflection in the mirror, I contemplate the image of God there. After a time, I ask myself how I might better reflect who I am.

I conclude in conversation, as with a friend, by sharing my thoughts and feelings with my Creator.

Our Father. [71]

SUGGESTED PRAYER TIME: 40 MINUTES

Preparation, Opening Prayer, Desire: 10 minutes. Prayer: 20 minutes. Colloquy of the Senses: 10 minutes. Listening Book after prayer: 10 minutes.

PRAYER TEXTS

God said, "Let us make humankind in our image, according to our likeness.". . . So God created humankind in his image, in the image of God he created them; male and female he created them. God saw everything that he had made, and indeed, it was very good. (Gn 1:26a, 27, 31a)

When I look at your heavens, the work of your fingers, the moon and the stars that you have established; what are human beings that you are mindful of them, mortals that you care for them? Yet you have made them a little lower than God, and crowned them with glory and honor. (Ps 8:3–5)

The Lord fashioned human beings from the earth,
to consign them back to it.
He gave them so many days and so much time,
he gave them authority over everything on earth.
He clothed them in strength, like himself,
and made them in his own image.
He made them a tongue, eyes and ears,
and gave them a heart to think with.
He filled them with knowledge and intelligence,
and showed them what was good and what evil.
He put his own light in their hearts
to show them the magnificence of his works,
so that they would praise his holy name
as they told of his magnificent works. (Sir 17:1–3, 5–10, NJB)

All of us, with unveiled faces, seeing the glory of the Lord as though reflected in a mirror, are being transformed into the same image from one degree of glory to another; for this comes from the Lord, the Spirit. (2 Cor 3:18)

Saturday   Awareness Examen

I Give Thanks	I give thanks for the graces, benefits, and good things of my day.
I Ask for Help	I ask the Holy Spirit for help to discern my day with openness.
I Review	I review my day, hour by hour, to see how God is working in my life.
I Respond	I respond to what I felt or learned in my review just made.
I Resolve	I resolve with hope and the grace of God to amend my life tomorrow. Our Father.[72]

SPIRITUAL DIRECTION

The Awareness Examen sifts my day with gratitude and seeks to discern the traces of God at work in my life. It also keeps my eyes open to the deep union I have with creation and life, to the creative friendship I have been living in this week. With the growth of such awareness I will discover the many ways, great and small, that my friendship with God is alive in my daily life.

The Awareness Examen is given here to learn and practice because I will be praying it most nights for the rest of my retreat. It is made with the above structure in five steps:

1. I become aware that I live in the stream of God's love—where all is gift. I review my day, recalling its gifts, large and small, and allow gratitude to well up in me.
2. I make a prayer to the Spirit for her discerning light in this examen.
3. I carefully search out how God is working in my life, moving hour by hour, through my day. After some weeks I also look for any pattern of events or relationships that console me or give me inner peace. Conversely, is there a pattern that desolates or deadens me? I begin to see how God works best through me. How may I work best with God?
4. I respond to what I experienced in the previous step. I might give thanks or express sorrow. I might feel wonder, sadness, or sheer delight with my Lord. We speak about this.

5. I consider the loving way forward tomorrow. I may desire growth or transformation. I may resolve to develop some virtue or grace or gift. I might seek to renew. So I act in response to my new awareness. I will do my best and surrender the outcome to God.

The prayer texts are words of Jesus that speak to each step.

SUGGESTED PRAYER TIME: 15 MINUTES

Thanks: 3 minutes. Help: 1 minute. Review: 7 minutes. Respond: 2 minutes. Resolve: 2 minutes.

PRAYER TEXTS

The Advocate, the Holy Spirit, whom the Father will send in my name, will teach you everything, and remind you of all that I have said to you. (Jn 14:26)

My Father is still working, and I also am working. Indeed, just as the Father raises the dead and gives them life, so also the Son gives life to whomever he wishes. (Jn 5:17, 21)

"The tax collector, standing far off, would not even look up to heaven, but was beating his breast and saying, "God, be merciful to me, a sinner!" I tell you, this man went down to his home justified rather than the other; for all who exalt themselves will be humbled, but all who humble themselves will be exalted. (Lk 18:13–14)

You did not choose me but I chose you. And I appointed you to go and bear fruit, fruit that will last, so that the Father will give you whatever you ask him in my name. (Jn 15:16)

Sunday	## I Desire Divine Relationship.
Preparation	At my prayer place, I consider how Jesus is looking at me as a friend. I make a gesture of reverence and humility. I read the prayer texts to anchor myself in the power of divine relationship.
Opening Prayer	In simple words, I offer my whole self to Jesus, Lord of heaven and earth.
Desire	I desire a divine relationship.
Prayer	With my imagination, I contemplate the Creator and all creatures.

First, the vision—Whenever evolution branches into two new species, those two species share a common ancestor. Here, I imagine the first, universal common ancestor of everything alive; then I see the network of life grow, the prokaryote cell, the world of bacteria, dividing from the eukaryote cell, with its nucleus and DNA. I see algae divide from sponges, vertebrates from invertebrates, insects from millipedes, plants and trees from slime.

Slowly and explosively, life blossoms. I see the amphibians branch from fish, dinosaurs from reptiles, birds from dinosaurs, monkeys from mammals, and so on, until apes and hominids divide from their common ancestor. I watch the whole tree of life growing, branching, dying, budding, reaching out.

Second, the relationships—I consider that I am related to every living creature, from protozoa to hominids, through incredible reaches of time, because I share a common ancestor with all of them. My birth line to the first life on earth is one unbroken chain of parent and child!

As a part of this ancestral life, I am intimately related to the Creator who lives mysteriously within this creation, embracing emergent life as it grows, dies, and changes—calling life itself forth into greater purpose.

What difference does this make to the way I relate to the Creator?

Colloquy of the Senses	In reverence, I place the four symbols of the week in a half circle before me—water, earth, grandparents' object, and mirror. I bless them.
	I sit before them to contemplate the true depth of my relationship with God.
	I conclude in conversation with Jesus my friend. I ask for the consolation of inner peace that comes in this relationship with him.
	Our Father.

SPIRITUAL DIRECTION

I take a little of the "water of creation" from my prayer symbols to a church. I go to the baptismal font and put a few drops on it. I reflect how the water of Baptism symbolizes the water of creation, liberation, and the heart of Jesus. I was baptized in such water.

SUGGESTED PRAYER TIME: AS NEEDED

PRAYER TEXTS

These are the generations of the heavens and the earth when they were created. In the day that the LORD God made the earth and the heavens, when no plant of the field was yet in the earth and no herb of the field had yet sprung up—for the LORD God had not caused it to rain upon the earth, and there was no one to till the ground; but a stream would rise from the earth, and water the whole face of the ground—then the LORD God formed man from the dust of the ground, and breathed into his nostrils the breath of life; and the man became a living being. (Gn 2:4–7)

God said, "See, I have given you every plant yielding seed that is upon the face of all the earth, and every tree with seed in its fruit; you shall have them for food. And to every beast of the earth, and to every bird of the air, and to everything that creeps on the earth, everything that has the breath of life, I have given every green plant for food." And it was so. God saw everything that he had made, and indeed, it was very good. (Gn 1:29–31a)

For you created my inmost being; you knit me together in my mother's womb. I praise you because I am fearfully and wonderfully made; your works are wonderful, I know that full well. (Ps 139:13–14, NIV)

Week Two   Jesus, a Friend for Every Day

Monday	Jesus shows me how friends accept.
Tuesday	Jesus shows me how friends receive.
Wednesday	Jesus shows me how friends share.
Thursday	Jesus shows me how friends heal.
Saturday	Healing Examen
Sunday	I desire divine life.
	Eucharist

SPIRITUAL DIRECTION

The structure of each exercise this week is the same. Each begins with preparation, including a morning-rise awareness prayer and the reading of prayer texts. In the prayer, there are four steps. This week I seek the simple experiences of friendship—accepting, receiving, and sharing. I end with the deeper experience of friendship in healing.

The first two prayer steps reflect that friendship is built on common desires. It grows when friends do things together, and new friendships are created when what is received is shared with another.

Step 1. **Jesus accepts me.** In this step I use the prayer form of Imaginative Contemplation. I choose *one* of the scripture texts and take the place of the one in relationship with Jesus. I set the scene, imaging the place, sounds, conversations, and people. I see the action as the scene unfolds. I imagine it all in my own way. With freedom, I allow the prayer scene to develop as it will.

Step 2. **As a friend of Jesus, I accept others.** Here, I respond to others as Jesus has responded to me. Using my imagination, I bring a person I already know before me. Or, I could bring a stranger, one I know who is in need because of his or her present situation.

Step 3. **I see my part in the great unfolding story of divine friendship—creation, the Incarnation, and eternal life.** I imagine, in detail, how one action in my life has great consequences. I see it set off a chain of relationships and events that reaches deep into the future. I imagine it rippling out for greater good into the mystery of God's continuing creation. This is friendship with Jesus in action.

Step 4. The Colloquy of the Senses. I continue using symbols to hold the heart of my prayer. This week I will need the next four:

1. Ointment (moisturizing cream)
2. Hand towel
3. Loaf of bread
4. Oil (scented massage oil)

The **Examen Prayer.** This week I pray the Awareness Examen. On Saturday I will be given the Healing Examen and encouraged to receive the Sacrament of the Anointing of the Sick.

Sunday Spiritual Exercise and Eucharist. To experience the progressive graces of the week, I bring together the four prayer symbols of the week. Then I take the "bread of sharing" symbol to my Sunday Eucharist or local church.

Monday   Jesus Shows Me How Friends Accept.

Preparation   Immediately on waking, I recall people I know who need acceptance and imagine bringing them to Jesus. I get dressed with thoughts like these.

At my prayer place, I make a gesture of reverence and humility.

Opening Prayer I ask for the grace to direct my whole self to the Jesus who accepts the burdened.

Desire   I desire to accept with Jesus.

Prayer   I read the prayer texts to see how Jesus accepts. Then, in three steps I pray.

1. Jesus accepts me. I choose *one* of the accepting relationships in the prayer texts. I use my imagination to enter the scene as the one in need. I fill in the details of people and conversation. I come to Jesus and let the scene unfold.

2. As a friend of Jesus, I accept others. I use my imagination to bring before me a person I know who yearns to be accepted. I imagine a place and what we might say. I let the scene unfold as I befriend and accept like Jesus.

3. I see my part in the great unfolding story of divine friendship, creation, salvation, and eternal life. Standing back, I imagine, in detail, the effects of my acceptance of the other radiating forward into the long future. I see more and more people, communities, and even earth and its creatures becoming utterly welcomed, accepted, and called into the living realm of God.

Colloquy   In reverence, I take a jar of ointment as a symbol of acceptance. I bless it.

Removing my shoes, I anoint and massage my feet with ointment. Then Jesus and I share how we feel about our friendship. We consider how to bring acceptance to those I have remembered in this prayer.

Our Father. [73]

SPIRITUAL DIRECTION
I pray the Awareness Examen this evening.

SUGGESTED PRAYER TIME: 40 MINUTES

Preparation and Desire: 5 minutes. Prayer step 1: 10 minutes. Step 2: 10 minutes. Step 3: 5 minutes. Colloquy of the Senses: 10 minutes. Listening Book after prayer: 10 minutes.

PRAYER TEXTS

A woman in the city, who was a sinner, having learned that [Jesus] was eating in the Pharisee's house, brought an alabaster jar of ointment. She stood behind him at his feet, weeping, and began to bathe his feet with her tears and to dry them with her hair. Then she continued kissing his feet and anointing them with the ointment. Now when the Pharisee who had invited him saw it, he said to himself, "If this man were a prophet, he would have known who and what kind of woman this is who is touching him—that she is a sinner."

Turning toward the woman, [Jesus] said to Simon, "Do you see this woman? I entered your house; you gave me no water for my feet, but she has bathed my feet with her tears and dried them with her hair. You gave me no kiss, but from the time I came in she has not stopped kissing my feet. You did not anoint my head with oil, but she has anointed my feet with ointment. Therefore, I tell you, her sins, which were many, have been forgiven; hence she has shown great love. But the one to whom little is forgiven, loves little." Then he said to her, "Your sins are forgiven. . . . Your faith has saved you; go in peace." (Lk 7:37–39, 44–48, 50)

Come to me, all you that are weary and are carrying heavy burdens, and I will give you rest. Take my yoke upon you, and learn from me; for I am gentle and humble in heart, and you will find rest for your souls. For my yoke is easy, and my burden is light. (Mt 11:28–30)

But you . . . my friend; you whom I took from the ends of the earth, and called from its farthest corners, saying to you, "You are my servant, I have chosen you and not cast you off"; do not fear, for I am with you, do not be afraid, for I am your God; I will strengthen you, I will help you." (Is 41:8–10a)

Tuesday — Jesus Shows Me How Friends Receive.

Preparation Immediately on waking, I recall people I know who have much to give me and imagine bringing them to Jesus. I get dressed with thoughts like these.

At my prayer place, I make a gesture of reverence and humility.

Opening Prayer I ask for the grace to direct myself to the Jesus who receives.

Desire I desire to receive with Jesus.

Prayer I read the prayer texts to see how Jesus receives. Then, in three steps I pray:

1. Jesus receives me. I choose *one* of the receiving relationships in the prayer texts. I use my imagination to enter the scene as one who receives. I fill in the details of people and conversation. I come to Jesus and let the scene unfold.

2. As a friend of Jesus, I receive others. I use my imagination to bring before me a person I know who has much to give me—either through who they are or with what they have. I fill in the details of place. I imagine what we might say. With humility, I let the scene unfold as I befriend and receive like Jesus.

3. I see my part in the great unfolding story of divine friendship, creation, salvation, and eternal life. I imagine, in detail, the effects of my openness to receive radiating forward into the long future. I see more and more people, communities, and even earth and its creatures receiving what is truly needed, and, in that, receiving the kingdom of God.

Colloquy of the Senses In reverence, I take a hand towel as a symbol of receiving. I bless it.

I place the towel on my lap. I rest both hands on it, palms open to receive. Now Jesus and I share how we feel about our friendship. Then we consider how to receive from those I have remembered in this prayer.

Our Father.[74]

SPIRITUAL DIRECTION

I pray the Awareness Examen this evening.

SUGGESTED PRAYER TIME: 40 MINUTES

Preparation and Desire: 5 minutes. Prayer step 1: 10 minutes. Step 2: 10 minutes. Step 3: 5 minutes. Colloquy of the Senses: 10 minutes. Listening Book after prayer: 10 minutes.

PRAYER TEXTS

Then Jesus poured water into a basin and began to wash the disciples' feet and to wipe them with the towel that was tied around him. He came to Simon Peter, who said to him, "Lord, are you going to wash my feet?" Jesus answered, "You do not know now what I am doing, but later you will understand." Peter said to him, "You will never wash my feet." Jesus answered, "Unless I wash you, you have no share with me." Simon Peter said to him, "Lord, not my feet only but also my hands and my head!" Jesus said to him, "One who has bathed does not need to wash, except for the feet, but is entirely clean. And you are clean, though not all of you."

After he had washed their feet . . . he said to them, "Do you know what I have done to you? You call me Teacher and Lord—and you are right, for that is what I am. So if I, your Lord and Teacher, have washed your feet, you also ought to wash one another's feet. For I have set you an example that you also should do as I have done to you. (Jn 13:3–10, 12–15)

The disciples came to Jesus and asked, "Who is the greatest in the kingdom of heaven?" He called a child, whom he put among them, and said, "Truly I tell you, unless you change and become like children, you will never enter the kingdom of heaven. Whoever becomes humble like this child is the greatest in the kingdom of heaven. Whoever welcomes one such child in my name welcomes me." (Mt 18:1–5)

If you ask anything of the Father in my name, he will give it to you. Until now you have not asked for anything in my name. Ask and you will receive, so that your joy may be complete. (Jn 16:23b–24)

Wednesday   Jesus Shows Me How Friends Share.

Preparation

Immediately on waking, I recall people I know who are in need and imagine bringing them to Jesus. I get dressed with thoughts like these.

At my prayer place, I make a gesture of reverence and humility.

Opening Prayer

I ask for the grace to direct my whole self toward Jesus who gives generously.

Desire

I desire to share with Jesus.

Prayer

I read the prayer texts to see how Jesus shares. Then, in three steps I pray:

1. Jesus shares with me. I choose *one* of the sharing relationships in the prayer texts. I use my imagination to enter the scene as the one receiving. I fill in the details of people and conversation. I come to Jesus and let the scene unfold.

2. As a friend of Jesus, I share with others. I use my imagination to bring before me a person I know in need. I fill in the details of place. I imagine what we might say. I let the scene unfold as I befriend and share like Jesus.

3. I see my part in the great unfolding story of divine friendship, creation, salvation, and eternal life. I imagine, in detail, the effects of my sharing radiating forward into the long future. I see more and more people, communities, and even earth and its creatures sharing with each other what is truly needed.

Colloquy of the Senses

In reverence, I take a loaf of bread as a symbol of sharing. I bless it.

With bread in my hands, Jesus and I say how we feel about our friendship. Then we consider how to share with those I have remembered in this prayer.

Our Father. [75]

SPIRITUAL DIRECTION

I pray the Awareness Examen this evening.

SUGGESTED PRAYER TIME: 40 MINUTES
Preparation and Desire: 5 minutes. Prayer step 1: 10 minutes. Step 2: 10 minutes. Step 3: 5 minutes. Colloquy of the Senses: 10 minutes. Listening Book after prayer: 10 minutes.

PRAYER TEXTS
The day was drawing to a close, and the twelve came to [Jesus] and said, "Send the crowd away, so that they may go into the surrounding villages and countryside, to lodge and get provisions; for we are here in a deserted place." But he said to them, "You give them something to eat." They said, "We have no more than five loaves and two fish—unless we are to go and buy food for all these people." For there were about five thousand men. And he said to his disciples, "Make them sit down in groups of about fifty each." They did so and made them all sit down. And taking the five loaves and the two fish, he looked up to heaven, and blessed and broke them, and gave them to the disciples to set before the crowd. And all ate and were filled. (Lk 9:12–17a)

[Jesus] looked up and saw rich people putting their gifts into the treasury; he also saw a poor widow put in two small copper coins. He said, "Truly I tell you, this poor widow has put in more than all of them; for all of them have contributed out of their abundance, but she out of her poverty has put in all she had to live on." (Lk 21:1–4)

Each of you must give as you have made up your mind, not reluctantly or under compulsion, for God loves a cheerful giver. And God is able to provide you with every blessing in abundance, so that by always having enough of everything, you may share abundantly in every good work.

He who supplies seed to the sower and bread for food will supply and multiply your seed for sowing and increase the harvest of your righteousness. You will be enriched in every way for your great generosity, which will produce thanksgiving to God through us. (2 Cor 9:7–8, 10–11)

Thursday   Jesus Shows Me How Friends Heal.

Preparation Immediately on waking, I recall people I know who need healing and imagine bringing them to Jesus. I get dressed with thoughts like these.

At my prayer place, I make a gesture of reverence and humility.

Opening Prayer I ask for the grace to direct my whole self toward Jesus the healer.

Desire I desire to heal with Jesus.

Prayer I read the prayer texts to see how Jesus heals. Then, in three steps I pray:

1. Jesus heals me. I choose *one* of the healing relationships in the prayer texts. I use my imagination to enter the scene as the one needing healing. I fill in the details of people and conversation. I come to Jesus and let the scene unfold.

2. As a friend of Jesus, I heal others. I use my imagination to bring before me a person I know in need of healing. I fill in the details of place. I imagine what we might say. I let the scene unfold as I befriend and heal like Jesus.

3. I see my part in the great unfolding story of divine friendship, creation, salvation, and eternal life. I imagine, in detail, the effects of my healing radiating forward into the long future. I see more and more people, communities, and even the earth and its creatures being healed.

Colloquy of the Senses In reverence, I take the scented oil, symbol of healing. I bless it.

I anoint and massage my hands, bring them to my face, and smell deeply.

Within the scent of healing, Jesus and I share how we feel about our friendship. Then we consider how to heal those I have remembered in this prayer.

Our Father. [76]

SPIRITUAL DIRECTION
I pray the Awareness Examen this evening.

SUGGESTED PRAYER TIME: 40 MINUTES

Preparation and Desire: 5 minutes. Prayer step 1: 10 minutes. Step 2: 10 minutes. Step 3: 5 minutes. Colloquy of the Senses: 10 minutes. Listening Book after prayer: 10 minutes.

PRAYER TEXTS

There was a woman who had been suffering from hemorrhages for twelve years. She had endured much under many physicians, and had spent all that she had; and she was no better, but rather grew worse. She had heard about Jesus, and came up behind him in the crowd and touched his cloak, for she said, "If I but touch his clothes, I will be made well." Immediately her hemorrhage stopped; and she felt in her body that she was healed of her disease. Immediately aware that power had gone forth from him, Jesus turned about in the crowd and said, "Who touched my clothes?" And his disciples said to him, "You see the crowd pressing in on you; how can you say, 'Who touched me?'" He looked all around to see who had done it. But the woman, knowing what had happened to her, came in fear and trembling, fell down before him, and told him the whole truth. He said to her, "Daughter, your faith has made you well; go in peace, and be healed of your disease." (Mk 5:25–34)

Just then some men came, carrying a paralyzed man on a bed. They were trying to bring him in and lay him before Jesus; but finding no way to bring him in because of the crowd, they went up on the roof and let him down with his bed through the tiles into the middle of the crowd in front of Jesus. When he saw their faith, he said, "Friend, your sins are forgiven you." Then the scribes and the Pharisees began to question, "Who is this who is speaking blasphemies? Who can forgive sins but God alone?" When Jesus perceived their questionings, he answered them, "Why do you raise such questions in your hearts? Which is easier, to say, 'Your sins are forgiven you,' or to say, 'Stand up and walk'? But so that you may know that the Son of Man has authority on earth to forgive sins"— he said to the one who was paralyzed—"I say to you, stand up and take your bed and go to your home." Immediately he stood up before them, took what he had been lying on, and went to his home, glorifying God. (Lk 5:18–25)

Saturday   Healing Examen

I Give Thanks   After reading the prayer texts, I stand before Jesus. He lays his hands on me. I sift the month with gratitude for times I have received or given healing.

I Ask for Help   I ask the Spirit to refresh, anoint, and heal me.

I Review   I move through the last month, day by day:

1. Where am I blind, deaf, dumb, or living a half life?

   Have I blinded or stolen the voice of another?

2. Where am I paralyzed by illness, a life situation, sinfulness, or fear?

   Have I paralyzed another?

3. Where am I tormented by demons, hurting myself?

   Have I demonized another?

4. Where am I dead, drained, grieving, or entombed?

   Have I taken life from another?

I Respond   In God's healing love, I humbly express my particular need, as revealed above.

I Resolve   I resolve to seek healing through one or more of the following paths:

1. To adjust my lifestyle, see a counselor or spiritual director, or deepen my personal, family, and church relationships, so the Lord may heal me through them.

2. To bring my wounds to Jesus in prayer, that he may clean, heal, and give them new meaning.

3. To take any needed healing action, for myself, or others I have hurt.

4. To receive the sacrament of healing now, and monthly if possible.

5. To make, by working with the Spirit, one small act of healing next month.

SPIRITUAL DIRECTION

Ignatius wrote no Healing Examen, but this new examen does mirror the Reconciliation Examen. Each examen reveals something about the other.

The two last prayer texts are from the Sacrament of the Anointing of the Sick. They remember the whole Christian story and make the connection between reconciliation and healing.

I am invited to receive the sacrament of healing this week. If possible, pray directly for healing or take a healing action. The Healing Examen can help prepare me for all these. In the "I Review" and "I Resolve" steps above, I spend more time on those questions or actions closest to my need.

SUGGESTED PRAYER TIME: AS NEEDED

PRAYER TEXTS

Is not this the fast that I choose: to loose the bonds of injustice, to undo the thongs of the yoke, to let the oppressed go free, and to break every yoke? Is it not to share your bread with the hungry, and bring the homeless poor into your house; when you see the naked, to cover them, and not to hide yourself from your own kin? Then your light shall break forth like the dawn, and your healing shall spring up quickly; your vindicator shall go before you, the glory of the LORD shall be your rear guard. Then you shall call, and the LORD will answer; you shall cry for help, and he will say, Here I am. (Is 58:6–9a)

The priest will lay hands on your head and anoint your forehead, saying: Through this holy anointing may the Lord in his love and mercy help you with the grace of the Holy Spirit. *Response*: Amen.

He anoints your hands, saying: May the Lord who frees you from sin, save you and raise you up. *Response*: Amen.

Concluding Prayer
Father in heaven, through this anointing grant us comfort in our suffering. When we are afraid, give us courage, when afflicted, give us patience, when dejected, afford us hope, and when alone, assure us of the support of your holy people. *Response*: Amen.[77]

Sunday   I Desire Divine Life.

Preparation	At my prayer place, I consider how Jesus is looking at me as a friend. I make a gesture of reverence and humility. I read the prayer texts to anchor myself in the power of divine life.
Opening Prayer	In simple words, I offer my whole self to Jesus, Lord of life.
Desire	I desire a deeper divine life.
Colloquy of the Senses	In reverence, I place the week's four prayer symbols in a half circle before me—ointment, towel, bread, and oil. I bless them.
	I sit in front of them and contemplate the depth of life from God.
	I conclude in conversation with Jesus my friend. I ask for the consolation of inner peace that comes in this life with him.
	Our Father.
Eucharist	I seek the same life in Sunday Eucharist.

SPIRITUAL DIRECTION

Moving from one symbol to another, I reflect upon how friendship with Jesus is built upon mutual acceptance, receiving, sharing, and healing. Then I consider the whole—how these relationships give life in abundance.

In the Sunday Eucharist, I imagine my "bread of sharing" placed on the offertory table. I see it offered with the bread of the Eucharist. I receive it back in Communion. During the Eucharist I link the personal graces of my prayer this week with the communal graces of Sunday Eucharist.

If I am unable to celebrate the Eucharist, I choose another sacred place, or place special to me, and creatively adapt the exercise for the same graces.

SUGGESTED PRAYER TIME: AS NEEDED

PRAYER TEXTS

Jesus said to them, "Very truly, I tell you, it was not Moses who gave you the bread from heaven, but it is my Father who gives you the true bread from heaven. For the bread of God is that which comes down from heaven and gives life to the world." They said to him, "Sir, give us this bread always."

Jesus said to them, "I am the bread of life. Whoever comes to me will never be hungry, and whoever believes in me will never be thirsty. This is indeed the will of my Father, that all who see the Son and believe in him may have eternal life; and I will raise them up on the last day." (Jn 6:32–38, 40)

[Jesus] said also to the one who had invited him [to dinner], "When you give a luncheon or a dinner, do not invite your friends or your brothers or your relatives or rich neighbors, in case they may invite you in return, and you would be repaid. But when you give a banquet, invite the poor, the crippled, the lame, and the blind. And you will be blessed, because they cannot repay you, for you will be repaid at the resurrection of the righteous." (Lk 14:12–14)

Jesus said to them, "Very truly, I tell you, unless you eat the flesh of the Son of Man and drink his blood, you have no life in you. Those who eat my flesh and drink my blood have eternal life, and I will raise them up on the last day; for my flesh is true food and my blood is true drink. Those who eat my flesh and drink my blood abide in me, and I in them." When many of his disciples heard it, they said, "This teaching is difficult; who can accept it?" (Jn 6:53–56, 60)

Week Three   Jesus, a Friend for Every Time

Monday	Jesus shows me how friends listen.
Tuesday	Jesus shows me how friends forgive.
Wednesday	Jesus shows me how friends work.
Thursday	Jesus shows me how friends love.
Saturday	Reconciliation Examen
Sunday	I desire divine intimacy.
	Eucharist

SPIRITUAL DIRECTION

The structure of each exercise this week is the same as last week. This week the spiritual exercises take my friendship with Jesus to another level. I pray through the powerful movements of listening, forgiving, working together, and love in friendship.

Step 1. **Jesus listens to me.** In this step I use the prayer form of Imaginative Contemplation. I choose *one* of the scripture texts and take the place of the one in relationship with Jesus. I set the scene, imagining the place, sounds, conversations, and people. I see the action as the scene unfolds. I imagine it all in my own way. With freedom, I allow the prayer scene to develop as it will.

Step 2. **As a friend of Jesus, I accept others.** Here, I respond to others as Jesus has responded to me. Using my imagination, I bring a person I already know before me. Or, I could bring a stranger, one I know who is in need because of his or her present situation.

Step 3. **I see my part in the great unfolding story of divine friendship, creation, salvation, and eternal life.** I imagine, in detail, how one action in my life has great consequences. I see it set off a chain of relationships and events that reaches deep into the future. I imagine it rippling out for greater good in the mystery of God's continuing creation. This is friendship with Jesus in action.

Step 4. **The Colloquy of the Senses.** I continue using symbols to hold the heart of my prayer. This week I will need the next four symbols at hand:

1. Seeds
2. Ring
3. Fruit
4. Cross.

The Examen Prayer. This week I will be given the Reconciliation Examen. I am also encouraged to receive the Sacrament of Reconciliation or make an act of reconciliation.

Sunday Spiritual Exercise and Eucharist. To experience the progressive graces of the week I bring together the four prayer symbols of the week. Then I take the "cross of love" symbol to my Sunday Eucharist or local church.

Monday   Jesus Shows Me How Friends Listen.

Preparation   Immediately on waking, I recall people I know who need a good listener and imagine bringing them to Jesus. I get dressed with thoughts like these.

At my prayer place, I make a gesture of reverence and humility.

Opening Prayer I ask for the grace to direct my whole self toward Jesus who listens.

Desire   I desire to listen with Jesus.

Prayer   I read the prayer texts to see how Jesus listens. Then, in three steps, I pray:

1. Jesus listens me. I choose *one* of the listening relationships in the prayer texts. I use my imagination to enter the scene as the one listening. I fill in the details of place, people, and conversation. I come to Jesus and let the scene unfold.

2. As a friend of Jesus, I listen to others. I use my imagination to bring before me a person I know who needs me, without judgment, to listen to them. I fill in the details of place. I imagine what we might say. I let the scene unfold as I befriend and listen like Jesus.

3. I see my part in the great unfolding story of divine friendship, creation, salvation, and eternal life. I imagine, in detail, the effects of my listening radiating forward into the long future. I see more and more people, communities, and even the earth and its creatures listening to each other and God's voice in all.

Colloquy of the Senses   In reverence, I take some seeds, symbol of listening with a good, honest heart. I bless them.

With seeds in my hands, Jesus and I share how we feel about our friendship. Then we consider how I may listen to those I have remembered in this prayer.

Our Father. [78]

SPIRITUAL DIRECTION
I pray the Awareness Examen this evening.

SUGGESTED PRAYER TIME: 40 MINUTES

Preparation and Desire: 5 minutes. Prayer step 1: 10 minutes. Step 2: 10 minutes. Step 3: 5 minutes. Colloquy of the Senses: 10 minutes. Listening Book after prayer: 10 minutes.

PRAYER TEXTS

[Martha] had a sister named Mary, who sat at the Lord's feet and listened to what he was saying. But Martha was distracted by her many tasks; so she came to him and asked, "Lord, do you not care that my sister has left me to do all the work by myself? Tell her then to help me." But the Lord answered her, "Martha, Martha, you are worried and distracted by many things; there is need of only one thing. Mary has chosen the better part, which will not be taken away from her." (Lk 10:39–42)

The parable [of the sower] is this: The seed is the word of God. The seeds on the path are those who have heard; then the devil comes and takes away the word from their hearts, so that they may not believe and be saved. As for what fell among the thorns, these are the ones who hear; but as they go on their way, they are choked by the cares and riches and pleasures of life, and their fruit does not mature. But as for that in the good soil, these are the ones who, when they hear the word, hold it fast in an honest and good heart, and bear fruit with patient endurance. (Lk 8:11–12, 14–15)

And Jesus looked upward and said, "Father, I thank you for having heard me. I knew that you always hear me, but I have said this for the sake of the crowd standing here, so that they may believe that you sent me." When he had said this, he cried with a loud voice, "Lazarus, come out!" The dead man came out, his hands and feet bound with strips of cloth, and his face wrapped in a cloth. Jesus said to them, "Unbind him, and let him go." (Jn 11:23–28, 32–44)

Tuesday   Jesus Shows Me How Friends Forgive.

Preparation

Immediately on waking, I recall people I know who need forgiveness and imagine bringing them to Jesus. I get dressed with thoughts like these.

At my prayer place, I make a gesture of reverence and humility.

Opening Prayer

I ask for the grace to direct myself to Jesus who forgives.

Desire

I desire to forgive with Jesus.

Prayer

I read the prayer texts to see how Jesus forgives. Then, in three steps I pray:

1. Jesus forgives me. I choose *one* of the forgiving relationships in the prayer texts. I use my imagination to enter the scene as the one needing loving mercy. I fill in the details of place, people, and conversation. I let the scene unfold.

2. As a friend of Jesus, I forgive others. I use my imagination to bring before me a person I need to forgive. I fill in the details of place. I imagine what we might say. I let the scene unfold as I befriend and forgive like Jesus.

3. I see my part in the great unfolding story of divine friendship, creation, salvation, and eternal life. I imagine, in detail, the effects of my forgiveness radiating forward into the long future. I see more and more people, communities, and even the earth and its creatures forgiving each other.

Colloquy of the Senses

In reverence, I take a ring, symbol of forgiveness and joy. I bless it.

With the ring on my finger, Jesus and I share how we feel about our friendship. Then we consider how to bring about the forgiveness of those I have remembered in this prayer.

Our Father. [79]

SPIRITUAL DIRECTION

I pray the Awareness Examen this evening.

SUGGESTED PRAYER TIME: 40 MINUTES

Preparation and Desire: 5 minutes. Prayer step 1: 10 minutes. Step 2: 10 minutes. Step 3: 5 minutes. Colloquy of the Senses: 10 minutes. Listening Book after prayer: 10 minutes.

PRAYER TEXTS

Jesus said, "There was a man who had two sons. The younger of them said to his father, 'Father, give me the share of the property that will belong to me.' So he divided his property between them. A few days later the younger son gathered all he had and traveled to a distant country, and there he squandered his property in dissolute living. When he had spent everything, a severe famine took place throughout that country, and he began to be in need. So he went and hired himself out to one of the citizens of that country, who sent him to his fields to feed the pigs. . . . But when he came to himself he said, 'How many of my father's hired hands have bread enough and to spare, but here I am dying of hunger! I will get up and go to my father, and I will say to him, 'Father, I have sinned against heaven and before you; I am no longer worthy to be called your son; treat me like one of your hired hands.' So he set off and went to his father. But while he was still far off, his father saw him and was filled with compassion; he ran and put his arms around him and kissed him. Then the son said to him, 'Father, I have sinned against heaven and before you; I am no longer worthy to be called your son.' But the father said to his slaves, 'Quickly, bring out a robe—the best one— and put it on him; put a ring on his finger and sandals on his feet. And get the fatted calf and kill it, and let us eat and celebrate; for this son of mine was dead and is alive again; he was lost and is found!' And they began to celebrate." (Lk 15:11–15, 17–24)

Peter went up to Jesus and said, "Lord, how often must I forgive my brother if he wrongs me? As often as seven times?" Jesus answered, "Not seven, I tell you, but seventy-seven times." (Mt 18:21–22, NJB)

Wednesday   Jesus Shows Me How Friends Work.

Preparation

Immediately on waking, I recall people I know who need God's action in their life, and imagine bringing them to Jesus. I get dressed with thoughts like these.

At my prayer place, my mind raised up, I consider how Jesus is looking at me as a friend. I make a gesture of reverence and humility.

Opening Prayer

I ask for the grace to direct my whole self to Jesus who does his Father's work.

Desire

I desire to work with Jesus.

Prayer

I read the prayer texts to see how Jesus works. Then, in three steps I pray:

1. Jesus works in me. I choose *one* of the work relationships in the prayer texts. I use my imagination to enter the scene as the one in need. I fill in the details of place, people, and conversation. I come to Jesus and let the scene unfold.

2. As a friend of Jesus, I work for others. I use my imagination to bring before me a person I know who needs God's work in their life and open myself to allow Jesus to work through me. I fill in the details of place. I imagine what we might say. I let the scene unfold as I befriend and work like Jesus.

3. I see my part in the great unfolding story of divine friendship, creation, salvation, and eternal life. I imagine, in detail, the effects of my work radiating forward into the long future. I see more and more people, communities, and even the earth and its creatures receiving life from this work of God.

Colloquy of the Senses

In reverence, I take a piece of fruit, symbol of fruitful work. I bless it.

With the fruit in my hands, Jesus and I share how we feel about our friendship. Then we consider how I might best work for those I have remembered in this prayer.

Our Father. [80]

SPIRITUAL DIRECTION

I also pray the Awareness Examen this evening.

SUGGESTED PRAYER TIME: 40 MINUTES

Preparation and Desire: 5 minutes. Prayer step 1: 10 minutes. Step 2: 10 minutes. Step 3: 5 minutes. Colloquy of the Senses: 10 minutes. Listening Book after prayer: 10 minutes.

PRAYER TEXTS

I am the vine, you are the branches. Those who abide in me and I in them bear much fruit, because apart from me you can do nothing. My Father is glorified by this, that you bear much fruit and become my disciples. Love one another as I have loved you. (Jn 15:5, 8, 12)

Jesus went about all the cities and villages, teaching in their synagogues, and proclaiming the good news of the kingdom, and curing every disease and every sickness. When he saw the crowds, he had compassion for them, because they were harassed and helpless, like sheep without a shepherd. Then he said to his disciples, "The harvest is plentiful, but the laborers are few; therefore ask the Lord of the harvest to send out laborers into his harvest." (Mt 9:35–38)

[Jesus] was teaching in one of the synagogues on the sabbath. And just then there appeared a woman with a spirit that had crippled her for eighteen years. She was bent over and was quite unable to stand up straight. When Jesus saw her, he called her over and said, "Woman, you are set free from your ailment." When he laid his hands on her, immediately she stood up straight and began praising God. But the leader of the synagogue, indignant because Jesus had cured on the sabbath, kept saying to the crowd, "There are six days on which work ought to be done; come on those days and be cured, and not on the sabbath day." But the Lord answered him and said, "You hypocrites! Does not each of you on the sabbath untie his ox or his donkey from the manger, and lead it away to give it water? And ought not this woman, a daughter of Abraham whom Satan bound for eighteen long years, be set free from this bondage on the sabbath day?" When he said this, all his opponents were put to shame; and the entire crowd was rejoicing at all the wonderful things that he was doing. (Lk 13:10–17)

Thursday   Jesus Shows Me How Friends Love.

Preparation

Immediately on waking, I recall people I know who need love and imagine bringing them to Jesus. I get dressed with thoughts like these.

At my prayer place, I make a gesture of reverence and humility.

Opening Prayer

I ask for the grace to direct my whole self toward Jesus who loves.

Desire

I desire to love with Jesus.

Prayer

I read the prayer texts to see how Jesus loves. Then, in three steps I pray:

1. Jesus loves me. I choose *one* of the loving relationships in the prayer texts. I use my imagination to enter the scene as the one needing love. I fill in the details of place, people, and conversation. I come to Jesus and let the scene unfold.

2. As a friend of Jesus, I love others. I use my imagination to bring before me a person I know in need of love. I fill in the details of place. I imagine what we might say. I let the scene unfold as I befriend and love like Jesus.

3. I see my part in the great unfolding story of divine friendship, creation, salvation, and eternal life. I imagine, in detail, the effects of my love radiating forward into the long future. I see more and more people, communities, and even the earth and its creatures loving one another and acting out of that love.

Colloquy of the Senses

In reverence, I take a cross, symbol of love. I bless it.

With the cross in my hands, Jesus and I share how we feel about our friendship. Then we consider how I might love those I have remembered in this prayer.

Our Father. [81]

SPIRITUAL DIRECTION

I pray the Awareness Examen this evening.

SUGGESTED PRAYER TIME: 40 MINUTES

Preparation and Desire: 5 minutes. Prayer step 1: 10 minutes. Step 2: 10 minutes. Step 3: 5 minutes. Colloquy of the Senses: 10 minutes. Listening Book after prayer: 10 minutes.

PRAYER TEXTS

It was nine o'clock in the morning when they crucified him. Those who passed by derided him. . . . In the same way the chief priests, along with the scribes, were also mocking him among themselves and saying, "He saved others; he cannot save himself. Let the Messiah, the King of Israel, come down from the cross now, so that we may see and believe." When it was noon, darkness came over the whole land until three in the afternoon. At three o'clock Jesus cried out with a loud voice, "Eloi, Eloi, lema sabachthani?" which means, "My God, my God, why have you forsaken me?" Then Jesus gave a loud cry and breathed his last. Now when the centurion, who stood facing him, saw that in this way he breathed his last, he said, "Truly this man was God's Son!" (Mk 15:25, 29–32a, 33–37, 39)

I say to you that listen, Love your enemies, do good to those who hate you, bless those who curse you, pray for those who abuse you. If anyone strikes you on the cheek, offer the other also; and from anyone who takes away your coat do not withhold even your shirt. Give to everyone who begs from you; and if anyone takes away your goods, do not ask for them again. Do to others as you would have them do to you. (Lk 6:27–31)

Love is patient; love is kind; love is not envious or boastful or arrogant or rude. It does not insist on its own way; it is not irritable or resentful; it does not rejoice in wrongdoing, but rejoices in the truth. It bears all things, believes all things, hopes all things, endures all things. (1 Cor 13:4–7)

The Lord, your God, is in your midst, a warrior who gives victory; he will rejoice over you with gladness, he will renew you in his love; he will exult over you with loud singing as on a day of festival. (Zep 3:17–18a)

Saturday   Reconciliation Examen

I Give Thanks   After reading the prayer texts, I stand for a few minutes before the Father, as son or daughter, and feel his compassion as he puts his arms around me.

I sift the month, with gratitude, for times I have received or given forgiveness.

I Ask for Help   I ask the Spirit to intercede for me with sighs too deep for words.

I Review   I move through the last month, day by day:

1. Before the Father of mercies, I recall if I have rejected or withheld love.

2. In the light of the Lord's forgiveness, I sift my thoughts, words, and actions.

3. With the Spirit, I examine the general direction of my life—my true self.

4. I explore one social structure I belong to, discerning good from the unjust.

5. I bring to Jesus any sin or sinful pattern that has real and deadly consequences in my life.

I Respond   I enter the mystery of the Trinity's reconciling and forgiving love. I humbly express my sorrow for what was revealed above, and ask for forgiveness.

I Resolve   I resolve to take one or more of the following paths to reconciliation:

1. To adjust my lifestyle or work, see a counselor or spiritual director, or deepen my personal, family, and church relationships, so that the Lord may forgive and reconcile me through them.

2. To bring where I need forgiveness to Jesus, and to call on his merciful love.

3. To take any needed reconciling action, for myself or others I have hurt.

4. To receive the Sacrament of Reconciliation, now and monthly if possible.

5. To make, as envoy for Christ, one small act of reconciliation next month.[82]

SPIRITUAL DIRECTION

The Reconciliation Examen above is broadened from the examination of thoughts, words, and deeds suggested by Ignatius. I spend more time on those questions or actions closest to my need.

Ignatius received a revelation on the road to Rome to begin his life-long service of God. "Before reaching Rome, I was at prayer in a church and experienced such a change in my soul and saw so clearly that God the Father placed me with Christ his Son that I would not dare doubt it."[83] The Christ before Ignatius is Jesus carrying his Cross. The love that he and Ignatius had for one another, their shared vision of God's kingdom, their desire to feed, liberate, and teach the needy, grew into a profound friendship and an effective, shared mission. Ignatius realized anything that fractured, enticed away, or hid this working relationship leaves one in need of loving reconciliation.

SUGGESTED PRAYER TIME: AS NEEDED

PRAYER TEXTS

[Jesus] said to Simon, "Do you see this woman? I entered your house; you gave me no water for my feet, but she has bathed my feet with her tears and dried them with her hair. You gave me no kiss, but from the time I came in she has not stopped kissing my feet. You did not anoint my head with oil, but she has anointed my feet with ointment. Therefore, I tell you, her sins, which were many, have been forgiven; hence she has shown great love. . . ." Then he said to her, "Your sins are forgiven. . . . Your faith has saved you; go in peace." (Lk 7:44–50)

The tax collector, standing far off, would not even look up to heaven, but was beating his breast and saying, "God, be merciful to me, a sinner!" (Lk 18:13)

If anyone is in Christ, there is a new creation: everything old has passed away; see, everything has become new! All this is from God, who reconciled us to himself through Christ, and has given us the ministry of reconciliation. (2 Cor 5:17–18)

Sunday	I Desire Divine Intimacy.
Preparation	At my prayer place, I consider how Jesus is looking at me as a friend. I make a gesture of reverence and humility.
	I read the prayer texts to anchor myself in the power of divine intimacy.
Opening Prayer	In simple words, I offer my whole self to Jesus, Lord of the heart.
Desire	I desire a divine intimacy.
Colloquy of the Senses	In reverence, I place in a half circle before me the week's four prayer symbols—seeds, ring, fruit, and cross. I bless them.
	I sit in front of them and contemplate the depth of intimacy with God.
	I conclude in conversation with Jesus my friend. I ask for the consolation of inner peace that comes in this intimacy with him.
	Our Father.
Eucharist	I seek the same intimacy in Sunday Eucharist.

SPIRITUAL DIRECTION

I slowly move my attention from one symbol to another, reflecting upon how my friendship with Jesus is grown through mutual listening, forgiveness, working together, and love.

I take the "cross of love" to Sunday Eucharist. In the church I hold my own cross as I contemplate the largest cross in the church, usually the one overlooking the altar. I reflect for a minute or two upon how the cross is a sign of great love. Through the two crosses, I feel the connection between the love offered to the world and the love offered to me.

During the Eucharist I look for how the cross is used and what it symbolizes. I link the personal graces of my retreat with the communal graces of Sunday Eucharist. If I am unable to celebrate the Eucharist, I choose another sacred place, or place in the city, and with the cross in my hands feel the connection between the love offered to me and the love offered to the world.

SUGGESTED PRAYER TIME: AS NEEDED

PRAYER TEXTS

I, [the LORD,] took [my people] up in my arms. . . . I led them with cords of human kindness, with bands of love. I was like those who lift infants to their cheeks. I bent down to them and fed them. (Hos 11:3–4)

Standing near the cross of Jesus were his mother, and his mother's sister, Mary the wife of Clopas, and Mary Magdalene. When Jesus saw his mother and the disciple whom he loved standing beside her, he said to his mother, "Woman, here is your son." Then he said to the disciple, "Here is your mother." And from that hour the disciple took her into his own home. (Jn 19:25–27)

[Father,] the glory that you have given me I have given them, so that they may be one, as we are one, I in them and you in me, that they may become completely one, so that the world may know that you have sent me and have loved them even as you have loved me. (Jn 17:22–23)

I sought him whom my soul loves; I sought him, but found him not. . . .
The sentinels found me, as they went about in the city.
"Have you seen him whom my soul loves?"
Scarcely had I passed them, when I found him whom my soul loves.
I held him, and would not let him go. (Sg 3:1, 3–4a)

Week Four   Jesus, a Friend for Life

Monday   The Father raises my friend to life.

Tuesday   The Spirit hovers over the friends of Jesus.

Wednesday   The Son calls his friends home.

Thursday   Program for Life

Saturday   Particular Examen

Sunday   I desire divine friendship.

Eucharist

SPIRITUAL DIRECTION

The exercises this week are similar to the first week. In them I explore how the promises of divine friendship unfold: I am given life from death, I am sent out to serve, I have a home in eternal life.

The first and last week of this retreat take me to the start and end of the story of creation. This week I complete the circle of creation, the Incarnation, friendship, death, resurrection, and eternal life.

Step 1. Promise Fulfilled. In this step 1 use the prayer form of Imaginative Contemplation. But rather than describing a whole event, each exercise will give me a starting place, a moment—like a flare of light—to pray from. Then, as directed, I simply allow the prayer scene to develop as it will.

Step 2. New Friends. In this step I use my imagination to set the scene, and then I rest in the Prayer of Contemplation. Each day Jesus introduces me to the Father and the Spirit in turn, and asks them to become my friend. Then, we sit in companionable quiet together, friends enjoying each other's presence.

Step 3. The Colloquy of the Senses. I continue using symbols to hold the heart of my prayer. This week I will need the next three symbols at hand:

1. New clothing (one inexpensive piece of clothing)
2. Candle flame (hand-width-sized candle)
3. House keys (front-door key).

Program for Life. This exercise carries my retreat relationship into my daily life. Here I plan how to nurture my friendship with Jesus.

The Examen Prayer. This week I pray the Awareness Examen. On Saturday, I will be given the Particular Examen.

Sunday Spiritual Exercise and Eucharist. In this last spiritual exercise, to experience the progressive graces of my whole retreat, I will use all fifteen prayer symbols. Then I will wear the "clothing of resurrection" to Sunday Eucharist or a local church.

Monday	## The Father Raises My Friend to Life.
Preparation	At my prayer place, I consider how the Father raises the dead to life. I make a gesture of reverence and humility.
	I read the prayer texts to understand the outcome of divine friendship.
Opening Prayer	With simple words, I offer my whole self to the Father.
Desire	I desire living hope from the Father.
Prayer	With my imagination, I see the consequences of friendship with Jesus:

First, a promise fulfilled—I use my imagination to stand in the small tomb of Jesus. It is pitch dark, yet as dawn breaks, beams of dusty, golden light slip past the round stone at my back. Gradually I make out the dead body of Jesus; his wounds are clear, his binding cloths folded at his feet. Suddenly, his whole back arches, ribs stretched, head thrown back, arms pressed to the stone. He takes the first great, shuddering breath of new life. His eyes snap open. He exhales slowly, settling down, deeply weighted in the here and now—alive.

He becomes aware of me, turns his head, and speaks my name.

I allow the rest of his resurrection to unfold around me.

Second, new friends—Next, I use my imagination to create a place of serenity to abide in—a place of peaceful habitation, a secure dwelling, a quiet resting place (see Is 32:18). It may be in a forest, garden, mountain, beach, or home. Here I sit with the risen Jesus and his Father. Jesus personally asks the Father to be my friend. The Father welcomes me with indescribable joy, and fills my heart with laughter. Then, as it is with closest friends, we sit in companionable quiet together, enjoying each other's presence.

Colloquy of the Senses	In reverence, I take an article of new clothing, symbol of resurrection. I bless it and put it on.

Then, clothed in Christ, Jesus and I share how we feel about our friendship.

I ask myself how I might join in his work of bringing new life from death.

Our Father. [84]

SPIRITUAL DIRECTION
I pray the Awareness Examen this evening.

SUGGESTED PRAYER TIME: 40 MINUTES
Preparation, Opening Prayer, Desire: 10 minutes. Prayer: 20 minutes. Conversation: 10 minutes. Listening Book after prayer: 10 minutes.

PRAYER TEXTS
Mary [Magdalene] stood weeping outside the tomb. As she wept, she bent over to look into the tomb; and she saw two angels in white, sitting where the body of Jesus had been lying, one at the head and the other at the feet. They said to her, "Woman, why are you weeping?" She said to them, "They have taken away my Lord, and I do not know where they have laid him." When she had said this, she turned around and saw Jesus standing there, but she did not know that it was Jesus. Jesus said to her, "Woman, why are you weeping? Whom are you looking for?" Supposing him to be the gardener, she said to him, "Sir, if you have carried him away, tell me where you have laid him, and I will take him away." Jesus said to her, "Mary!" She turned and said to him in Hebrew, "Rabbouni!" (which means Teacher). Jesus said to her, "Do not hold on to me, because I have not yet ascended to the Father. But go to my brothers and say to them, 'I am ascending to my Father and your Father, to my God and your God.'" (Jn 20:11–17)

As many of you as were baptized into Christ have clothed yourselves with Christ. There is no longer Jew or Greek, there is no longer slave or free, there is no longer male and female; for all of you are one in Christ Jesus. (Gal 3:27–28)

Do you not know that all of us who have been baptized into Christ Jesus were baptized into his death? Therefore we have been buried with him by baptism into death, so that, just as Christ was raised from the dead by the glory of the Father, so we too might walk in newness of life. For if we have been united with him in a death like his, we will certainly be united with him in a resurrection like his. (Rom 6:3–5)

Tuesday   The Spirit Hovers over the Friends of Jesus.

Preparation

At my prayer place, I consider how the Spirit hovers over me, kindling in me the fire of God's love. I make a gesture of reverence and humility.

I read the prayer texts to understand the gifts of divine friendship.

Opening Prayer   With simple words, I offer my whole self to the Spirit.

Desire   I desire fire from the Spirit.

Prayer   With my imagination, I see the consequences of friendship with Jesus.

First, a promise fulfilled—I use my imagination to re-create the upper room of a house in the old city of Jerusalem. I see men and women, disciples of Jesus, and Mary his mother. I am there too. I imagine the conversations—some calm, some agitated, some fearful. Then I hear a sound like the rush of a strong wind. I see tongues of fire descend on everyone, and feel one dancing on my head. I am filled with the Spirit—love and gift and courage race through the core of my being.

Second, new friends—Next, I use my imagination to return to the special place I created in the previous prayer, the quiet resting place. I am sitting with Jesus and the Father when a third person joins us. Jesus introduces me personally to the Spirit and asks her to be my friend. The Spirit, with great joy, fills my hands with gifts and my heart with her fire. Then, as it is with closest friends, we sit in companionable quiet together, enjoying each other's presence.

Colloquy of the Senses

In reverence, I take a large candle, symbol of the fire of the Spirit. I light it and bless it.

With the candle in my hands, Jesus and I share how we feel about our friendship. I thank him for the particular gifts that shine in me.

I ask myself how I might serve, where I might be sent with such gifts.

Our Father. [85]

SUGGESTED PRAYER TIME: 50 MINUTES

Preparation, Opening Prayer, Desire: 10 minutes. Prayer: 30 minutes. Conversation: 10 minutes. Listening Book after prayer: 10 minutes.

PRAYER TEXTS

When the day of Pentecost had come, [the disciples] were all together in one place. And suddenly from heaven there came a sound like the rush of a violent wind, and it filled the entire house where they were sitting. Divided tongues, as of fire, appeared among them, and a tongue rested on each of them. All of them were filled with the Holy Spirit and began to speak in other languages, as the Spirit gave them ability. (Acts 2:1–4)

The fruit of the Spirit is love, joy, peace, patience, kindness, generosity, faithfulness, gentleness, and self-control. If we live by the Spirit, let us also be guided by the Spirit. (Gal 5:22–23, 25)

We also boast in our sufferings, knowing that suffering produces endurance, and endurance produces character, and character produces hope, and hope does not disappoint us, because God's love has been poured into our hearts through the Holy Spirit that has been given to us. (Rom 5:3–5)

Jesus said to [the disciples] again, "Peace be with you. As the Father has sent me, so I send you." When he had said this, he breathed on them and said to them, "Receive the Holy Spirit." (Jn 20:21–22)

Wednesday   The Son Calls His Friends Home.

Preparation

At my prayer place, I consider how I am created to live for eternity. I make a gesture of reverence and humility.

I read the prayer texts to see the promises of divine friendship.

Opening Prayer   With simple words, I offer my whole self to Jesus.

Desire   I desire resurrection with Jesus.

Prayer

With my imagination, I see the consequences of friendship with Jesus.

First, a promise fulfilled—Throughout the world about 150,000 people die each day. I imagine these people in a small valley leading into heaven. In small groups, they walk up this valley toward me. A tree line of shady woods behind them hides the mystery of their death and resurrection, but now, in clear, bright sunlight, they walk into the kingdom of God.

I cannot turn around, yet I sense the gentle pressure of eternal light pressing on my back. Instead I wonder at the different people, watch their faces, imagine their thoughts and feelings. Then, I see myself—and I hear the voice of Jesus calling me home.

I allow the rest of my walk to unfold as it will in my prayer.

Second, new friends—Next, I use my imagination to return to the special place I created in the previous prayers, the place of peaceful consolation. Jesus, the Father, the Spirit, and I sit here—four good friends together. They introduce me to the men, women, and children of heaven, the Communion of Saints, who desire to help and support me.

Friendship with Jesus draws me into friendship with them and every living creature that has existed or will exist. So, as it is with closest friends, we sit in companionable quiet together, the whole kingdom of God, all life, enjoying each other's presence. The circle is complete.

Colloquy of the Senses	In reverence, I take my house keys, symbol of the home prepared for me. I bless them.

With the front-door key in my hands, Jesus and I share how we feel about our friendship. I ask myself how I might live now, knowing my destination, knowing that the kingdom of God has already begun to grow.

Our Father. [86]

SPIRITUAL DIRECTION
I pray the Awareness Examen this evening.

SUGGESTED PRAYER TIME: 40 MINUTES
Preparation, Opening Prayer, Desire: 10 minutes. Prayer: 20 minutes. Conversation: 10 minutes. Listening Book after prayer: 10 minutes.

PRAYER TEXTS
In my Father's house there are many dwelling places. If it were not so, would I have told you that I go to prepare a place for you? And if I go and prepare a place for you, I will come again and will take you to myself, so that where I am, there you may be also. (Jn 14:1–3)

The kingdom of God is not coming with things that can be observed; nor will they say, "Look, here it is!" or "There it is!" For, in fact, the kingdom of God is among you. (Lk 17:20b–21)

Blessed be the God and Father of our Lord Jesus Christ! By his great mercy he has given us a new birth into a living hope through the resurrection of Jesus Christ from the dead, and into an inheritance that is imperishable, undefiled, and unfading, kept in heaven for you, who are being protected by the power of God through faith for a salvation ready to be revealed in the last time. Although you have not seen [Jesus Christ], you love him; and even though you do not see him now, you believe in him and rejoice with an indescribable and glorious joy, for you are receiving the outcome of your faith, the salvation of your souls. (1 Pt 1:3–5, 8–9)

Thursday   Program for Life

Preparation   Immediately on waking up, I rouse myself to joy by imagining Jesus delighted with my program for life. I will get dressed with thoughts like these.

Opening Prayer   I ask for the grace to direct my whole self toward the Trinity.

Desire   I desire to create a program for life.

Prayer   I read the prayer texts. Then, I draw up an outline of a program for life:

1. What time can I take for enhancing family life? For children? For parents?

2. What time can I take for enhancing work life? For finding God at work in it?

3. What time can I take for enhancing personal life? Recreation? Exercise? Vacation or holiday?

4. What time can I take for prayer life? How often? Personal prayer? Communal prayer?

5. What time can I take for engagement in my church? When? For Eucharist?

6. What time can I take for engagement in my community? What service? When?

7. What time can I take for engagement in my faith life? A retreat? A little pilgrimage?

8. Is there a particular spiritual desire, awaiting action, that I have always felt?

9. Is there a particular work of Jesus that I desire to imitate?

10. Is there a particular opportunity I can use in the service of God?

Conclusion   After writing my program for life, I examine it as a whole.

I consider my whole self and life in regard to it. Do they enliven each other?

I end by explaining my program for life to Jesus, asking his help.

Our Father. [87]

SPIRITUAL DIRECTION

My program will need to be realistic and sustainable. I want to integrate small actions into my life. I will receive more encouragement and consolation in this than in a huge, unworkable project. I can expect some excitement, joy, or sense of rightness with this exercise. I should let these feelings guide me. I can be confident Jesus will supply the strength for and fruit of my program.

With life's journey ahead of me, Ignatius proposes I set off in the right direction, like a pilgrim's ship, "to set ourselves at the arrival port of our pilgrimage, that is in the supreme love of God."[88]

SUGGESTED PRAYER TIME: AS NEEDED

PRAYER TEXTS

I must remind you to frequent the sacraments, to read spiritual books, and to pray with as much recollection as you possibly can. Every day set aside some time so that the soul will not be without its food and, thus, you will not be induced to complain like the one who said "My heart has withered because I have forgotten to eat my bread" (Ps 102:4).[89]

Beloved, whatever is true, whatever is honorable, whatever is just, whatever is pure, whatever is pleasing, whatever is commendable, if there is any excellence and if there is anything worthy of praise, think about these things. Keep on doing the things that you have learned . . . and the God of peace will be with you. (Phil 4:8–9)

In the reform of one's life, one should seek nothing other than the greater praise and glory of God our Lord in and through everything. So it must be borne in mind that a person will make progress in things of the spirit to the degree to which they divest themselves of self-love, self-will, and self-interest. (*Spiritual Exercises* 21)

Be serious and discipline yourselves for the sake of your prayers. Like good stewards of the manifold grace of God, serve one another with whatever gift each of you has received. Whoever speaks must do so as one speaking the very words of God; whoever serves must do so with the strength that God supplies, so that God may be glorified in all things through Jesus Christ. (1 Pt 4:7, 10–11)

Saturday   Particular Examen

Start of day

I Resolve   Upon rising, I firmly resolve to carefully practice my particular desire today.

During the day

I Mark   I mark each experience of my desire with a simple, symbolic action.

End of day

I Ask for Help   I ask God to help me see clearly in my review.

I Review   I review the day to see how God has been working in my particular desire.

I Compare   I compare hour by hour, day by day, week by week, my progress in my desire.

I Resolve   I firmly resolve to act with my desire tomorrow.

Our Father.[90]

SPIRITUAL DIRECTION

The Particular Examen is given at this point of my retreat as a way of praying after my retreat. It is an effective way to keep to my program for life because it focuses on particular desires and action. Following Ignatius, "I ask for what I desire more earnestly in connection with particular things" (*Spiritual Exercises* 199). It may be any holy desire directed to my good or the service of others. So I might choose this examen if I have a particular desire but have never known a way to nourish it or bring it into action. Or, I might have a particular desire that is revealed through its opposite; for instance, I may notice a destructive pattern of selfishness in a certain relationship, and now I desire to practice generosity in it.

Today I make my Particular Examen on the desire to be wholehearted in my friendships.

It is good to realize that while I strive to embody my particular desire, I can also ask God to act through it. In this way, for example, God's generosity acts through my generosity. I allow God to complete all I have been doing through faith (see 2 Thes 1:11). With such a wonderful possibility, my day rightly begins and ends with firm and joyful resolve.

To progress more quickly, whenever I realize my particular desire in the day, I make a small, symbolic body gesture of gratitude. This need not be public or long, just a symbol that expresses that I have received or practiced my particular desire.

SUGGESTED PRAYER TIME: 15 MINUTES
Desire: 1 minute. Review: 10 minutes. Compare: 2 minutes. Resolve: 2 minutes.

PRAYER TEXTS
Pursue love and strive for the spiritual gifts. (1 Cor 14:1a)

Ask, and it will be given you; search, and you will find; knock, and the door will be opened for you. For everyone who asks receives, and everyone who searches finds, and for everyone who knocks, the door will be opened. (Lk 11:9)

We always pray for you, asking that our God will make you worthy of his call and will fulfil by his power every good resolve and work of faith. (2 Thes 1:11)

SPIRITUAL DIRECTION
It is worth considering the "particular" in life. If I want to dance with another person, I need to learn particular steps. If I need to be healed, I go to a particular doctor, look at particular symptoms, and have a particular treatment. If I find a particular thing utterly desirable, I might sell or abandon all I have to get it. If I am lost, I use a particular map to find my way home. When I grieve, it is because I have lost someone I particularly love. Indeed, if I desire to progress in any activity, be it intellectual, musical, sporting, artistic, or spiritual, I need to do particular exercises.

"Particular" is the way I live in depth, the way I search with focus, the way I heal, the way I find, the way I enjoy, the way I choose, and the way I act in union with Christ and others. All these shapes of "particular" are held in the Particular Examen.

Sunday   I Desire Divine Friendship.

Preparation   At my prayer place, I consider how Jesus is looking at me as a friend. I make a gesture of reverence and humility.

I read the prayer texts to fan my desire for divine friendship.

Opening Prayer   In simple words, I offer my whole self to Jesus, a friend for all times.

Desire   I desire a divine friendship.

Colloquy   In reverence, I place in a circle large enough to hold me the twelve prayer symbols of water, earth, grandparents' object, and mirror; ointment, towel, bread, and oil; seeds, ring, fruit, and cross.

I space each symbol in turn, like the twelve numbers of a clock face, water being one o'clock and ending with the cross at twelve o'clock.

Then I place the symbols of the candle flame and house keys to the left and right of where I will sit in the center.

To complete the symbols of my retreat, I put on the symbol of new clothing, and I light the candle. Then I bless them all.

Finally, I sit in the center of the circle, facing the cross. Held in my circle of life, I contemplate the depth of divine friendship.

I conclude in conversation with Jesus my friend. I ask for the consolation of inner peace that comes in this friendship with him, now and forever.

When I am ready, I offer to Jesus my program for life.

Our Father.

Eucharist   I seek the same friendship in Sunday Eucharist.

SPIRITUAL DIRECTION

I gaze at one symbol then another, remembering the truth held in each. Sometimes my eyes linger on one; other times my hands caress one. I remember those that mark the more powerful graces of my retreat, and smile for the places where I got stuck. Thus I move from the simple gifts of friendship with Jesus, to the great universal story beneath them, and back to the intimacy of my friend wishing me to be one with him. Such is the life of my friendship with Jesus.

On Sunday, I wear the "clothing of resurrection" to church.

At the offertory of my Sunday Eucharist, I use my imagination to place my program for life with the bread and wine as they are taken to the altar. In Communion, my friendship is renewed. In the deepest way possible, I receive the body and blood of my friend.

At the end of the Eucharist, I imagine God giving me back my program for life, blessing me, and saying with the minister, "Go in peace, glorifying the Lord by your life."

If I am unable to celebrate the Eucharist, I choose another sacred place, or a place special to me, make my offering, and ask Jesus for a blessing. This I receive in deepest friendship.

SUGGESTED PRAYER TIME: AS NEEDED

PRAYER TEXTS

I do not call you servants any longer, because the servant does not know what the master is doing; but I have called you friends, because I have made known to you everything that I have heard from my Father. You did not choose me but I chose you. And I appointed you to go and bear fruit, fruit that will last, so that the Father will give you whatever you ask him in my name. (Jn 15:15–16)

Clothe yourselves with love, which binds everything together in perfect harmony. And let the peace of Christ rule in your hearts, to which indeed you were called in the one body. And be thankful. Let the word of Christ dwell in you richly; teach and admonish one another in all wisdom; and with gratitude in your hearts sing psalms, hymns, and spiritual songs to God. And whatever you do, in word or deed, do everything in the name of the Lord Jesus, giving thanks to God the Father through him. (Col 3:14–17)

The mountains may depart and the hills be removed, but my steadfast love shall not depart from you, my covenant of peace shall not be removed, says the LORD, who has compassion on you. (Is 54:10)

A friend loves at all times. (Prv 17:17)

INNER PEACE IN THE SERVICE OF GOD

Let love be genuine;
hate what is evil, hold fast to what is good;
love one another with mutual affection;
outdo one another in showing honor.
Do not lag in zeal, be ardent in spirit,
serve the Lord.
Rejoice in hope, be patient in suffering, persevere in prayer.
Contribute to the needs of the saints; extend hospitality to strangers.
Bless those who persecute you; bless and do not curse them.
Rejoice with those who rejoice, weep with those who weep.
Live in harmony with one another;
do not be haughty, but associate with the lowly;
do not claim to be wiser than you are.
Do not repay anyone evil for evil,
but take thought for what is noble in the sight of all.
If it is possible, so far as it depends on you,
live peaceably with all.
"If your enemies are hungry, feed them;
if they are thirsty, give them something to drink.". . .
Do not be overcome by evil,
but overcome evil with good.
Romans 12:9–18, 20–21

Ignatius was a master of the art of conversation. People like Maria, Leonor, and Beatriz, whose stories we hear below, were greatly encouraged by him. In their spiritual conversations they felt the desire rise in their hearts to work in the service of God. At this point, Ignatius would offer them the First Spiritual Exercises—this he freely gave to anyone who desired it.

> She told Yñigo that she would like to speak with him, and so she did speak with him and asked him to explain the service of God. And Yñigo told her that he would have to talk with her over the period of a month . . . and he told her how she should love God. (Maria de la Flor, May 10, 1527)

> And he asked her whether she had listened to Yñigo and what he had taught her. She replied that Yñigo had taught her the commandments of the Church and the five senses and other things for the service of God. (Leonor, daughter of Ana de Mena, March 6, 1527)

> Yñigo was giving doctrine on the first two commandments, how it was necessary to know and love God, etc., and about this he spoke at length; and that this witness found herself amongst these people, and was overwhelmed in seeing that what the said Yñigo talked about were things, not new to this witness, but about loving God and one's neighbor, etc. (Beatriz Ramirez, November, 1527)

The word "service" abounds in the First Spiritual Exercises. This particular retreat aims to free sacred desires and loosen my feet for the service of God. It hopes to bring me the peace that comes from knowing my work with Jesus in a particular service is deeply right to who I am.

Yet, it will be done in a gentle and simple way. The first-week exercises offer a way to discover meaning and find relish in my faith. Using the rhythm of breath, the second-week exercises take me into deeper divine relationships. The third and fourth weeks provide whole days to seek a gift of the Spirit, or special virtue, or to ponder a work of mercy.

The four Sundays pray with the Body of Christ in different ways. So, each week of my retreat builds on the next. Finally, in response to the graces of the whole retreat, I consider how I may bear greater fruit in the service of God by creating a program for life.

THE RETREAT STRUCTURE

This retreat is a twenty-one-day retreat in daily life. Prayer is made four days a week, preferably Monday to Thursday, for four weeks. Each prayer day includes a time for prayer and reflection after prayer. Together they add up to a daily commitment of about fifty minutes. There are some weekend exercises, and Sunday Eucharist is recommended.

THE RETREAT DYNAMIC

My retreat is to be experienced as a whole, with a dynamic that moves through all four weeks. The daily prayer texts of each exercise have been carefully chosen, as single texts and as an ecology of texts. As single texts, they are part of the spiritual exercise. They provide the content and context of my exercise and my relationship with God. They also shed light on central elements of my faith.

As an ecology of texts, where there is more than one text, each text illuminates the others, offering a progression of meaning, or a contrast of content, or a balance of masculine and feminine experience.

Furthermore, the daily texts provide a meaningful progression throughout the week. They are balanced as a weekly group and are to be prayed in a weekly dynamic. Certain images, actions of God, or sets of grace and desire are developed throughout a week.

In like manner, the exercises of each week as a whole are chosen to guide me through certain movements that are only experienced when I make the full four-week retreat. They deliberately introduce me to many different images of God, inviting a variety of divine relationships and giving me a taste of the extraordinary richness in knowing and loving God.

SPIRITUAL JOURNALING

Ignatius directs: "After finishing the exercise I will either sit down or walk around for a quarter of an hour while I see how things have gone for me during the contemplation or meditation" (*Spiritual Exercises* 77).

For the First Spiritual Exercises, a special journal called the Listening Book is used. It will be essential for remembering and discerning the graces I receive in prayer. The Ignatian Guide to Spiritual Journaling (page 349) outlines how to do this.

SPIRITUAL CONVERSATION

Spiritual conversation, personal or group, is very highly recommended. See the Ignatian Guide to Spiritual Conversation found at the end of this book.

Retreat Map Inner Peace in the Service of God

WEEK ONE PROGRESS THROUGH DELIGHT

Monday Awareness Examen

Tuesday Delight and meaning in the Father

Wednesday Delight and meaning in Mary

Thursday Delight and meaning in my faith

Sunday Food in the Body of Christ

WEEK TWO PROGRESS THROUGH RELATIONSHIP

Monday Breathing in the Father

Tuesday Breathing in the Soul of Christ

Wednesday Breathing in the Spirit

Thursday Breathing in the Creator

Sunday Life in the Body of Christ

WEEK THREE PROGRESS THROUGH DESIRE

Monday Particular Examen

Tuesday Progress through the new commandments

Wednesday Progress through the Beatitudes

Thursday Progress through the virtues

Saturday Reconciliation Examen

Sunday Ligament in the Body of Christ

WEEK FOUR PROGRESS THROUGH SERVICE

Monday Progress through the gifts of the Spirit

Tuesday Progress through the gifts of the body

Wednesday Progress through the works of mercy

Thursday Program for Life

Sunday Service in the Body of Christ

Week One   Progress through Delight

Monday   Awareness Examen

Tuesday   Delight and meaning in the Father

Wednesday   Delight and meaning in Mary

Thursday   Delight and meaning in my faith

Sunday   Food in the Body of Christ

                  Eucharist

SPIRITUAL DIRECTION

This week begins with learning the Awareness Examen. I will pray it most evenings in the first two weeks of my retreat. The rest of the first week contemplates the meaning of each word in five ancient Christian prayers. Ignatius calls this "The Second Way of Praying."

The single biggest challenge with these exercises is that they appear too simple and so can be easily dismissed. But in this retreat there is a vast difference between knowing how to pray the exercise and doing that exercise. It is as great as the difference between knowing how to pan for gold on the one hand and doing it: desiring to find gold, searching for the right river, working hard to pan the gravel with the same repetitive motions, accepting days of no result, and feeling the utter delight of finding what I seek.

In the exercises this week, Ignatius invites me to find "meanings, comparisons, relish, and consolation" in each word. This is how I pan or work each word. I pray both word and whole prayer, and with increasing fertility each word or prayer grows from the previous. Sometimes I find unexpected relish, sometimes a wonderful insight, and sometimes spiritual consolation. But the real power of these exercises comes when the grace of one word in one ancient prayer spills into the other ancient prayers. Then phrases and delights and meanings begin to sing to each other.

Another power of the five traditional prayers prayed this way is that I am immersing myself in the love of the Father and his kingdom (Our Father), in the mystery of God becoming human (Hail Mary), in my core Christian beliefs (Apostles' Creed), in the death and resurrection of Jesus (Soul of Christ), and in the gifts of the Spirit (Come, Holy Spirit). The whole of God's history with humanity is traversed. Ultimately, these exercises reveal "where I am going and to what purpose."[91]

To better understand the dynamic of praying these exercises I might consider formal dancing. There is formal movement, structure, progression, and particular steps. Each partner mirrors the other. Yet, each dance is a unique union of dancers, free, alive, and always moving. This way of praying and the one taught next week are a dance with God, a dance that for Ignatius reveals "the inner feeling and relish of things that fills and satisfies the soul" (*Spiritual Exercises* 2).

The words to the five ancient prayers are found after the first exercise on the Our Father.

Monday   Awareness Examen

I Give Thanks	I give thanks for the graces, benefits, and good things of my day.
I Ask for Help	I ask the Holy Spirit for help to discern my day with openness.
I Review	I review my day, hour by hour, to see how God is working in my life.
I Respond	I respond to what I felt or learned in my review just made.
I Resolve	I resolve with hope and the grace of God to amend my life tomorrow.
	Our Father.[92]

SPIRITUAL DIRECTION

I spend the day going over and learning the five-point structure of the Awareness Examen above. I pray it in the evening and review the day just ended.

The Awareness Examen sifts my day with gratitude and seeks to discern the traces of God at work in my life. It guides me with consolations, understanding, and inner peace and is made in five steps:

1. I become aware that I live in the stream of God's love—where all is gift. I review my day, recalling its gifts, large and small, and allow gratitude to well up in me.
2. I make a prayer to the Spirit for her discerning light in this examen.
3. I carefully search out how God is working in my life, moving hour by hour, through my day. After some weeks I also look for any pattern of events or relationships that console me or give me inner peace. Conversely, is there a pattern that desolates or deadens me? I begin to see how God works best through me. How may I work best with God?
4. I respond to what I experienced in the previous point. I might give thanks or express sorrow. I might feel wonder, sadness, or sheer delight with my Lord. We speak about this.
5. I consider the loving way forward tomorrow. I may desire growth or transformation. I may resolve to develop some virtue or grace or

gift. I might seek to renew. So I act in response to my new awareness. I will do my best and surrender the outcome to God.

The prayer texts are words of Jesus that speak to each step.

SUGGESTED PRAYER TIME: 15 MINUTES

Thanks: 3 minutes. Help: 1 minute. Review: 7 minutes. Respond: 2 minutes. Resolve: 2 minutes.

PRAYER TEXTS

The Advocate, the Holy Spirit, whom the Father will send in my name,
will teach you everything, and remind you of all that I have said to you.
(Jn 14:26)

My Father is still working, and I also am working. Indeed, just as the
Father raises the dead and gives them life, so also the Son gives life to
whomever he wishes. (Jn 5:17, 21)

The tax collector, standing far off, would not even look up to heaven, but
was beating his breast and saying, "God, be merciful to me, a sinner!" I
tell you, this man went down to his home justified rather than the other;
for all who exalt themselves will be humbled, but all who humble themselves will be exalted. (Lk 18:13–14)

You did not choose me but I chose you. And I appointed you to go and
bear fruit, fruit that will last, so that the Father will give you whatever
you ask him in my name. (Jn 15:16)

Tuesday — Delight and Meaning in the Father

Preparation	I will allow my spirit to rest a little and consider where I am going and for what purpose. I make a gesture of reverence and humility. I read the prayer texts.
Opening Prayer	I ask the Father for the grace to direct my whole self toward him.
Desire	I desire to find delight and meaning in the Father.
Prayer	Keeping my eyes closed, or fixed on one spot without wandering, I say the word "Our," staying with this word for as long as I find meanings, comparisons, relish, and consolation in considerations related to it. I do this for each word or sense phrase of the Our Father.
	I spend my whole prayer time on the Our Father. When I am finished I say the Our Father, Hail Mary, Apostles' Creed, Soul of Christ, and Come, Holy Spirit, aloud or silently, in the usual way.
Conversation	I ask the Father for the virtues or graces for which I feel the greatest need.[93]

SPIRITUAL DIRECTION

I need to give myself a minute or so for each of the considerations, "meaning, comparisons, relish, and consolation," that I make of each word. With practice, each one of these considerations will deepen, engaging both my lived experience and my desires.

Ignatius adds the following two notes:

> If I find in one or two words rich matter for reflection, relish, and consolation, I will have no anxiety to go further, even though the whole prayer time is spent on what has been found. When my prayer time is up, I will say the remainder of the Our Father in the usual way. And then the other prayers as named above. (*Spiritual Exercises* 254)

> If a complete prayer time has been spent on one or two words and I want to go back to the same prayer on another day, I will say those one or two words in the usual way, and then begin the contemplation on the word immediately following them. (*Spiritual Exercises* 255)

I pray the Awareness Examen this evening, to see how the Father has been at work in my day.

SUGGESTED PRAYER TIME: 30 MINUTES
Preparation: 5 minutes. Opening Prayer: 1 minute. Desire: 1 minute. Prayer: 20 minutes. Conversation: 3 minutes. Listening Book after prayer: 10 minutes.

PRAYER TEXTS

Our	Father,	who art in	heaven,
hallowed be	your name.	Your	kingdom
come;	your will	be done	on earth
as it is in heaven.	Give us	this day	our
daily bread;	and forgive us	our	sins
as we forgive	those who sin	against us;	and lead us not
into temptation	but deliver us	from evil.	Amen.

[Jesus] was praying in a certain place, and after he had finished, one of his disciples said to him, "Lord, teach us to pray, as John taught his disciples." He said to them, "When you pray, say:

> Father, hallowed be your name.
> Your kingdom come.
> Give us each day our daily bread.
> And forgive us our sins,
> for we ourselves forgive everyone indebted to us.
> And do not bring us to the time of trial."

And he said to them, "Suppose one of you has a friend, and you go to him at midnight and say to him, 'Friend, lend me three loaves of bread; for a friend of mine has arrived, and I have nothing to set before him.' And he answers from within, 'Do not bother me; the door has already been locked, and my children are with me in bed; I cannot get up and give you anything.' I tell you, even though he will not get up and give him anything because he is his friend, at least because of his persistence he will get up and give him whatever he needs." (Lk 1:1–8)

Five Ancient Christian Prayers

Our Father

Our Father, who art in heaven,
hallowed be your name.
Your kingdom come;
your will be done on earth as it is in heaven.
Give us this day our daily bread;
and forgive us our sins as we forgive those who sin against us;
and lead us not into temptation but deliver us from evil. Amen. [94]

Hail Mary

Hail Mary, full of grace,
the Lord is with you.
Blessed are you among women,
and blessed is the fruit of your womb, Jesus.
Holy Mary, Mother of God,
pray for us sinners, now,
and at the hour of our death. Amen. [95]

Apostles' Creed

I believe in God, the Father almighty,
Creator of heaven and earth,
and in Jesus Christ, his only Son, our Lord,
who was conceived by the Holy Spirit,
born of the Virgin Mary,
suffered under Pontius Pilate,
was crucified, died, and was buried;
he descended into hell;
on the third day he rose again from the dead;
he ascended into heaven,
and is seated at the right hand of God the Father almighty;
from there he shall come to judge the living and the dead.
I believe in the Holy Spirit,
the holy catholic Church,
the communion of saints,
the forgiveness of sins,
the resurrection of the body,
and life everlasting. Amen. [96]

Soul of Christ

Soul of Christ, sanctify me.
Body of Christ, save me.
Blood of Christ, inebriate me.
Water from Christ's side, wash me.
Passion of Christ, strengthen me.
O good Jesus, hear me;
within your wounds hide me.
Suffer me not to be separated from thee;
from the malicious enemy defend me.
In the hour of my death call me
and bid me come unto thee that I may praise you
with your saints and with your angels,
forever and ever. Amen. [97]

Come, Holy Spirit — Veni, Sancte Spiritus

Come, Holy Spirit,
fill the hearts of your faithful
and kindle in them the fire of your love.
Send forth your Spirit
and they shall be created.
And you shall renew the face of the earth.
O God, who by the light of the Holy Spirit
did instruct the hearts of the faithful,
grant that by the same Holy Spirit
we may be truly wise
and ever enjoy his consolations,
through Christ our Lord. Amen. [98]

Wednesday　　Delight and Meaning in Mary

Preparation	I will allow my spirit to rest a little and consider where I am going and for what purpose. I make a gesture of reverence and humility. I read the prayer texts.
Opening Prayer	I ask for the grace to direct my whole self toward Mary.
Desire	I desire to find delight and meaning in Mary.
Prayer	Keeping my eyes closed, or fixed on one spot without wandering, I say the word "Hail," staying with this word for as long as I find meanings, comparisons, relish, and consolation in considerations related to it. I do this for each word or sense phrase of the Hail Mary.
	I spend my whole prayer time on the Hail Mary. When I am finished I say the Hail Mary, Apostles' Creed, Soul of Christ, Come, Holy Spirit, and Our Father, aloud or silently, in the usual way.
Conversation	I ask Mary for the virtues or graces for which I feel the greatest need.[99]

SPIRITUAL DIRECTION

With each word, I pray the four considerations: "meaning, comparisons, relish, and consolation." For depth of understanding and feeling, I need to give myself a minute or so for each consideration.

I continue to keep in mind the directions Ignatius gave:

> If I find in one or two words rich matter for reflection, relish, and consolation, I will have no anxiety to go further, even though the whole prayer time is spent on what has been found. When my prayer time is up, I will say the remainder of the Our Father in the usual way. And then the other prayers as named above. (*Spiritual Exercises* 254)

Spiritual consolations are sought in this prayer. Ignatius calls them

> any interior movement produced in the soul which leads her to become inflamed with the love of her Creator and Lord . . . every increase of hope, faith and charity . . . to all interior happiness which calls and attracts to heavenly things . . . leaving the soul quiet and at peace in her Creator and Lord. (*Spiritual Exercises* 316)

I pray the Awareness Examen this evening, to see how Mary has been at work in my day.

SUGGESTED PRAYER TIME: 30 MINUTES

Preparation: 5 minutes. Opening Prayer: 1 minute. Desire: 1 minute. Prayer: 20 minutes. Conversation: 3 minutes. Listening Book after prayer: 10 minutes.

PRAYER TEXTS

Hail	Mary,	full	of grace,
the Lord	is	with	you.
Blessed	are you	among	women, and
blessed	is the fruit of	your womb,	Jesus.
Holy	Mary,	Mother	of God,
pray	for us	sinners,	now,
and at the hour	of our	death.	Amen.

In the sixth month the angel Gabriel was sent by God to a town in Galilee called Nazareth, to a virgin engaged to a man whose name was Joseph, of the house of David. The virgin's name was Mary. And he came to her and said, "Greetings, favored one! The Lord is with you."

But she was much perplexed by his words and pondered what sort of greeting this might be. The angel said to her, "Do not be afraid, Mary, for you have found favor with God. And now, you will conceive in your womb and bear a son, and you will name him Jesus. He will be great, and will be called the Son of the Most High, and the Lord God will give to him the throne of his ancestor David.

In those days Mary set out and went with haste to a Judean town in the hill country, where she entered the house of Zechariah and greeted Elizabeth. When Elizabeth heard Mary's greeting, the child leaped in her womb. And Elizabeth was filled with the Holy Spirit and exclaimed with a loud cry, "Blessed are you among women, and blessed is the fruit of your womb." (Lk 1:26–32, 39–42)

Thursday	**Delight and Meaning in My Faith**
Preparation	I will allow my spirit to rest a little and consider where I am going and for what purpose. I make a gesture of reverence and humility. I read the prayer texts.
Opening Prayer	I ask for the grace to direct my whole self toward the Trinity.
Desire	I desire to find delight and meaning in my faith.
Prayer	Keeping my eyes closed, or fixed on one spot without wandering, I say the words "I believe in," staying with this phrase for as long as I find meanings, comparisons, relish, and consolation in considerations related to it. I do this for each word or sense phrase of the Apostles' Creed.
	I spend my whole prayer time on the Apostles' Creed. When I am finished I say the Apostles' Creed, Soul of Christ, Come, Holy Spirit, Our Father, and Hail Mary, aloud or silently, in the usual way.
Conversation	I ask the Trinity for the virtues or graces for which I feel the greatest need.[100]

SPIRITUAL DIRECTION

I spend a minute each for meaning, comparisons, relish, and consolation. With practice, each one of these considerations will obtain for me a deeper and richer reflection than first experienced.

I continue to keep in mind the directions Ignatius gave:

> If I find in one or two words rich matter for reflection, relish, and consolation, I will have no anxiety to go further, even though the whole prayer time is spent on what has been found. When my prayer time is up, I will say the remainder of the Our Father in the usual way. And then the other prayers as named above. (*Spiritual Exercises* 254)

The first creeds all began with a relationship and response to Jesus. After the resurrection, they found a natural place in evangelization, baptismal rites, and liturgy. They were important to communal belief, to the union of hearts and minds across cultures and times. Creeds grew with experience and understanding, and today all churches share the Apostles' and Nicene Creeds.

The Ignatian Guide to Christian Belief (page 339) offers longer exercises to pray the creeds.

I pray the Awareness Examen this evening, to see how the Trinity has been at work in my day.

SUGGESTED PRAYER TIME: 30 MINUTES

Preparation: 5 minutes. Opening Prayer: 1 minute. Desire: 1 minute. Prayer: 20 minutes. Conversation: 3 minutes. Listening Book after prayer: 10 minutes.

PRAYER TEXTS

I believe in	God	the Father	almighty,
Creator	of heaven	and earth.	I believe in
Jesus	Christ,	his	only
Son	our	Lord,	who was
conceived	by the power	of the Holy	Spirit,
born of	the Virgin	Mary,	suffered under
Pontius Pilate,	was crucified,	died,	and was buried.
He descended	into hell;	on the third day	he rose again
from the dead;	he ascended	into heaven	and sits
at the right hand	of God	the Father,	almighty
from thence	he shall come	again to judge	the living
and the dead.	I believe in	the Holy	Spirit,
the holy	catholic	Church,	the communion
of saints,	the forgiveness	of sins,	the resurrection
of the body,	and life	everlasting.	Amen.

Jesus asked the twelve, "Do you also wish to go away?" Simon Peter answered him, "Lord to whom can we go? You have the words of eternal life. We have come to believe and know that you are the Holy One of God." (Jn 6:67–69)

Sunday   Food in the Body of Christ

Desire   I desire living bread in the Body of Christ.

Preparation   I read the prayer texts about the Body of Christ.

In My Home   Keeping my eyes closed, or fixed upon an image of Jesus, I say the words "Take this," the first words of the Institution Narrative from the second Eucharistic Prayer, given in the first prayer text.

I stay with each word for as long as I find meanings, comparisons, relish, and consolations in it. I do this for each word or sense phrase in the Institution Narrative. I spend all my prayer time on these words.

When finished, I say the whole of the Institution Narrative in the usual way.

I conclude giving thanks for the retreat graces of this week.

In the Eucharist I hear the words of the Creed, Institution Narrative, and Our Father in a fresh way. I experience how the Eucharist brings the three together and how my prayer this week enlightens them all. What other meanings can I find in the celebration of the Eucharist?

After receiving the living bread in Communion, I open myself to new consolations and relish.

SPIRITUAL DIRECTION

The words Jesus spoke at the Last Supper, with the actions of "take, eat, and drink," are referred to as the words of institution, and they are central in the Eucharistic liturgy. They are what Jesus asked us to remember and enact so that we might understand what he is offering, and why.

If I am unable to celebrate the Eucharist, I may profitably spend more time in the home exercise offered above.

SUGGESTED PRAYER TIME: AS NEEDED

PRAYER TEXTS

Take this,	all of you,	and eat	of it,
for this is	my Body	which will be	given up for you.
Take this,	all of you,	and drink	from it,
for this is	the chalice	of my	Blood,
the Blood	of the new	and eternal	covenant,
which will be	poured out	for you	and for many
for the	forgiveness	of sins.	
Do	this	in memory	of me. [101]

"Very truly, I tell you, it was not Moses who gave you the bread from heaven, but it is my Father who gives you the true bread from heaven. For the bread of God is that which comes down from heaven and gives life to the world." [The Jews] said to him, "Sir, give us this bread always." Jesus said to them, "I am the bread of life. Whoever comes to me will never be hungry, and whoever believes in me will never be thirsty. I am the living bread that came down from heaven. Whoever eats of this bread will live forever; and the bread that I will give for the life of the world is my flesh. Those who eat my flesh and drink my blood have eternal life, and I will raise them up on the last day; for my flesh is true food and my blood is true drink. Those who eat my flesh and drink my blood abide in me, and I in them. Just as the living Father sent me, and I live because of the Father, so whoever eats me will live because of me." (Jn 6:32–35, 51, 54–57)

The cup of blessing that we bless, is it not a sharing in the blood of Christ? The bread that we break, is it not a sharing in the body of Christ? Because there is one bread, we who are many are one body, for we all partake of the one bread. (1 Cor 10:15–17)

Week Two   Progress through Relationship

Monday   Breathing in the Father

Tuesday   Breathing in the Soul of Christ

Wednesday   Breathing in the Spirit

Thursday   Breathing in the Creator

Sunday   Life in the Body of Christ

                  Eucharist

SPIRITUAL DIRECTION

"I have life within me, the breath of God in my nostrils" (see Jb 27:3). This week continues with praying each word in the five traditional prayers—now moving from the first three to include the Soul of Christ and the Come, Holy Spirit. The way of praying is also changed this week. Now I will use my breath and its natural rhythm to pray. Ignatius calls this prayer "The Third Way of Praying" (*Spiritual Exercises* 258–60). Thursday and Sunday will take me deeper into union with the Trinity and the Body of Christ.

If I am praying and a particular word moves me or is full of meaning for my relationship with God, then at a later time, I could pray that single word with rhythmic breathing for the whole prayer.

The word *ruah* in Aramaic means Spirit, breath, wind, breeze, life, and life of God. The one who hovers over creation is *ruah*. The breath that Jesus breathes into his disciples is *ruah*. The Spirit that the Lord sends forth to renew the earth is *ruah*.

There is a beautiful Israelite belief that when a child is born, the child's first breath takes in the breath that the Creator has just breathed out. When that person dies, and breathes his or her last breath out, the Creator breathes it in and eternal life begins (see Ps 104:27–30). This understanding of breath as life-giving, life renewing, and life divine moves beneath all of the exercises this week.

Monday   Breathing in the Father

Preparation   I will allow my spirit to rest a little and consider where I am going and for what purpose. I make a gesture of reverence and humility. I read the prayer texts.

Opening Prayer   I ask for the grace to direct my whole self toward the Father.

Desire   I desire to breathe in the Father.

Prayer   I pray silently on each intake or expulsion of my breath, by saying one word of the Our Father, so that only a single word is pronounced between one breath and the next. I do this with the natural rhythm of my normal breathing.

Contemplatively, I pay special attention to the meaning of that word or to the Father to whom I am praying. In this way I deepen my relationship with the Father. I make myself ready for his action in me.

I spend my whole prayer time on the Our Father. When I am finished I say the Our Father, Hail Mary, Apostles' Creed, Soul of Christ, and Come, Holy Spirit aloud or silently, in the usual way.

Conversation   I ask the Father for the virtues or graces for which I feel the greatest need. [102]

SPIRITUAL DIRECTION

In practice, it is important to keep my breathing normal, neither deeper nor shallower than usual. At times I may pray a sense phrase on a breath or one word on several breaths.

I pray the Awareness Examen this evening, to see how the Father has been at work in my day.

SUGGESTED PRAYER TIME: 15 MINUTES

Preparation: 3 minutes. Opening Prayer: 1 minute. Desire: 1 minute. Prayer: 10 minutes or as desired. Conversation: 1 minute. Listening Book after prayer: 10 minutes.

PRAYER TEXTS

Our	Father,	who art in	heaven,
hallowed be	your name.	Your	kingdom
come;	your will	be done	on earth
as it is in heaven.	Give us	this day	our
daily bread;	and forgive us	our	sins
as we forgive	those who sin	against us;	and lead us not
into temptation	but deliver us	from evil.	Amen. [103]

Righteous Father, the world does not know you, but I know you; and these know that you have sent me. I made your name known to them, and I will make it known, so that the love with which you have loved me may be in them, and I in them. (Jn 17:25–26)

Very truly, I tell you, if you ask anything of the Father in my name, he will give it to you. Until now you have not asked for anything in my name. Ask and you will receive, so that your joy may be complete. (Jn 16:23b–24)

I am no longer in the world, but they are in the world, and I am coming to you. Holy Father, protect them in your name that you have given me, so that they may be one, as we are one. I am not asking you to take them out of the world, but I ask you to protect them from the evil one. (Jn 17:11, 15)

Tuesday   Breathing in the Soul of Christ

Preparation	I will allow my spirit to rest a little and consider where I am going and for what purpose. I make a gesture of reverence and humility. I read the prayer texts.
Opening Prayer	I ask for the grace to direct my whole self toward Jesus.
Desire	I desire to breathe in the soul of Christ.
Prayer	I pray silently on each intake or expulsion of my breath, by saying one word of the Soul of Christ, so that only a single word is pronounced between one breath and the next. I do this with the natural rhythm of my normal breathing.
	Contemplatively, I pay special attention to the meaning of that word or to Jesus to whom I am praying. In this way I deepen my relationship with Jesus. I make myself ready for his action in me.
	I spend my whole prayer time on the Soul of Christ. When I am finished I say the Soul of Christ, Come, Holy Spirit, Our Father, Hail Mary, and Apostles' Creed aloud or silently, in the usual way.
Conversation	I ask Jesus for the virtues or graces for which I feel the greatest need.[104]

SPIRITUAL DIRECTION

I remember to keep my breathing normal, neither faster nor slower than usual. On occasions, I may prefer to use a sense phrase rather than a single word or pray one word on several breaths.

Suffering, vulnerability, or powerlessness can leave me with little choice but to come to the Cross—the place and event—and person where life is born through death. At such a time in my life, breathing in the soul of the passionate Lord may bring me comfort and life.

Or again, I may feel wounded and, like Thomas, desire to put my hand into Christ's wounds and allow him to do the same with mine— standing close enough to share a healing breath.

I pray the Awareness Examen this evening, to see how Christ has been at work in my day.

SUGGESTED PRAYER TIME: 15 MINUTES

Preparation: 3 minutes. Opening Prayer: 1 minute. Desire: 1 minute. Prayer: 10 minutes or as desired. Conversation: 1 minute. Listening Book after prayer: 10 minutes.

PRAYER TEXTS

Soul	of Christ,	sanctify	me.
Body	of Christ,	save	me.
Blood	of Christ,	inebriate	me.
Water	from Christ's side,	wash	me.
Passion	of Christ,	strengthen	me.
O good	Jesus,	hear	me;
within	your wounds	hide	me.
Suffer me	not to be	separated	from thee;
from the malicious	enemy	defend	me.
In the hour of	my death	call	me
and bid	me	come unto	thee
that I	may praise	you	with your saints
and with	your angels,	forever and ever.	Amen.

They crucified [Jesus], and with him two others, one on either side, with Jesus between them. When Jesus had received the wine, he said, "It is finished." Then he bowed his head and gave up his spirit. But when they came to Jesus and saw that he was already dead, they did not break his legs. Instead, one of the soldiers pierced his side with a spear, and at once blood and water came out. (Jn 19:18, 30, 33–34)

[Thomas] said to [the disciples], "Unless I see the mark of the nails in his hands, and put my finger in the mark of the nails and my hand in his side, I will not believe." A week later his disciples were again in the house, and Thomas was with them. Although the doors were shut, Jesus came and stood among them and said, "Peace be with you." Then he said to Thomas, "Put your finger here and see my hands. Reach out your hand and put it in my side. Do not doubt but believe." Thomas answered him, "My Lord and my God!" (Jn 20:25b–28)

Wednesday	Breathing in the Spirit
Preparation	I will allow my spirit to rest a little and consider where I am going and for what purpose. I make a gesture of reverence and humility. I read the prayer texts.
Opening Prayer	I ask for the grace to direct my whole self toward the Spirit.
Desire	I desire to breathe in the Spirit.
Prayer	I pray silently on each intake or expulsion of my breath, by saying one word of the Come, Holy Spirit, so that only a single word is pronounced between one breath and the next. I do this with the natural rhythm of my normal breathing.
	Contemplatively, I pay special attention to the meaning of that word or to the Spirit to whom I am praying. In this way I deepen my relationship with the Spirit. I make myself ready for her action in me.
	I spend my whole prayer time on the Come, Holy Spirit. When I am finished I say the Come, Holy Spirit, Our Father, Hail Mary, Apostles' Creed, and Soul of Christ aloud or silently, in the usual way.
Conversation	I ask the Spirit for the virtues or graces for which I feel the greatest need. [105]

SPIRITUAL DIRECTION

The Come, Holy Spirit or *Veni, Sancte Spiritus*, as it is traditionally known, is a prayer asking for the grace of the Holy Spirit. It has been used for centuries in private devotion and appears in the Mass for the feast of Pentecost.

My breathing remains normal, the rhythm unforced. And if it helps, I may pray a sense phrase on a breath or one word on many breaths.

At another time, as a variation, I may breathe in a gift of the spirit, for instance, to breathe the fire of love, the spirit of courage, the light of understanding, the gift of wisdom, the joy of consolation, etc.

I pray the Awareness Examen this evening, to see how the Spirit has been at work in my day.

SUGGESTED PRAYER TIME: 15 MINUTES

Preparation: 3 minutes. Opening Prayer: 1 minute. Desire: 1 minute. Prayer: 10 minutes or as desired. Conversation: 1 minute. Listening Book after prayer: 10 minutes.

PRAYER TEXTS

Come,	Holy	Spirit,	fill
the hearts	of your	faithful	and kindle
in them	the fire	of your	love.
Send	forth	your	Spirit
and they	shall be	created.	
And you	shall renew	the face	of the earth.
O God, who	by the light	of the Holy	Spirit
did instruct	the hearts	of the faithful,	grant
that by the same	Holy	Spirit	we
may be truly	wise	and ever enjoy	his
consolations,	through Christ	our Lord.	Amen.

When the day of Pentecost had come, [the disciples] were all together in one place. And suddenly from heaven there came a sound like the rush of a violent wind, and it filled the entire house where they were sitting. Divided tongues, as of fire, appeared among them, and a tongue rested on each of them. All of them were filled with the Holy Spirit and began to speak in other languages, as the Spirit gave them ability. (Acts 2:1–4)

The Counselor, the Holy Spirit, whom the Father will send in my name, will teach you all things and will remind you of everything I have said to you. Peace I leave with you; my peace I give you. I do not give to you as the world gives. Do not let your hearts be troubled and do not be afraid. (Jn 14:25–27, NIV-G/K)

Thursday   Breathing in the Creator

Preparation   I will allow my spirit to rest a little and consider where I am going and for what purpose. I make a gesture of reverence and humility. I read the prayer texts.

Opening Prayer I ask for the grace to direct my whole self toward the Creator.

Desire   I desire to breathe in the Creator.

Prayer   I become aware of my breath passing through my nostrils. For five minutes, I feel and focus on the sensation of my breath flowing in and out of my nostrils.

Then I imagine, with each breath that I breathe out, that all the trees, plants, and flowers respond by breathing in. When they breathe out to offer oxygen, I breathe in. For five minutes I remain with this awareness of my breathing in and plants breathing out, of my breathing out and plants breathing in.

So I experience the rhythm of creation and creature breathing to live.

Now I imagine the same relationship between Creator and creature, God and myself. God breathes the Spirit into me, and I breathe out to renew the face of the earth. God breathes the Spirit into me, and I am re-created. I breathe the Spirit out to re-create life in my relationships, home, work, etc. I do this for five minutes.

So I experience the rhythm of Creator and creature breathing to renew the face of earth.

Conversation   I ask the Creator for the virtues or graces for which I feel the greatest need. [106]

SPIRITUAL DIRECTION

This prayer is outside the five prayers suggested by Ignatius, but it does increase an awareness of the whole of creation, something Ignatius does several times throughout the Spiritual Exercises. Here, the awareness of Creator and creature serves well to conclude my week.

I pray the Awareness Examen this evening, to see how the Creator has been at work in my day.

SUGGESTED PRAYER TIME: 25 MINUTES

Preparation: 5 minutes. Opening Prayer: 1 minute. Desire: 1 minute. Prayer: 15 minutes. Conversation: 3 minutes. Listening Book after prayer: 10 minutes.

PRAYER TEXTS

The spirit of God has made me,
and the breath of the Almighty gives me life. (Jb 33:4)

The LORD God formed the man from the dust of the ground,
and breathed into his nostrils the breath of life;
and the man became a living being. (Gn 2:7)

Thus says God, the LORD,
who created the heavens and stretched them out,
who spread out the earth and what comes out of it,
who gives breath to the people upon it
and spirit to those who walk in it. (Is 42:5)

These all look to you to give them their food in due season;
when you give to them, they gather it up;
when you open your hand, they are filled with good things.
When you hide your face, they are dismayed;
when you take away their breath,
they die and return to their dust.
When you send forth your spirit, they are created;
and you renew the face of the ground. (Ps 104:27–30)

Sunday	Life in the Body of Christ
Desire	I desire life in the Body of Christ.
Preparation	I read the prayer texts about the Body of Christ.
In My Home	Using my imagination, I close my eyes and enter into the Body of Christ. Then, with my normal breathing, I breathe as the breath of Christ in the Body of Christ. I imagine myself as the breath that animates his body. He breathes in and takes me into himself. This is my prayer, that we give each other life.
	I conclude giving thanks for the retreat graces of this week.
In the Eucharist	I begin by repeating my home prayer, breathing in the Body of Christ. I do this for a few minutes. Then, still breathing in the Body of Christ, I widen my awareness to hear the sounds of community gathering around me for the Eucharist. I imagine and see myself breathing at one with them as we make up more of the Body of Christ.
	Finally, I widen my awareness to all Christians in the world breathing today. I experience the full and complete Body of Christ. I remain breathing in this sacred reality as long as I may.

SPIRITUAL DIRECTION

If I am unable to celebrate the Eucharist, I may profitably spend more time in the home exercise offered above.

For prayer by breath after my retreat, I may be guided by this suggestion of Ignatius: "Whoever wants to remain longer on the prayer by rhythm can recite all the five prayers mentioned above, or fewer of them, but keeping the same system of rhythmic breathing already explained" (*Spiritual Exercises* 260).

SUGGESTED PRAYER TIME: AS NEEDED

PRAYER TEXTS

No one ever hates his own body, but he nourishes and tenderly cares for it, just as Christ does for the church, because we are members of his body. "For this reason a man will leave his father and mother and be joined to his wife, and the two will become one flesh." This is a great mystery, and I am applying it to Christ and the church. (Eph 5:29–32)

The body does not consist of one member but of many. If the foot would say, "Because I am not a hand, I do not belong to the body," that would not make it any less a part of the body. And if the ear would say, "Because I am not an eye, I do not belong to the body," that would not make it any less a part of the body. If the whole body were an eye, where would the hearing be? If the whole body were hearing, where would the sense of smell be? But as it is, God arranged the members in the body, each one of them, as he chose. If all were a single member, where would the body be? As it is, there are many members, yet one body. The eye cannot say to the hand, "I have no need of you," nor again the head to the feet, "I have no need of you." If one member suffers, all suffer together with it; if one member is honored, all rejoice together with it. (1 Cor 12:14–21, 26)

For just as the body is one and has many members, and all the members of the body, though many, are one body, so it is with Christ. For in the one Spirit we were all baptized into one body—Jews or Greeks, slaves or free—and we were all made to drink of one Spirit. (1 Cor 12:12–13)

Week Three   Progress through Desire

Monday	Particular Examen
Tuesday	Progress through the new commandments
Wednesday	Progress through the Beatitudes
Thursday	Progress through the virtues
Saturday	Reconciliation Examen
Sunday	Ligament in the Body of Christ
	Eucharist

SPIRITUAL DIRECTION

This week I pray the new commandments, Beatitudes, and virtues. The method is the Prayer of Consideration. Ignatius calls it "The First Way of Praying" (*Spiritual Exercises* 258–60).

Ignatius suggests that, "for a better knowledge of each gift, I could look at their contraries; and similarly, and more surely to progress in a particular gift, I could resolve and endeavor by means of devout exercises to acquire the good and avoid the contrary evil" (*Spiritual Exercises* 245). The exercises of the coming weeks all do this.

Again, he directs, "If I find I am not much engaged with one commandment as I pray, there is no need for me to spend long over it. But according to how I live or desire each one, more or less, so I should spend more or less time in the consideration and examination of it" (*Spiritual Exercises* 242). This refers to an adaptation of this exercise where I may spend more time on a particular beatitude, virtue, gift, etc.

In the Awareness Examen of Week One I sought God's love and power at work in all things. During the next two weeks, I will seek God's love and power at work in one particular thing. To help me to do this I will first learn to pray the Particular Examen and practice it for the remainder of my retreat.

Monday   Particular Examen

Start of day

I Resolve   Upon rising, I firmly resolve to carefully practice my
                     particular desire today.

During the day

I Mark   I mark each experience of my desire with a simple,
                     symbolic action.

End of day

I Ask for Help   I ask God to help me see clearly in my review.

I Review   I review the day to see how God has been working in
                     my particular desire.

I Compare   I compare hour by hour, day by day, week by week, my
                     progress in my desire.

I Resolve   I firmly resolve to act with my desire tomorrow.

                     Our Father.[107]

SPIRITUAL DIRECTION

The Particular Examen focuses on a particular desire. Following Ignatius, "I ask for what I desire more earnestly in connection with particular things" (*Spiritual Exercises* 199). It may be any holy desire directed to my good or the service of others. So I might choose this examen if I have a particular desire but have never known a way to nourish it or bring it into action.

Or, I might have a particular desire that is revealed through its opposite; for instance, I may notice a destructive pattern of selfishness in a certain relationship, and now I desire to practice generosity in it.

In either case, while I strive to embody my particular desire, I also ask God to act through it. This way, God's generosity acts through my generosity. I allow God to complete all I have been doing through faith (see 2 Thes 1:1). With such wonderful possibility, my day begins and ends with firm resolve.

To progress more quickly, whenever I realize my particular desire in the day, I make a small, symbolic body gesture of gratitude. This need not be public or long, just a symbol that expresses that I have received or practiced my particular desire.

Today, I make my particular desire the desire to express gratitude to those who help me. Then my Particular Examen is made nightly in the following weeks, as directed, on the particular action chosen in the conversation at the end of each prayer.

SUGGESTED PRAYER TIME: 15 MINUTES
Desire: 1 minute. Review: 10 minutes. Compare: 2 minutes. Resolve: 2 minutes.

PRAYER TEXTS
Pursue love and strive for the spiritual gifts. (1 Cor 14:1a)

Ask, and it will be given you; search, and you will find; knock, and the door will be opened for you. For everyone who asks receives, and everyone who searches finds, and for everyone who knocks, the door will be opened. (Lk 11:9)

We always pray for you, asking that our God will make you worthy of his call and will fulfil by his power every good resolve and work of faith. (2 Thes 1:11)

SPIRITUAL DIRECTION
It is worth considering the "particular" in life. If I want to dance with another person, I need to learn particular steps. If I need to be healed, I go to a particular doctor, look at particular symptoms, and have a particular treatment. If I find a particular thing utterly desirable, I might sell or abandon all I have to get it. If I am lost, I use a particular map to find my way home. When I grieve, it is because I have lost someone I particularly love. Indeed, if I desire to progress in any activity, be it intellectual, musical, sporting, artistic, or spiritual, I need to do particular exercises.

"Particular" is the way I live in depth, the way I search with focus, the way I heal, the way I find, the way I enjoy, the way I choose, and the way I act in union with Christ and others. All these shapes of "particular" are held in the Particular Examen.

Tuesday	## Progress through the New Commandments

Preparation   I will allow my spirit to rest a little and consider where I am going and for what purpose. I make a gesture of reverence and humility. I read the prayer texts.

Opening Prayer   I ask Jesus for understanding of the new commandments that I may live them better for his greater service.

Desire   I desire spiritual progress in the new commandments.

Prayer
1. I consider loving God with all my heart. What is Jesus teaching here?

2. Where is this heartfelt love present in my life?

3. Where is it absent in my life?

4. I reflect on the contrary of this new commandment.

After 3 minutes of consideration, I ask Jesus for what I desire now.

Our Father.

The same procedure is repeated for each of the seven commandments.

Conversation   Now I examine the commandments as a whole. I ask:
1. Which commandment do I live the best, more than any other?

2. Which commandment do I desire to live for greater service of God?

3. Which commandment would give me the greatest inner peace now?

In conversation with Jesus, I ask for grace and help. Then I choose one new commandment to live well today.[108]

SPIRITUAL DIRECTION

In this prayer, I take each new commandment in turn. I consider its meaning, ponder where it is present or absent in my life, and then reflect on its contrary. It is very important I take half a minute to answer the four questions in turn, and not take them as examples of one question. The same is true of the three questions in the conversation with Jesus.

In practicing a particular commandment today, I can do it when I choose or, with alertness, open myself for the Spirit to enact that commandment through me. I pray the Particular Examen this evening, to see how God has been at work in my chosen new commandment.

SUGGESTED PRAYER TIME: 40 MINUTES

Preparation: 5 minutes. Opening Prayer: 1 minute. Desire: 1 minute. Prayer: 30 minutes. Conversation: 3 minutes, or as needed. Listening Book after prayer: 10 minutes.

PRAYER TEXTS

The New Commandments

1. To love God with all my heart.
2. To love God with all my soul.
3. To love God with all my mind.
4. To love my neighbor as myself.
5. To love others as Jesus loves me.
6. To surrender my possessions and follow Jesus.
7. To abide in the love and joy of God.

"You shall love the Lord your God with all your heart, and with all your soul, and with all your mind." This is the greatest and first commandment. And a second is like it: "You shall love your neighbor as yourself." On these two commandments hang all the law and the prophets. (Mt 22:37–40)

I give you a new commandment, that you love one another. Just as I have loved you, you also should love one another. By this everyone will know that you are my disciples. (Jn 13:34–35a)

Jesus, looking at him, loved him and said, "You lack one thing; go, sell what you own, and give the money to the poor, and you will have treasure in heaven; then come, follow me." When he heard this, he was shocked and went away grieving, for he had many possessions. (Mk 10:21–22)

As the Father has loved me, so I have loved you; abide in my love. If you keep my commandments, you will abide in my love, just as I have kept my Father's commandments and abide in his love. I have said these things to you so that my joy may be in you, and that your joy may be complete. (Jn 15:9–11)

Wednesday   Progress through the Beatitudes

Preparation	I will allow my spirit to rest a little and consider where I am going and for what purpose. I make a gesture of reverence and humility. I read the prayer texts.
Opening Prayer	I ask Jesus for understanding of the Beatitudes that I may live them better for his greater service.
Desire	I desire spiritual progress through the Beatitudes.
Prayer	1. I consider being poor in spirit. What is Jesus promising here?

2. Where is this beatitude present in my life?

3. Where is it absent in my life?

4. I reflect on the contrary of blessing the poor in spirit.

After 3 minutes, I ask Jesus for what I desire now.

Our Father.

The same procedure is repeated for each of the eight Beatitudes.

Conversation   Now I examine the Beatitudes as a whole. I ask myself:

1. Which beatitude do I live in the greatest measure, more than any other?

2. Which beatitude do I desire to live for the greater service of God?

3. Which beatitude would give me the greatest inner peace now?

In conversation with Jesus, I ask for grace and help. Then I choose one beatitude to live well today.[109]

SPIRITUAL DIRECTION

I take each beatitude and consider its meaning, ponder where it is present or absent in my life, and then reflect on the contrary. I need to take about half a minute with each of the four questions. The same time is necessary with the three questions at the end.

To practice a particular beatitude, I can act it when I decide or allow the Spirit to gently blow that beatitude through me.

I pray the Particular Examen this evening, to see how God has been at work in my chosen beatitude.

SUGGESTED PRAYER TIME: 40 MINUTES

Preparation: 5 minutes. Opening Prayer: 1 minute. Desire: 1 minute. Prayer: 30 minutes. Conversation: 3 minutes or as needed. Listening Book after prayer: 10 minutes.

PRAYER TEXTS

The Beatitudes

1. Blessed are the poor in spirit,
   for theirs is the kingdom of heaven.
2. Blessed are those who mourn,
   for they will be comforted.
3. Blessed are the meek,
   for they will inherit the earth.
4. Blessed are those who hunger and thirst for righteousness,
   for they will be filled.
5. Blessed are the merciful,
   for they will receive mercy.
6. Blessed are the pure in heart,
   for they will see God.
7. Blessed are the peacemakers,
   for they will be called children of God.
8. Blessed are those who are persecuted for righteousness' sake,
   for theirs is the kingdom of heaven. (Mt 5:3–10)

You have heard that it was said to those of ancient times, "You shall not murder"; and "whoever murders shall be liable to judgment." But I say to you that if you are angry with a brother or sister, you will be liable to judgment.

You have heard that it was said, "You shall not commit adultery." But I say to you that everyone who looks at a woman with lust has already committed adultery with her in his heart.

But if anyone strikes you on the right cheek, turn the other also; and if anyone forces you to go one mile, go also the second mile. Give to everyone who begs from you, and do not refuse anyone who wants to borrow from you.

You have heard that it was said, "You shall love your neighbor and hate your enemy." But I say to you, Love your enemies and pray for those who persecute you. (Mt 5:21–22a, 27–28, 38–39, 42–44)

Thursday	**Progress through the Virtues**
Preparation	I will allow my spirit to rest a little and consider where I am going and for what purpose. I make a gesture of reverence and humility. I read the prayer texts.
Opening Prayer	I ask God for understanding of the virtues, that I may live them better for his greater service.
Desire	I desire spiritual progress through the virtues.
Prayer	1. I consider faith. What is the Christian community encouraging here?
	2. Where is it present in my life?
	3. Where is it absent in my life?
	4. I reflect on the contrary of faith.
	After 3 minutes, I ask God for what I desire now.
	Our Father.
	The same procedure is repeated for each of the seven virtues.
Conversation	Now I examine the virtues as a whole. I ask:
	1. Which virtue do I have in the greatest measure, more than any other?
	2. Which virtue do I desire for greater service of God?
	3. Which virtue would give me the greatest inner peace now?
	In conversation with God, I ask for grace and help. Then I choose one virtue to live well today.[110]

SPIRITUAL DIRECTION

As I pray each virtue in turn, I use the four questions to consider its meaning, ponder where it is present or absent in my life, and then reflect on its contrary. I have to take about thirty seconds to answer each question. The same time applies to the three questions in the conversation with Jesus.

I can practice my chosen virtue throughout the day as I wish, or be ready for the Spirit to enact that virtue through me.

I pray the Particular Examen this evening, to see how God has been at work in my chosen virtue.

Virtues have been described as the firm and habitual disposition to do the good. Today spiritual guides suggest new virtues like self-esteem, hospitality, gratitude, humility, vigilance, serenity, empathy, humor, restraint, tolerance, generosity, fitness, forgiveness, integrity, and compassion. One of these might be prayed when needed in the future.

SUGGESTED PRAYER TIME: 40 MINUTES

Preparation: 5 minutes. Opening Prayer: 1 minute. Desire: 1 minute. Prayer: 30 minutes. Conversation: 3 minutes or as needed. Listening Book after prayer: 10 minutes.

PRAYER TEXTS
The Seven Virtues
1. Faith
2. Hope
3. Love
4. Self-control
5. Wisdom
6. Justice
7. Courage

Faith, hope, and love abide, these three; and the greatest of these is love. (1 Cor 13:13)

You will understand righteousness and justice and equity, every good path; for wisdom will come into your heart, and knowledge will be pleasant to your soul; prudence will watch over you; and understanding will guard you. It will save you from the way of evil. (Prv 2:9–12a)

[Wisdom] renews all things; in every generation she passes into holy souls and makes them friends of God, and prophets. Her labors are virtues; for she teaches self-control and prudence, justice and courage; nothing in life is more profitable for mortals than these. Therefore I determined to take her to live with me, knowing that she would give me good counsel and encouragement in cares and grief. (Wis 7:27b, 8:7, 9)

In 1523 Ignatius set out for Barcelona to take ship to Jerusalem. Although there were some offers of company, he wanted to go quite alone, for his whole idea was to have God alone as refuge: One day when some were urging strongly, because he did not know either the Italian or the Latin languages, that he have a certain companion . . . he said that he would not go even in the company of the son or the brother of the Duke of Cardona, because he wanted to practice three virtues, love, faith, and hope. If he took a companion, he would expect help from him when he was hungry; if he fell down, the man would help him get up; and so also he would trust him and feel attachment to him on this account; but he wanted to place that trust, attachment, and expectation in God alone. What he said in this way, he felt just so in his heart.[111]

Faith. I will take you for my wife in righteousness and in justice, in steadfast love, and in mercy. I will take you for my wife in faithfulness; and you shall know the LORD. (Hos 2:19b–20)

Hope. We also boast in our sufferings, knowing that suffering produces endurance, and endurance produces character, and character produces hope, and hope does not disappoint us, because God's love has been poured into our hearts through the Holy Spirit that has been given to us. (Rom 5:3–5)

Love. If I speak in the tongues of mortals and of angels, but do not have love, I am a noisy gong or a clanging cymbal. If I have prophetic powers, and understand all mysteries and all knowledge, and if I have all faith, so as to remove mountains, but do not have love, I am nothing. If I give away all my possessions, if I hand over my body so that I may boast, but do not have love, I gain nothing.

Love is patient; love is kind; love is not envious or boastful or arrogant or rude. It does not insist on its own way; it is not irritable or resentful; it does not rejoice in wrongdoing, but rejoices in the truth. It bears all things, believes all things, hopes all things, endures all things. Love never ends. (1 Cor 13:1–8a)

Justice. Return to your God, hold fast to love and justice, and wait continually for your God. (Hos 12:6)

Wisdom/Prudence. My child, do not let these escape from your sight: keep sound wisdom and prudence, and they will be life for your soul and adornment for your neck. Then you will walk on your way securely and your foot will not stumble. If you sit down, you will not be afraid; when you lie down, your sleep will be sweet. Do not be afraid of sudden panic, or of the storm that strikes the wicked; for the Lord will be your confidence and will keep your foot from being caught. (Prv 3:21–26)

Self-control/Temperance. His divine power has bestowed on us everything that makes for life and devotion, through the knowledge of him who called us by his own glory and power. For this very reason, make every effort to supplement your faith with virtue, virtue with knowledge, knowledge with self-control, self-control with endurance, endurance with devotion, devotion with mutual affection, mutual affection with love. (2 Pt 1:3, 5–7, NAB)

Courage. Be strong and of good courage, and act. Do not be afraid or dismayed; for the Lord God, my God, is with you. He will not fail you or forsake you, until all the work . . . . is finished. (1 Chr 28:20)

Every virtue—The Mind of Christ. Be of the same mind. . . . Do nothing from selfish ambition or conceit, but in humility regard others as better than yourselves. Let each of you look not to your own interests, but to the interests of others. Let the same mind be in you that was in Christ Jesus, who, though he was in the form of God, did not regard equality with God as something to be exploited, but emptied himself, taking the form of a slave, being born in human likeness. And being found in human form, he humbled himself and became obedient to the point of death—even death on a cross. Therefore God also highly exalted him and gave him the name that is above every name. (Phil 2:2b–9)

Saturday

Reconciliation Examen

I Give Thanks

After reading the prayer texts, I stand for a few minutes before the Father, as son or daughter, and feel his compassion as he puts his arms around me.

I sift the month, with gratitude, for times I have received or given forgiveness.

I Ask for Help

I ask the Spirit to intercede for me with sighs too deep for words.

I Review

I move through the last month, day by day:

1. Before the Father of mercies, I recall if I have rejected or withheld love.

2. In the light of the Lord's forgiveness, I sift my thoughts, words, and actions.

3. With the Spirit, I examine the general direction of my life—my true self.

4. I explore one social structure I belong to, discerning good from the unjust.

5. I bring to Jesus any sin or sinful pattern that has real and deadly consequences in my life.

I Respond

I enter the mystery of the Trinity's reconciling and forgiving love. I humbly express my sorrow for what was revealed above, and ask for forgiveness.

I Resolve

I resolve to take one or more of the following paths to reconciliation:

1. To adjust my lifestyle or work, see a counselor or spiritual director, or deepen my personal, family, and church relationships, so that the Lord may forgive and reconcile me through them.

2. To bring where I need forgiveness to Jesus, and to call on his merciful love.

3. To take any needed reconciling action, for myself or others I have hurt.

4. To receive the Sacrament of Reconciliation, now and monthly if possible.

5. To make, as envoy for Christ, one small act of reconciliation next month.[112]

SPIRITUAL DIRECTION

The Reconciliation Examen above is broadened from the examination of thoughts, words, and deeds suggested by Ignatius. I spend more time on those questions or actions closest to my need.

Ignatius received a revelation on the road to Rome to begin his life-long service of God. "Before reaching Rome, I was at prayer in a church and experienced such a change in my soul and saw so clearly that God the Father placed me with Christ his Son that I would not dare doubt it."[113] The Christ before Ignatius is Jesus carrying his Cross. The love that he and Ignatius had for one another, their shared vision of God's kingdom, their desire to feed, liberate, and teach the needy, grew into a profound friendship and an effective, shared mission. Ignatius realized anything that fractured, enticed away, or hid this working relationship leaves one in need of loving reconciliation.

SUGGESTED PRAYER TIME: AS NEEDED

PRAYER TEXTS

[Jesus] said to Simon, "Do you see this woman? I entered your house; you gave me no water for my feet, but she has bathed my feet with her tears and dried them with her hair. You gave me no kiss, but from the time I came in she has not stopped kissing my feet. You did not anoint my head with oil, but she has anointed my feet with ointment. Therefore, I tell you, her sins, which were many, have been forgiven; hence she has shown great love. . . . " Then he said to her, "Your sins are forgiven. . . . Your faith has saved you; go in peace." (Lk 7:44–50)

The tax collector, standing far off, would not even look up to heaven, but was beating his breast and saying, "God, be merciful to me, a sinner!" (Lk 18:13)

If anyone is in Christ, there is a new creation: everything old has passed away; see, everything has become new! All this is from God, who reconciled us to himself through Christ, and has given us the ministry of reconciliation. (2 Cor 5:17–18)

Sunday   Ligament in the Body of Christ

Desire I desire to be a ligament in the Body of Christ.

Preparation I read the prayer texts about the Body of Christ.

In My Home I lift one arm to consider my bone, muscle, and ligaments. Very slowly, in turn, I rotate my wrist, bend my elbow, and flex my upper arm. I roll my lower arm, clench and open my hand, and touch my thumb to each finger.

Continuing such movements, I feel and watch the play of muscle, tendon, and ligament in my arm. I consider how each part is joined to the other and how each needs to work properly to complete the desired action in my mind.

I reflect how I am made for movement, how prolonged inaction leads to the shriveling of muscle and choice. I wonder at my whole body in this way. I tell the Lord how much I desire to be a ligament in his body, the Christian community, helping it to move in a more loving way.

I give thanks for the retreat graces of this week that will help me to do so.

In the Eucharist Before or after Eucharist, I walk the nave and transepts of the church. Most cross-shaped churches image the Body of Christ. The head is the eastern end behind the altar. The heart is where the altar is. The left and right arms are the left and right transepts respectively. The body of Christ is the nave, and his feet end at the western end of the church. So, as an exercise, I walk and trace in the body of Christ for a few minutes in the sacred space of the church, reflecting upon him, myself, and the body of Christ today.

After the church is filled, I may properly see the living Body of Christ, with all its wonderful parts. Then I am joined to Christ in the Eucharist, where the one becomes many and many become one.

SPIRITUAL DIRECTION

Belonging, union, and communion are related. In Reconciliation, Communion, and Eucharist I touch the heart of this mystery. In a sacred, sacramental way I experience true belonging in God. This is why the natural flow of reconciliation is into communion, and the natural flow of communion is into love given out. And the natural flow of love given out is into action, and the natural flow of this action is into the building up of the household of God in love.

If I am unable to celebrate the Eucharist, I may profitably spend more time in the home exercise.

SUGGESTED PRAYER TIME: AS NEEDED

PRAYER TEXTS
We must no longer be children, tossed to and fro and blown about by every wind of doctrine, by people's trickery, by their craftiness in deceitful scheming. But speaking the truth in love, we must grow up in every way into him who is the head, into Christ, from whom the whole body, joined and knit together by every ligament with which it is equipped, as each part is working properly, promotes the body's growth in building itself up in love. (Eph 4:14–16)

Do not let anyone disqualify you, insisting on self-abasement and worship of angels, dwelling on visions, puffed up without cause by a human way of thinking, and not holding fast to the head, from whom the whole body, nourished and held together by its ligaments and sinews, grows with a growth that is from God. (Col 2:18–19)

So [Jesus] came and proclaimed peace to you who were far off and peace to those who were near; for through him both of us have access in one Spirit to the Father. So then you are no longer strangers and aliens, but you are citizens with the saints and also members of the household of God, built upon the foundation of the apostles and prophets, with Christ Jesus himself as the cornerstone. In him the whole structure is joined together and grows into a holy temple in the Lord; in whom you also are built together spiritually into a dwelling-place for God. (Eph 2:17–22)

Week Four   Progress through Service

Monday   Progress through the gifts of the Spirit

Tuesday   Progress through the gifts of the body

Wednesday   Progress through the works of mercy

Thursday   Program for Life

Sunday   Service in the Body of Christ

                Eucharist

SPIRITUAL DIRECTION

The heart of this retreat's prayer, and the way it moves me forward, is that I join my desire with God's desire and place my best action in God's loving action. My action cooperates with God's action. My particular desire is filled with the same desire in God; his desiring love floods this particular desire in us both. Mysteriously, I act my desire within God's action through me.

This week I will begin to see and feel the cumulative effect of how divine relationship, particular desires, Beatitudes, commandments, and virtues all join to support my service of God.

The exercises of this week are orientated to particular service. I pray the gifts of the Spirit, the gifts of the body, and the works of mercy. I ask for grace, help, and understanding that I may use these gifts better for the greater glory, praise, and service of God (*Spiritual Exercises* 240).

The Particular Examen continues at night this week, focusing on the particular gift of the Spirit, gift of the body, or work of mercy that I want to practice in each respective day.

At the end of this week I am invited to create a program for life. This will give me a way to order my energies and commitments, and help to integrate my daily life with my spiritual life. Ignatius saw the Spiritual Exercises as the opportunity for "ordering of one's life on the basis of a decision made in freedom from any disordered attachment" (*Spiritual Exercises* 21). At this point in my retreat, I am ordering my life with the gifts and desires I have found in my retreat.

Monday   Progress through the Gifts of the Spirit

Preparation   I will allow my spirit to rest a little and consider where I am going and for what purpose. I make a gesture of reverence and humility. I read the prayer texts.

Opening Prayer I ask the Spirit for understanding of the gifts, that I may use them better for her greater service.

Desire   I desire spiritual progress through the gifts of the Spirit.

Prayer   1. I consider wisdom. What is the Spirit offering me here?

                   2. Where is it present in my life?

                   3. Where is it absent in my life?

                   4. I reflect on the contrary of wisdom.

                   After 3 minutes, I ask the Spirit for what I desire now.

                   Our Father.

                   The same procedure is repeated for each of the seven gifts.

Conversation   Now I examine the gifts of the Spirit as a whole. I ask myself:

                   1. Which gift do I have in the greatest measure, more than any other?

                   2. Which gift do I desire for greater service of God?

                   3. Which gift would give me the greatest inner peace now?

                   In conversation with the Spirit, I ask for grace and help. Then I choose one gift to live well today.[114]

SPIRITUAL DIRECTION

I may pray either the gifts of the Spirit or the fruits of the Spirit.

Four questions will guide my consideration of each gift or fruit. I consider its meaning, ponder where it is present or absent in my life, and then identify its contrary. It is necessary to spend half a minute with each question in turn. I must do the same with the last three questions.

In practicing a particular gift or fruit, I can act when I desire, or I can surrender myself to the Spirit, to allow that gift or fruit to pour through me.

I pray the Particular Examen this evening, to see how God has been at work in my chosen gift or fruit of the Spirit.

SUGGESTED PRAYER TIME: 40 MINUTES

Preparation: 5 minutes. Opening Prayer: 1 minute. Desire: 1 minute. Prayer: 30 minutes. Conversation: 3 minutes or as needed. Listening Book after prayer: 10 minutes.

PRAYER TEXTS

Gifts of the Spirit	**Fruits of the Spirit**
1. Wisdom	1. Love
2. Understanding	2. Joy
3. Counsel	3. Peace
4. Fortitude	4. Patience
5. Knowledge	5. Kindness
6. Piety	6. Generosity
7. Fear of the Lord	7. Gentleness

The Spirit of the LORD shall rest on him, the spirit of wisdom and understanding, the spirit of counsel and might, the spirit of knowledge and the fear of the LORD. (Is 11:2)

The fruit of the Spirit is love, joy, peace, patience, kindness, generosity, faithfulness, gentleness, and self-control. If we live by the Spirit, let us also be guided by the Spirit. (Gal 5:22–23, 25)

Now there are varieties of gifts, but the same Spirit; and there are varieties of services, but the same Lord; and there are varieties of activities, but it is the same God who activates all of them in everyone. To each is given the manifestation of the Spirit for the common good. (1 Cor 12:4–7)

Tuesday   Progress through the Gifts of the Body

Preparation I will allow my spirit to rest a little and consider where I am going and for what purpose. I make a gesture of reverence and humility. I read the prayer texts.

Opening Prayer I ask the Creator for understanding of my senses, that I may use them better for the greater service of God.

Desire I desire spiritual progress through the gifts of my body.

Prayer
1. I consider my sense of sight. What has the Creator given me here?

2. Where do I see best in my life?

3. Where do I see least in my life?

4. I reflect on the contrary of my sight.

After 3 minutes, I ask the Lord for what I desire now.

Our Father.

The same procedure is repeated for each of the senses.

Conversation Now I examine the gifts of the body as a whole. I ask myself:

1. Which sense do I excel in, more than any other?

2. Which sense do I desire to use for greater service of God?

3. Which sense would give me the greatest inner peace now?

In conversation with my Creator, I ask for grace and help. Then I choose one sense to serve with today, or one sense to imitate Jesus with today.[115]

SPIRITUAL DIRECTION

In this prayer, I take each sense in turn. I consider its meaning, see where it is present or absent in my life, and then become aware of its contrary. I need to take about half a minute to answer each of the four questions. This reflective pace is also necessary in the three questions at the end.

In serving with a sense of my body today, I can consciously choose particular times to do so, or I can allow the Spirit to enhance that sense and service through me.

There is a second way to pray the senses of my body. It is to imitate Jesus, Mary, or a living saint. Thus, for a day, I can strive to use my hands in the way Jesus would, or see with the eyes of Jesus, or hear with the ears of Mary, or taste reality the way the living saint does. I could then move through each sense, imagining how I might imitate these people in each of these senses. I would be embodying their desires.

I pray the Particular Examen this evening, to see how God has been at work in my chosen sense.

SUGGESTED PRAYER TIME: 40 MINUTES

Preparation: 5 minutes. Opening Prayer: 1 minute. Desire: 1 minute. Prayer: 30 minutes. Conversation: 3 minutes or as needed. Listening Book after prayer: 10 minutes.

PRAYER TEXTS
The Five Gifts of the Body
1. Sight
2. Hearing
3. Smell
4. Taste
5. Touch

Sensual God. [In the promised land] you will serve other gods made by human hands, objects of wood and stone that neither see, nor hear, nor eat, nor smell. From there you will seek the Lord your God, and you will find him if you search after him with all your heart and soul. (Dt 4:28–29)

Sensual humanity. God created humankind in his image, in the image of God he created them; God saw everything that he had made, and indeed, it was very good. (Gn 1:27a, 31a)

Sensual witness. We are afflicted in every way, always carrying in the body the death of Jesus, so that the life of Jesus may also be made visible in our bodies. While we live, we are always being given up to death for Jesus' sake, so that the life of Jesus may be made visible in our mortal flesh. (2 Cor 4:8a, 10–11)

Wednesday　　Progress through the Works of Mercy

Preparation　I will allow my spirit to rest a little and consider where I am going and for what purpose. I make a gesture of reverence and humility. I read the prayer texts.

Opening Prayer　I ask the Lord God for understanding of the works of mercy, that I may act for his greater service.

Desire　I desire spiritual progress through the works of mercy.

Prayer
1. I consider feeding the hungry. What does the Lord desire here?

2. Where is this work present in my life?

3. Where is it absent in my life?

4. I reflect on the contrary of feeding the hungry.

After 3 minutes, I ask the Lord for what I desire now.

Our Father.

The same procedure is repeated for each of the works of mercy.

Conversation　Now I examine the works of mercy as a whole. I ask myself:

1. Which work do I excel in, more than any other?

2. Which work do I desire for greater service of God?

3. Which work would give me the greatest inner peace now?

In conversation with my Lord, I ask for grace and help. Then I choose one work of mercy to serve with today, or one work of mercy to imitate Jesus with today.[116]

SPIRITUAL DIRECTION

I may pray either the bodily or spiritual works of mercy.

The reflections on each work of mercy, considering its meaning, its presence or absence in my life, and its contrary, will break open my personal experience of each work of mercy. So it is vital I take about half a minute with each of the four questions. The same method is followed with the three questions in the conversation with Jesus.

In practicing a work of mercy today, I organize a particular action, or I can open myself to the Spirit to direct that work through me in God's time.

I pray the Particular Examen this evening, to see how God has been at work in my chosen work of mercy.

SUGGESTED PRAYER TIME: 40 MINUTES

Preparation: 5 minutes. Opening Prayer: 1 minute. Desire: 1 minute. Prayer: 30 minutes. Conversation: 3 minutes or as needed. Listening Book after prayer: 10 minutes.

PRAYER TEXTS

Mercy for the body	**Mercy for the spirit**
1. To feed the hungry	1. To instruct
2. To shelter the homeless	2. To advise
3. To clothe the naked	3. To console
4. To visit the sick	4. To comfort
5. To visit the imprisoned	5. To forgive
6. To bury the dead	6. To bear wrongs patiently
7. To give alms to the poor	7. To pray for the living and the dead

The king will say to those at his right hand, "Come, you that are blessed by my Father, inherit the kingdom prepared for you from the foundation of the world; for I was hungry and you gave me food, I was thirsty and you gave me something to drink, I was a stranger and you welcomed me, I was naked and you gave me clothing, I was sick and you took care of me, I was in prison and you visited me." (Mt 25:34–36)

Rejoice with those who rejoice, weep with those who weep. Live in harmony with one another; do not be haughty, but associate with the lowly; do not claim to be wiser than you are. Do not repay anyone evil for evil, but take thought for what is noble in the sight of all. If it is possible, so far as it depends on you, live peaceably with all. (Rom 12:15–19)

For we are what he has made us, created in Christ Jesus for good works, which God prepared beforehand to be our way of life. (Eph 2:10)

Thursday   Program for Life

Preparation   Immediately on waking up, I rouse myself to joy by imagining Jesus delighted with my program for life. I will get dressed with thoughts like these.

Opening Prayer   I ask for the grace to direct my whole self toward the Trinity.

Desire   I desire to create a program for life. [117]

Prayer   I read the prayer texts. Then, I draw up an outline of a program for life:

1. What time can I take for enhancing family life? For children? For parents?

2. What time can I take for enhancing work life? For finding God at work in it?

3. What time can I take for enhancing personal life? Recreation? Exercise? Vacation or holiday?

4. What time can I take for prayer life? How often? For personal prayer? Communal prayer?

5. What time can I take for engagement in my church? When? For Eucharist?

6. What time can I take for engagement in my community? What service? When?

7. What time can I take for engagement in my faith life? For a retreat? For a little pilgrimage?

8. Is there a particular spiritual desire, awaiting action, that I have always felt?

9. Is there a particular work of Jesus that I desire to imitate?

10. Is there a particular opportunity I can use in the service of God?

Conclusion   After writing my program for life, I examine it as a whole.

I consider my whole self and life in regard to it. Do they enliven each other?

I end by explaining my program for life to Jesus, asking his help.

Our Father.

SPIRITUAL DIRECTION

My program will need to be realistic and sustainable. I want to integrate small actions into my life. I will receive more encouragement and consolation in this than in a huge, unworkable project.

I can expect some excitement, joy, or sense of rightness with this exercise. I should let these feelings guide me. I can be confident Jesus will supply the strength and fruit of my program.

With life's journey ahead of me, Ignatius proposes I set off in the right direction, like a pilgrim's ship, "to set ourselves at the arrival port of our pilgrimage, that is in the supreme love of God."[118]

SUGGESTED PRAYER TIME: AS NEEDED

PRAYER TEXTS

I must remind you to frequent the sacraments, to read spiritual books, and to pray with as much recollection as you possibly can. Every day set aside some time so that the soul will not be without its food and, thus, you will not be induced to complain like the one who said "My heart has withered because I have forgotten to eat my bread." (Ps 102:4)[119]

Beloved, whatever is true, whatever is honorable, whatever is just, whatever is pure, whatever is pleasing, whatever is commendable, if there is any excellence and if there is anything worthy of praise, think about these things. Keep on doing the things that you have learned . . . and the God of peace will be with you. (Phil 4:8–9)

In the reform of one's life, one should seek nothing other than the greater praise and glory of God our Lord in and through everything. So it must be borne in mind that a person will make progress in things of the spirit to the degree to which they divest themselves of self-love, self-will, and self-interest. (*Spiritual Exercises* 21)

Be serious and discipline yourselves for the sake of your prayers. Like good stewards of the manifold grace of God, serve one another with whatever gift each of you has received. Whoever speaks must do so as one speaking the very words of God; whoever serves must do so with the strength that God supplies, so that God may be glorified in all things through Jesus Christ. (1 Pt 4:7, 10–11)

Sunday   Service in the Body of Christ

Desire   I desire to serve in the Body of Christ.

Preparation   I read the prayer texts about the Body of Christ.

In My Home   I place myself before the risen Lord, body to body, face-to-face. Jesus breathes out into me and I breathe in, receiving the Spirit. I feel the fullness of the Spirit within me, in every crevice, in the heart of who I am.

With the Spirit, I go over the graces I have received in my retreat. When I recall a grace, I picture it within myself. Then, on the breath that is Spirit, I breathe that gift out into my relationships, work, and world.

With the help of the Spirit, I name another gift I received in my retreat. I feel it in myself, then breathe it out to renew the face of the earth. I repeat this naming, holding, and breathing out of my retreat graces as long as I desire.

In the Eucharist At the offertory, I use my imagination to place my program for life with the bread and wine as they are taken to the altar. With the prayer of the people, I offer it humbly to God, asking for the strength to carry it out.

At the end of the Eucharist, I imagine God giving me back my program for life, blessing me, and saying with the minister, "Go in peace, glorifying the Lord by your life."

SPIRITUAL DIRECTION
If I am unable to celebrate the Eucharist, I may profitably spend more time in the home exercise.

SUGGESTED PRAYER TIME: AS NEEDED

PRAYER TEXTS
Jesus said to them again, "Peace be with you. As the Father has sent me, so I send you." When he had said this, he breathed on them and said to them, "Receive the Holy Spirit." (Jn 20:21–22)

After Jesus had washed their feet, had put on his robe, and had returned to the table, he said to them, "Do you know what I have done to you? You call me Teacher and Lord—and you are right, for that is what I am. So if I, your Lord and Teacher, have washed your feet, you also ought to wash one another's feet. For I have set you an example, that you also should do as I have done to you. (Jn 13:12–15)

We have gifts that differ according to the grace given to us: prophecy, in proportion to faith; ministry, in ministering; the teacher, in teaching; the exhorter, in exhortation; the giver, in generosity; the leader, in diligence; the compassionate, in cheerfulness. (Rom 12:6–8)

I therefore, the prisoner in the Lord, beg you to lead a life worthy of the calling to which you have been called, with all humility and gentleness, with patience, bearing with one another in love, making every effort to maintain the unity of the Spirit in the bond of peace. There is one body and one Spirit, just as you were called to the one hope of your calling, one Lord, one faith, one baptism, one God and Father of all, who is above all and through all and in all. (Eph 4:1–6)

SPIRITUAL PROGRESS

KEEPING THE GRACES RECEIVED

[God] has made with me an everlasting covenant,
ordered in all things and secure.
Will he not cause to prosper
all my help and
my desire?
—2 Samuel 23:5

[Some] seed fell on rocky ground, where it did not have much soil, and it sprang up quickly, since it had no depth of soil. And when the sun rose, it was scorched; and since it had no root, it withered away. Other seed fell among thorns, and the thorns grew up and choked it, and it yielded no grain. Other seed fell into good soil and brought forth grain, growing up and increasing and yielding thirty and sixty and a hundredfold. (Mk 4:5–8)

How do I keep the graces I have received in my retreat? Ignatius gave a lot of thought to this because he was familiar with the experience of how difficult it is to move from retreat time to ordinary time and keep the graces received. He added ways of praying and various guides to the back of the Spiritual Exercises for this purpose. He also kept each exercise in the retreat simple in method so it would be memorable for use in daily life.

The clearest way to keep a grace is to return to the exercise that provided the grace in the first place. The Ignatian Guide to Twelve Ways of Prayer found in this book will also help. The other great help is the one Ignatius called our "supremely generous" God.

On May 7, 1547, St. Ignatius wrote a letter of encouragement to young Jesuit students at Coimbra:

> As every good thing, every grace, flows from the generosity of our Creator and Redeemer, may he be constantly blessed and praised for it all, and may it please him each day to open more widely the fountain of his graciousness in order thus to increase and carry forward what he has begun in your minds and hearts.[120]

Retreat graces are generous gifts from my Creator, deserving praise and gratitude (*Spiritual Exercises* 21). Ignatius wishes me to be filled with the utter certainty of God's overflowing graciousness. It is this fountain of grace that will keep graces within me. But is more grace really possible? Ignatius continues:

> I have no doubt that God's generosity and love will indeed bring this about. The supreme generosity of God is so supremely eager to spread its own riches; and the eternal love, with which God wants to give us our final fulfillment, is a desire to give far greater than ours to receive.[121]

God's "supreme" generosity and "supreme" eagerness have two key implications. The first is for the nature of God. I need to keep this creative, gracious, generous, eager, eternally loving God before me and have no other God. The second is for keeping grace. I must try to stay in this relationship.

Remaining in relationship

How did I relate to God in my retreat? Do I remember being with the Father as Creator, lover, or merciful one? Did I meet Jesus as friend, healer, or teacher, or all three? Did I see him vulnerable and powerless, or strong and powerful? Did I feel the Spirit move with me in every exercise? Has the Trinity engaged with me in particular and personal ways? To remain in grace-filled relationship, I need to recall the most intimate, desirable face of God that I experienced during my retreat and bring that relationship into my daily life.

Growing in friendship

To grow in friendship with God, I do what I do for any friendship—I give the Lord both time and commitment. I share my affection and trust. I ask for forgiveness when necessary. I seek help when I need it. I share my vulnerabilities. I allow acceptance and openness to grow between us. In other words, I enjoy our relationship, and this keeps me filled with grace.

The daily Awareness Examen will be especially helpful in this. If I stay in touch, sharing the joys and concerns of life, I will not drift apart from God. If I pray regularly, friendship will take root. Moreover, I can gather with other friends of God to build a community of friendship. Ignatius advocated regular Eucharist and Reconciliation as sure ways to "keep on increasing in grace."[122]

Sharing what I have received

In the Spiritual Exercises, Ignatius asks me to give what I have received from God (cf. Rom 8:35–39). He asserts God is eager to increase what he has begun in my heart and mind. He is forthright:

> If this were not so, Jesus Christ would not say, Be perfect, as your heavenly Father is perfect, encouraging us to strive for what we can receive from His hand alone. It is certainly the case that he for his part is ready, if only we for ours have a humility and desire capacious enough to receive His graces, and if only He can see us using

well the graces we have received, and asking eagerly and lovingly
for His grace.[123]

If I take a few minutes to hold any retreat grace and ask myself what
this grace tells me about the giver of it, I will appreciate it all the more.
If I examine my grace very closely, with love and humility, and turn it
around in my hand like a diamond, I will see all its facets. I will catch
how God's light moves through it—in scintillations of love, reflections of
compassion, the flash of new life, and more. Retreat graces are wonderfully complex.

So I may ask, what does God desire in giving me this exact grace in
my present circumstances? Is it a grace that works well because of special gifts I already have, a grace joined to my strengths? Or is it a grace
for something I know I am utterly powerless with on my own—a grace
joined to God's power? Is it a grace for me or for someone else, to be
given through me? Am I now called to be supremely generous like God?
Reflections like these will sustain my retreat graces.

Having a large desire

Ignatius encourages us to have a desire capacious enough to receive
great gifts. He sees God on one side, who waits ready to give, and me on
the other side, eager and open to receive.[124] This relationship lies under
every exercise in my retreat—a keel to give me balance and direction, or
a keel to size the boat of my desires.

Taking a guide for the road

The first road guide is spiritual reading. I can explore how beautifully
my grace is revealed in a particular person, or how different understand-
ings of this grace have enriched particular communities, or how this
grace has been expressed in action by others. Similarly, I may look for
my grace in poetry, art, or music—I may be surprised as the Spirit sings
my grace out in these special ways. A retreat grace has a great many
songs.

The second road guide can be found in spiritual conversation. Here I
share with a Spiritual Conversation Guide or another at the level of faith.
We become comfortable talking about our spiritual life, our relationship
with God, and our concerns. A regular spiritual conversation can energize retreat graces. A related help is my spiritual journal, the Listening

Book. I can "listen" again to the graces I received for new meanings and fresh feelings.

The third road guide is spiritual direction. Meeting with a spiritual director is a truly effective way to keep and carry forward my retreat graces. A spiritual director is best defined as one who helps another nurture the graces that they have received from God.

Putting grace into action

Finally, Ignatius suggests that to progress with a retreat grace I need to use it. He firmly believed that love is best shown in action. The last exercise of my First Spiritual Exercises was to create a program for life. Putting this program into action will be an excellent way to keep my grace alive.

RECEIVING FURTHER EXERCISES

According to the grace of God given to me, like a skilled master builder I laid a foundation, and someone else is building on it. Each builder must choose with care how to build on it. For no one can lay any foundation other than the one that has been laid; that foundation is Jesus Christ. (1 Cor 3:10–11)

When St. Ignatius gave his Spiritual Exercises he was aware that a person's faith life began well before he met that person and would continue long after he or she made the retreat. Divine relationships, love, and service are living things. So he wanted to help people to keep moving forward in them.

This concern is not new in Christian communities. Jesus himself used images of growth and trust. Paul spoke of building upon the foundation. The early church felt itself alive, gifted, and active in the Spirit, filled with a momentum of desire to do good.

In Barcelona, on December 6, 1524, Ignatius wrote a letter to Inés Pascual, a woman who was like a mother to him and who provided room and board for him. Inés's friend and servant had died; she was ill, depressed, and her former friends in high society were giving her a hard time because she was begging with Ignatius for food and alms to give to the poor.

With great heart, Iñigo (Ignatius) wrote:

I have decided to write you this because of the desires to serve the Lord that I have seen in you. . . . For the love of God our Lord try to keep going forward. Always avoid whatever things are harmful. If you avoid them, temptation will have no power against you. This is what you should be doing always, placing the Lord's praise ahead of everything else. All the more so since the Lord does not require you to do anything exhausting or harmful to your person. He wants you to live taking joy in him and granting the body whatever it needs. Let all your words, thoughts, and behavior be in him, and attend to your bodily necessities for his sake, always placing the observance of God's commandments first. This is what he wants and what he commands us.

Iñigo continued:

> So, for the love of our Lord let us make every effort in him, since we owe him so much. For we tire of receiving his gifts much sooner than he tires of giving. May Our Lady intercede between us poor sinners and her Son and Lord; may she obtain for us the grace that, with the cooperation of our own toil and effort, our weak and sorry spirits may be made strong and joyful in his praise.
>
> The Poor Pilgrim, Iñigo.[125]

Ignatius invites Inés to try to keep moving forward, to live taking joy in the Lord, to make every effort in the Lord, and to remain open to receiving more gifts. It is worth reading the last sentence again, because these four simple invitations from Ignatius are a beautiful way to build on the graces of my retreat: I try to keep moving forward, I live taking joy in the Lord, I make every effort in the Lord, and I remain open to receiving more gifts from God.

How else may I "keep moving forward?" Many people, upon finishing a First Spiritual Exercises retreat, feel drawn to receive further exercises. Each suggestion below offers a next step.

Annual First Spiritual Exercises retreat

Four retreats are offered as First Spiritual Exercise retreats. Having experienced one of them, why not schedule one of the other three next year? This is a natural progression. Indeed, there may be experiences that I had in my first retreat that I wish to explore in a second retreat.

Ignatian prayer day

Here are two ways to build on my retreat experience. The first is to free up a day in my diary, say every four to six weeks. This will be my prayer day. I choose where I wish to be, undistracted and comfortable. In this day, I begin by reading through my spiritual journal, the Listening Book, from my First Spiritual Exercises retreat. When the book reminds me of a spiritual exercise that moved me deeply, I look for that exercise in this book. Then I take myself through that spiritual exercise again. Ignatius calls this powerful form of prayer the "Prayer of Repetition."[126]

The second way is to seek out a spirituality center, retreat house, or church community that is offering a prayer day, preferably Ignatian.

Having made the First Spiritual Exercises, I would be more experienced than those coming for a first time of extended prayer. Indeed, I may well bring many gifts to a day like this.

Ignatian weekend retreat

After making the First Spiritual Exercises, another excellent step forward would be to make a weekend retreat at an Ignatian spirituality center. I would already possess all I need to make such a retreat, and I will find the move from a twenty-two-day retreat in daily life to a two-day, live-in retreat quite natural. The Ignatian spirituality underpinning such a weekend would be familiar to me, as would the movements of prayer and reflection, retreat topics, and much else.

If an Ignatian center is not a realistic possibility, then I can look for any retreat center or parish offering a weekend retreat. In either case, one advantage is that it will be guided by an experienced director and made in the company of others with similar desires.

Ignatian individually directed retreat

In the individually directed retreat, I have a spiritual director assigned to meet with me each day. A directed retreat is a gentle and kindly way to make a retreat because my director will be guided by my own prayer. The pace will be mine and no other's. The Spirit, who knows and loves me intimately, will point the way forward. I can trust my own heart in this. There are no outside expectations, and I will have the attentive ear of my very own director—something to enjoy and profit from during my retreat. Such a retreat could be any time from two days to eight days.

An individually guided retreat is usually silent. I may fear that a retreat like this is only for very experienced people. But, having made the First Spiritual Exercises, I am already very experienced! Consider this: every Ignatian director in the world will have prayed the same Spiritual Exercises I have prayed in my First Spiritual Exercises. This is a bond that will prove fruitful in any spiritual direction.

Full Spiritual Exercises retreat

After my First Spiritual Exercises, I may feel strongly moved or attracted to do more over a greater length of time. It could be a transition time in my life or, mysteriously, I just feel deeply called to spend more time with God. If this is so, my first step is to sit down with an Ignatian spiritual director and have a conversation about this desire and the spiritual movements within myself.

Then, after a period of spiritual direction, the decision may be made whether I am to undertake the Full Spiritual Exercises. This is no ordinary commitment, and I would still need to find a trained Giver of the Exercises for this length of retreat, which is usually either thirty days enclosed or thirty weeks in daily life. The introduction to the First Spiritual Exercises in the front of this book explains the differences between these forms of the Spiritual Exercises.

These retreats are offered at Ignatian spirituality centers or by individual Ignatian directors working independently. This form of the Exercises is listed here because, although it is not common, some people have moved from the First Spiritual Exercises to the Full Spiritual Exercises. Furthermore, they have made them and made them well.

GIVING THE FIRST EXERCISES TO OTHERS

> [Jesus] cried out, "Let anyone who is thirsty come to me, and let the one who believes in me drink. As the scripture has said, 'Out of the believer's heart shall flow rivers of living water.'" (Jn 7:37b–38)

When I experience something really wonderful, profound, or liberating I often feel an immediate desire to share that experience with someone else. It is as if I cannot keep my good news secret. It seems the best gifts in life are for giving, not keeping. Although given personally in a retreat, my spiritual gifts seem to move through me like a great river, seeking a way to flow out and give life elsewhere.

One of the secret graces hidden in the First Spiritual Exercises is that once received, the Exercises desire to be passed on. In them are methods of prayer, intimacy with the Trinity, exercises about mercy and conversion, exercises for love and freedom, and much more. And every one of these exercises can be learned and taught with reasonable ease. Ignatius felt this too:

> Still, let me repeat once and twice and as many more times as I am able: I implore you, out of a desire to serve God our Lord, to do what I have said to you up to now. May His Divine Majesty never ask me one day why I did not ask you as strongly as I possibly could! The Spiritual Exercises are all the best that I have been able to think out, experience and understand in this life, both for helping somebody to make the most of themselves, as also for being able to bring advantage, help, and profit to many others. So, even if you don't feel the need for the first, you will see that they are much more helpful than you might have imagined for the second.[127]

Who shall teach them? Anyone who has prayed one of the spiritual exercises and received the graces of that exercise can teach that exercise to another. While I need training to give a First Spiritual Exercises retreat, I need no training to instruct someone in an exercise. The qualification is one of knowledge (how to do it), one of experience (I have felt God at work in this exercise), and one of grace (I know what it is like to receive the desired grace). This very likely means me. I can teach these exercises.

In September 1540, Blessed Peter Favre, a first companion of Ignatius, wrote to Ignatius about giving the Exercises in Parma, Italy. He tells how he gave the First Spiritual Exercises to a few, and then the few taught others, and the others taught more others—the First Spiritual Exercises rippling out into the lives of people in Parma and then spreading into the surrounding towns.

Among these who first received the First Spiritual Exercises were teachers, influential women, parish priests, families in the court, widows, preachers, and lay fraternities. And they taught others. These people, and groups of people, were all moved to a "good life." Peter was astonished. He writes:

> Indeed, some of the parish priests are giving the Exercises to their subjects. We taught the commandments right from the beginning when we came to Parma. Since then they have spread by way of the school masters, some of whom have even given the initial Exercises to a number of their capable students. Likewise there are women who make it their business to go from house to house teaching the girls and other women who cannot go out freely.
>
> The first thing they give is always the ten commandments, the seven deadly sins, and then the material for a general confession. The results obtained by this method here inside Parma and outside it I neither know how nor am able to explain; neither am I able to say how much good has come in, both in the city and outside it, because of frequent confession. By now no one is considered anything in Parma who does not confess at least once a month. I was told a few days ago that in one town, on the past feast of our Lady in August, more than three hundred persons received communion.
>
> The sermons have also been a considerable factor in these results, beyond what can be known, and not only those preached by the two of us but also by three others who, after making the Exercises, have preached throughout the region, so that ten or twelve of the main towns in the Parmesan territory have been moved to a good life.
>
> I shall not repeat the fruits that have been achieved with little difficulty in Sissa, the residence of that Orlando who constantly hears confessions, gives exercises, teaches children, and preaches

on every feast day, sometimes preaching in three or four villages
on a given feast day.[128]

Peter's language is that of the sixteenth century, and some of the exercises reflect the religious sensibility of the day. Still, the basic content and dynamic of the First Spiritual Exercises has not changed since he gave them, and I will have experienced exactly the same First Spiritual Exercises as the people of Parma. If I could talk to them, I would quickly find I share similar desires, graces, and experience.

One of Orlando's ministries was giving exercises, and those given "initial exercises" felt the need to teach, renew, and spread the Gospel through the same Exercises. As it was for them, so it can be for me. I can teach these "initial "or First Spiritual Exercises to others.

This is not to be a spiritual director or retreat Giver. I would need formation for those roles. Rather, I now possess the experience and grace of many spiritual exercises. I know their structure, the desire sought and how to enter into prayerful relationship with God. I could teach others exercises in the context of a personal relationship or in small groups.

In a personal relationship, if the situation arises in a conversation where I realize that the person has a particular desire and would benefit from a particular exercise, then I might share my experience and offer to teach them how to make that exercise. Such possibilities often arise when an ordinary conversation deepens naturally into a spiritual conversation—a sharing where deeper desires, confusions, or spiritual needs are raised. This is precisely how Ignatius gave the First Spiritual Exercises himself. There is an original connection between spiritual conversation and the First Spiritual Exercises. Furthermore, Ignatius was a layman without any special training when he did so.

Similarly, in a prayer, formation, support, or ministry group, if I recognize a desire being expressed that I prayed in my retreat, I could offer to teach them that exercise, as a way to receive what is desired. Such a group may even be a group of friends who meet regularly. In these, and many other fertile places, God desires to work through me as I teach the exercises I know.

How do I do it? Once I realize what may suit the person or group, I copy the relevant exercise from the relevant retreat in this book. Then I go through the exercise with them, explaining the prayer structure and pointing out the prayer texts. After they make the exercise, I might offer to listen to what they experienced. I could share my own experience and continue the original spiritual conversation that sparked the suggestion of making an exercise. And that is it—nothing more complicated!

While it might require a little courage to first teach an exercise, I will soon find what others have found, what Peter Favre found, that people in need will truly be grateful for my understanding, the clear structure of the exercise, and someone to help them pray it.

Indeed, the ministry of the First Spiritual Exercises and spiritual conversation could become a part of my life. For at some time in the future, I could well do the training to become a Giver of the First Spiritual Exercises and a Spiritual Conversation Guide. This training is much less than that for a spiritual director and, having made the retreats myself, I have already received the greater part of the training required. The lovely thing about such a service is that God will supply the strength for it.

> Like good stewards of the manifold grace of God, serve one another with whatever gift each of you has received. Whoever speaks must do so as one speaking the very words of God; whoever serves must do so with the strength that God supplies, so that God may be glorified in all things through Jesus Christ. (1 Pt 4:10–11)

Guides AND Helps

Spiritual Life

You should always take care
to maintain your soul
in peace,
in quiet,
and in readiness
for whatever Our Lord might wish to do within it.
There is no doubt that it is a greater virtue in the soul
and a greater grace for it to be able to relish its Lord
in a variety of duties
and in a variety of places,
rather than simply in one.
—Letter of Ignatius Loyola, Epistle 466

THE IGNATIAN AWARENESS EXAMEN

I Give Thanks	I give thanks for the graces, benefits, and good things of my day.
I Ask for Help	I ask the Holy Spirit for help to discern my day with openness.
I Review	I review my day, hour by hour, to see how God is working in my life.
I Respond	I respond to what I felt or learned in my review just made.
I Resolve	I resolve with hope and the grace of God to amend my life tomorrow.
	Our Father.[128]

SPIRITUAL DIRECTION

The story is told that an exhausted Jesuit wrote to Ignatius, saying his day was completely full—working day and night, saying Mass, and begging for alms—so he asked if he might drop the examens and shorten his meditation time. Ignatius wrote back, saying that he could drop everything else except the examens!

The Awareness Examen sifts my day with gratitude and seeks to discern the traces of God at work in my life. It guides me along the right path with understanding. My awareness of God at work will grow with practice as I become sensitive to the divine presence. It is prayed in five easy points:

1. I become aware that I live in the stream of God's love—where all is gift. I review my day, recalling its gifts, large and small, and allow gratitude to well up in me.
2. I make a prayer to the Spirit for her discerning light in this examen.
3. I carefully search out how God is working in my life, moving hour by hour, through my day. After some weeks I also look for any pattern of events or relationships that console me or give me inner peace. Conversely, is there a pattern that desolates or deadens me?

4. I respond to what I experienced in the previous point. I might give thanks or express sorrow. I might feel wonder, sadness, or sheer delight with my Lord. We speak about this.

5. I consider the loving way forward tomorrow. I may desire growth or change. I may want to live some virtue. I resolve to do my best and surrender the outcome to God.

The best time to pray the examen is at midday or the end of the day. I can be confident that over time this prayer will root my life in God's life. The prayer texts speak to each step.

SUGGESTED PRAYER TIME: 15 MINUTES

Thanks: 3 minutes. Help: 1 minute. Review: 7 minutes. Respond: 2 minutes. Resolve: 2 minutes.

AWARENESS EXAMEN TEXTS

The Advocate, the Holy Spirit, whom the Father will send in my name, will teach you everything, and remind you of all that I have said to you. (Jn 14:26)

My Father is still working, and I also am working. The Father loves the Son and shows him all that he himself is doing; and he will show him greater works than these, so that you will be astonished. Indeed, just as the Father raises the dead and gives them life, so also the Son gives life to whomever he wishes. (Jn 5:17, 20–21)

The tax collector, standing far off, would not even look up to heaven, but was beating his breast and saying, "God, be merciful to me, a sinner!" I tell you, this man went down to his home justified rather than the other; for all who exalt themselves will be humbled, but all who humble themselves will be exalted. (Lk 18:13–14)

You did not choose me but I chose you. And I appointed you to go and bear fruit, fruit that will last, so that the Father will give you whatever you ask him in my name. (Jn 15:16)

THE IGNATIAN PARTICULAR EXAMEN

Start of day

I Resolve	Upon rising, I firmly resolve to carefully practice my particular desire today.

During the day

I Mark	I mark each experience of my desire with a simple, symbolic action.

End of day

I Ask for Help	I ask God to help me see clearly in my review.
I Review	I review the day to see how God has been working in my particular desire.
I Compare	I compare hour by hour, day by day, week by week, my progress in my desire.
I Resolve	I firmly resolve to act with my desire tomorrow.
	Our Father.[130]

SPIRITUAL DIRECTION

The Particular Examen focuses on a particular desire. Following Ignatius, "I ask for what I desire more earnestly in connection with particular things" (*Spiritual Exercises* 199). It is worth considering the "particular" in life. If I want to dance with another person, I need to learn particular steps. If I need to be healed, I go to a particular doctor, look at particular symptoms, and have a particular treatment. If I find a particular thing utterly desirable, I might sell or abandon all I have to get it. If I am lost, I use a particular map to find my way home. When I grieve, it is because I have lost someone I particularly love. Indeed, if I desire to progress in any activity, be it intellectual, musical, sporting, artistic, or spiritual, I need to do particular exercises.

"Particular" is the way I live in depth, the way I search with focus, the way I heal, the way I find, the way I enjoy, the way I choose, and the way

I act in union with Christ and others. All these shapes of "particular" are held in the Particular Examen.

While I strive to enact my particular desire, I also ask God to act through it. In this way, for example, God's generosity acts through my generosity. I allow God to complete all I have been doing through faith (see 2 Thes 1:1). With such wonderful possibility, my day begins and ends with firm resolve.

To progress more quickly, whenever I realize my particular desire in the day, I make a small, symbolic body gesture of gratitude. This need not be public or long—just a symbol that I have received or practiced my particular desire.

SUGGESTED PRAYER TIME: 15 MINUTES
Desire: 1 minute. Review: 10 minutes. Compare: 2 minutes. Resolve: 2 minutes.

PARTICULAR EXAMEN TEXTS
Pursue love and strive for the spiritual gifts. (1 Cor 14:1a)

Ask, and it will be given you; search, and you will find; knock, and the door will be opened for you. For everyone who asks receives, and everyone who searches finds, and for everyone who knocks, the door will be opened. (Lk 11:9)

A new heart I will give you, and a new spirit I will put within you; and I will remove from your body the heart of stone and give you a heart of flesh. (Ez 36:26)

The kingdom of heaven is like a merchant in search of fine pearls; on finding one pearl of great value, he went and sold all that he had and bought it. (Mt 13:45–46)

We always pray for you, asking that our God will make you worthy of his call and will fulfil by his power every good resolve and work of faith. (2 Thes 1:11)

THE IGNATIAN
RECONCILIATION EXAMEN

I Give Thanks   After reading the prayer texts, I stand for a few minutes before the Father, as son or daughter, and feel his compassion
as he puts his arms around me.

I sift the month, with gratitude, for times I have received or
given forgiveness.

I Ask for Help   I ask the Spirit to intercede for me with sighs too deep for
words.

I Review   I move through the last month, day by day:

1. Before the Father of mercies, I recall if I have rejected or
   withheld love.

2. In the light of the Lord's forgiveness, I sift my thoughts,
   words, and actions.

3. With the Spirit, I examine the general direction of my
   life—my true self.

4. I explore one social structure I belong to, discerning
   good from the unjust.

5. I bring to Jesus any sin or sinful pattern that has real and
   deadly consequences in my life.

I Respond   I enter the mystery of the Trinity's reconciling and forgiving love. I humbly express my sorrow for what was re-
vealed above, and ask for forgiveness.

I Resolve	I resolve to take one or more of the following paths to reconciliation:

1. To adjust my lifestyle or work, see a counselor or spiritual director, or deepen my personal, family, and church relationships, so that the Lord may forgive and reconcile me through them.

2. To bring where I need forgiveness to Jesus, and to call on his merciful love.

3. To take any needed reconciling action, for myself or others I have hurt.

4. To receive the Sacrament of Reconciliation, now and monthly if possible.

5. To make, as envoy for Christ, one small act of reconciliation next month.[131]

SPIRITUAL DIRECTION

The Reconciliation Examen above is broadened from the examination of thoughts, words, and deeds suggested by Ignatius. I spend more time on those questions or actions closest to my need.

Ignatius received a revelation on the road to Rome to begin his lifelong service to God. "Before reaching Rome, I was at prayer in a church and experienced such a change in my soul and saw so clearly that God the Father placed me with Christ his Son that I would not dare doubt it."[132] The Christ before Ignatius is Jesus carrying his Cross. The love that he and Ignatius had for one another, their shared vision of God's kingdom, their desire to feed, liberate, and teach the needy, grew into a profound friendship and an effective, shared mission. Ignatius realized anything that fractured, enticed away, or hid this working relationship leaves one in need of loving reconciliation.

SUGGESTED PRAYER TIME: AS NEEDED

RECONCILIATION EXAMEN TEXT

If anyone is in Christ, there is a new creation: everything old has passed away; see, everything has become new! All this is from God, who reconciled us to himself through Christ, and has given us the ministry of reconciliation. (2 Cor. 5:17–18)

THE IGNATIAN HEALING EXAMEN

I Give Thanks   After reading the prayer texts, I stand before Jesus. He lays his hands on me. I sift the month with gratitude for times I have received or given healing.

I Ask for Help   I ask the Spirit to refresh, anoint, and heal me.

I Review   I move through the last month, day by day:

1. Where am I blind, deaf, dumb, or living a half life?

   Have I blinded or stolen the voice of another?

2. Where am I paralyzed by illness, a life situation, sinfulness, or fear?

   Have I paralyzed another?

3. Where am I tormented by demons, hurting myself?

   Have I demonized another?

4. Where am I dead, drained, grieving, or entombed?

   Have I taken life from another?

I Respond   In God's healing love, I humbly express my particular need, as revealed above.

I Resolve   I resolve to seek healing through one or more of the following paths:

1. To adjust my lifestyle, see a counselor or spiritual director, or deepen my personal, family, and church relationships, so that the Lord may heal me through them.

2. To bring my wounds to Jesus in prayer, that he may clean, heal, and give them new meaning.

3. To take any needed healing action, for myself or others I have hurt.

4. To receive the sacrament of healing now and monthly, if possible.

5. To make, working with the Spirit, one small act of healing next month.

SPIRITUAL DIRECTION

Ignatius wrote no Healing Examen, but this new Examen does mirror the Reconciliation Examen. Each of these examens reveals something about the other. The two last prayer texts are from the Sacrament of the Anointing of the Sick. They make the connection between reconciliation and healing.

I am invited to receive the Sacrament of the Anointing of the Sick this week. If possible, pray directly for healing or take a healing action. The Healing Examen can help prepare me for all these. In the "I Review" and "I Resolve" steps above, I spend more time on those questions or actions closest to my need.

SUGGESTED PRAYER TIME: AS NEEDED

HEALING EXAMEN TEXTS

Is not this the fast that I choose: to loose the bonds of injustice, to undo the thongs of the yoke, to let the oppressed go free, and to break every yoke? Is it not to share your bread with the hungry, and bring the homeless poor into your house; when you see the naked, to cover them, and not to hide yourself from your own kin? Then your light shall break forth like the dawn, and your healing shall spring up quickly; your vindicator shall go before you, the glory of the LORD shall be your rear guard. Then you shall call, and the LORD will answer; you shall cry for help, and he will say, Here I am. (Is 58:6–9a)

During the sacrament of anointing the priest lays his hands on your head and anoints your forehead, saying: Through this holy anointing may the Lord in his love and mercy help you with the grace of the Holy Spirit. *Response*: Amen.

He anoints your hands, saying: May the Lord who frees you from sin, save you and raise you up. *Response*: Amen.

Concluding Prayer

Father in heaven, through this anointing grant us comfort in our suffering. When we are afraid, give us courage, when afflicted, give us patience, when dejected, afford us hope, and when alone, assure us of the support of your holy people. *Response*: Amen.[133]

Spiritual Guides

THE IGNATIAN GUIDE
TO ENHANCE EXERCISES

The Lord is near. Do not worry about anything, but in everything by prayer and supplication with thanksgiving let your requests be made known to God. And the peace of God, which surpasses all understanding, will guard your hearts and your minds in Christ Jesus. (Phil 4:5b–7)

This Guide is in two parts. Part one is a set of individual guides to enhance prayer. Part two has several sets of guides for making better exercises. Ignatius provides this assistance, "to find more readily what I want," in the annotations, additions, and notes of *The Spiritual Exercises*. Both part one and two use his text or, divided for greater simplicity, are offered in simple paraphrase. The number at the end of each particular guide refers to the number of the annotation in the Exercises.[134] There are fifty in total.

The first set of guides "to enhance prayer" will be of use straight away in my retreat and personal prayer.

The second set of guides to "make better exercises" wait for when they will do the greatest good. A read through the lot will make me familiar with the different sets. The "best approach" set will be of use quite early in my retreat. The "during the exercise." "during the retreat" and "in general" sets find their place after the first or second week of my retreat, or when I judge they may best help, earlier or later.

The "during desolation" set is only to be acted upon if I experience spiritual desolation, otherwise left alone. The "for the future" set is for the last week of my retreat.

If I have a Giver of the First Spiritual Exercises or Spiritual Conversation Guide, then that person can more usefully introduce the sets of guides to me at the best time. In any case, I can always seek and trust my wisest counselor and guide, the Holy Spirit.

Part 1. Guide for Enhancing Prayer

1. Prepare the prayer space

Creating a prayer space will keep me focused during the First Spiritual Exercises. For my retreat, I could make a small home altar with an image, flower, and cross. I may add symbols of light, water, or desire as I experience a grace or need during my retreat (*Spiritual Exercises* 79, 130).

2. Think before sleep

I take twenty seconds, before I sleep, to recall the time I have to get up, and for what purpose, going over the exercise I have to make (*Spiritual Exercises* 73).

3. Remember upon waking

Before I allow my thoughts to wander, I bring to mind the subject of the exercise for the day. I then rouse my feelings by imagining the relationship I desire with the Lord. I desire to know him more intimately so as to better serve and follow him (*Spiritual Exercises* 24, 74, 130, 131).

4. Consider while dressing

Dress or dressing can be used in symbolic gestures of imagination and desire. I imagine myself as I wish to be before the God of my spiritual exercise today. The preparation step of most exercises will guide me in this (*Spiritual Exercises* 74).

5. Rehearse beforehand

When the time for my spiritual exercise is approaching, I remember that I am going to enter the presence of God, and then I run briefly over the spiritual exercise ahead of me (*Spiritual Exercises* 131).

6. Reverence to begin

I stand before my prayer place for a minute, and with my mind raised up I consider how God our Lord is looking at me with tender love. In response, I make a genuflection or another gesture of reverence and humility (*Spiritual Exercises* 75, 131).

7. Body at rest

For prayer I may kneel or sit, lie face down or face up, or stand. Ignatius adds, "Two things should be noted: first, if I find what I want whilst kneeling, I will go no further, and similarly if prostrate, etc. Second, where I find what I want, I will settle down, without any anxiety to move on" (*Spiritual Exercises* 76).

8. Express your generosity and desire

It is highly profitable for the receiver to begin with great generosity and freedom, and to offer all his or her powers of desire. This is in the preparation prayer and desire of each exercise. [5]

9. Pray the exercise

Pray the full amount of time chosen beforehand. [12, 13]

10. Journal with the Listening Book after the exercise

After prayer, Ignatius instructs, "I will either sit down or walk around for a quarter of an hour while I see how things have gone for me during the prayer." The First Spiritual Exercises spiritual journal, the Listening Book, does this at depth (*Spiritual Exercises* 77).

11. My physical world

I adapt the physical world to mirror the desire of the spiritual exercise. So I darken or lighten a room, I place a bowl of water, I wear certain colored clothes, and so on (*Spiritual Exercises* 77).

12. My emotional world

I remain in the emotional world of an exercise by keeping my whole day in serenity, joy, sorrow, etc., so matching the desired emotions of each particular exercise (*Spiritual Exercises* 80).

13. My inner world

I sustain the inner world of my spiritual exercise with thoughts and memories that keep the climate of my retreat throughout the day (*Spiritual Exercises* 78, 130).

14. My imaginative world

I enhance the imaginative world of the spiritual exercise by choosing what I look at, what I touch, what I smell, how I eat, where I am during the day. So I try to remain in harmony with the particular exercise of that day (*Spiritual Exercises* 81).

15. My symbolic world

I use the power of the symbolic world by creating body actions that mark special graces or desires. The sign of the cross or a hand over my heart is traditional. Discretely, I may use similar gestures throughout the day (*Spiritual Exercises* 27).

Part 2. Guide to Make Better Exercises

THE BEST APPROACH

16. Be at peace
I need not be anxious about knowing enough of prayer, Bible, or church life to make a First Spiritual Exercises retreat. I do not need to be churched. Nor do I need to be concerned about my past. None are necessary to meet God. My desire itself is more than enough (*Spiritual Exercises* 2).

17. Value personal experience
My own prayer will be more fruitful than anything I may read in a book or be taught by an expert. In making the First Exercises, I can relax and be confident in my own graces and insights (*Spiritual Exercises* 2).

18. Seek inner relish
Ignatius felt strongly that "the inner feeling and the relish of things" will fill and satisfy my soul more than knowledge (*Spiritual Exercises* 2).

19. Practice reverence
As my retreat advances, I will become aware of a growing intimacy in my relationship with each person in the Trinity. This will call for deeper reverence (*Spiritual Exercises* 3).

20. Go with the dynamic of the four weeks
The First Spiritual Exercises take four weeks. Each week opens a new theme, progressively guiding me forward. I will be guided, step by step, in each new exercise (*Spiritual Exercises* 4).

21. Look for fruit in the right place
I look for the fruit appropriate to the exercise I am making now. Everything else is a distraction (*Spiritual Exercises* 4).

22. Adjust the prayer time if needed
I may adjust my exercises by making them a little longer or shorter, or by moving a day if I need to. But I do not move them for ordinary convenience. Each retreat week has its own integrity (*Spiritual Exercises* 4).

23. Have a largeness of heart
I begin every exercise with generosity and a magnanimous spirit—for this is how my Creator and Lord approaches me (*Spiritual Exercises* 5).

24. Offer God everything

I offer God all my desires and every freedom. I do so that he may avail himself of me and all that I possess. This offering is made in the preparation prayer of each exercise (*Spiritual Exercises* 5).

DURING DESOLATION

25. Be gentle

In times of spiritual desolation, I will be kind and gentle to myself (*Spiritual Exercises* 7).

26. Ask for courage and strength

In desolation, I ask the Spirit for courage and strength. I may also talk to my retreat Giver, a spiritual conversation guide, spiritual director, or a prayerful, nonjudgmental friend (*Spiritual Exercises* 7).

27. Reveal the tricks of the enemy

In times of desolation, I ask the Holy Spirit to lay bare the tricks of the enemy of human nature (*Spiritual Exercises* 7).

28. Trust the rhythm of consolation

Spiritual consolation always follows desolation. Knowing this, I will take heart (*Spiritual Exercises* 7).

29. Discern the two spirits

If I experience various agitations and thoughts brought about by different spirits, the good and the bad, I will seek out the Giver of my Exercises. If I am by myself, I may study the Ignatian Guide to the Discernment of Spirits in this book. This will help me to identify where I am and how to move in the direction of the good spirit (*Spiritual Exercises* 7–8, 17).

30. Face suspicious obstacles

If I experience temptations, such as disheartening hardships, worrying about what people think of me, a lost status, or fear of the unknown, I should be suspicious. In a person moving from good to better, such confusion is likely the work of the bad spirit (*Spiritual Exercises* 9).

31. Expect resistance

I need to be aware that the enemy will try anything to disrupt my retreat. In times of consolation it is easy to keep to my commitments, but in desolation it is difficult to last out. So, I might add a little to my usual commitment, so as to "get into the way not only of resisting the enemy, but even of defeating him completely" (*Spiritual Exercises* 12–13).

32. Surrender to God
In times of desolation, when I have done my best, and sought the help of my Giver of the First Exercises, I will surrender and leave everything else to God. I make ready for the consolation which is surely to come (*Spiritual Exercises* 7).

DURING THE EXERCISE AND IN CONVERSATION AFTER

33. Focus on the present exercise
I focus on what is sought in the exercise before me rather than reading ahead. Each exercise, day, and week has its own particular order and dynamic. It is very important to stay in the place given in the exercise and not be drawn anywhere else (*Spiritual Exercises* 11).

34. Communicate directly with God
As strongly stated by Ignatius, it is "much better that my Creator and Lord communicates directly with me, inflaming me in his love and praise, and disposing me toward the way in which I will be better able to serve him in the future" (*Spiritual Exercises* 15).

35. Know the role of the Giver of the Exercises
The above truth is a reminder that the role of the Giver of my Exercises, or Spiritual Conversation Guide, is not to sway or encourage me toward any choice or preference, but to leave the Creator to deal directly with me, and me to deal with my Creator and Lord (*Spiritual Exercises* 15).

36. Be open with the Giver of the Exercises
A faithful account of my prayer experience is useful not only for myself but also for the Giver of my First Spiritual Exercises. With my Listening Book, I ask, where was I moved? What happened? Have I received what I desired? Detail here is very important. This is shared with my Giver (*Spiritual Exercises* 17).

37. Apply the exercises to one's disposition and energies
I apply the timetable of the retreat to my disposition and temperament, making more or less exercises if helpful. Similarly, I may adapt them to my age and health, making an exercise a little shorter or in several parts

over a number of days. Some days, I may have the energy to pray a little longer or repeat the exercise (*Spiritual Exercises* 18, 72, 129, 133, 209).

DURING THE RETREAT

38. Choose the right retreat
I choose the First Spiritual Exercises retreat likely to give me the most help. I match my desires with the desires sought in each retreat. There is absolutely no profit to be gained from doing a retreat that does not meet my desires or disposition at the present time (*Spiritual Exercises* 18).

39. Reject unrealistic expectations
There is nothing in the First Spiritual Exercises, either of content or process, that I cannot do. I do not need particular education, great intelligence, or perfect health. Unlike the Full Spiritual Exercises, the First Spiritual Exercises are for everyone. The only thing I need is the generosity to take the practical steps and the faith to open myself to the God who loves me (*Spiritual Exercises* 18).

40. Be genuine and committed
Making a retreat is not about being driven; it is more about surrender. While each retreat has four weeks of daily prayer and Sunday Eucharist, there is no deadline inherent in them. My life will have its own rhythms; I need to find the balance between making a real sacrifice and commitment and doing what is sustainable (*Spiritual Exercises* 18).

41. Complete all the steps
The First Spiritual Exercises have a deliberate order and progressive dynamic. I need to be faithful, to trust the order and leave out no steps— even if they seem obvious. Each exercise seeks, not only to bring me to God, but also to have me do so habitually (*Spiritual Exercises* 18–20).

42. When to stop
If a retreat is draining me and leaving me overly fatigued, then I should stop—it is likely I am trying to make a retreat that is not suitable for me, or not suitable at this time. I am a free, responsible adult; I can choose another time to make my retreat, or try a different retreat, or seek advice from a Spiritual Conversation Guide or director. Or I may choose to make a few exercises that really do attract and help. This may be all I need to do at this time (*Spiritual Exercises* 18).

IN GENERAL

43. Let questions for information wait until later

During the course of the First Spiritual Exercises I may discover that I would like some particular information or instruction on the gospels, Church teaching, spirituality, and so on. To follow this urge with immediate research or reading during my retreat will take me out of it and away from God. I will do better to note my questions and follow up on them after my retreat (*Spiritual Exercises* 18).

44. Let the examens guide you in the background

There are four examens in the First Spiritual Exercises, the Awareness, Particular, Reconciliation, and Healing Examens. Each is introduced precisely, in rhythm and beat, with the exercises made that week. The Reconciliation and Healing Examens may be preparation for the Sacraments of Reconciliation and the Anointing of the Sick, or similar ritual and action. The Awareness and Particular Examens bed my daily life into God's action in the world. After learning these examens, I can pray them, without fuss in the background, and they will support me and all my exercises (*Spiritual Exercises* 18).

45. Let adult faith grow in the background

The First Spiritual Exercises do not have faith formation as a primary aim, but they do, quietly in the background, teach me most of the important Christian beliefs and values (*Spiritual Exercises* 18).

46. Let the sacred word speak in the background

With the solid scriptural foundation of each exercise, I will receive a very good overview of the gospels and their content, as well as insight into Christian relationships, action, and community from the rest of the scriptures (*Spiritual Exercises* 2, 4, 18).

47. Let the sacraments feed you in the background

Each retreat has a Sunday Eucharist exercise. During my retreat, I will also be invited to receive the Sacraments of Reconciliation, Anointing of the Sick, and even Baptism. Ignatius makes the sacraments an integral part of the First Spiritual Exercises because he experienced God powerfully through the synergy of sacrament, prayer, and Christian service. See the Program for Life (*Spiritual Exercises* 18).

FOR THE FUTURE

48. Take one realistic step forward

The goal of the First Spiritual Exercises is to take just one generous step in the right direction, not necessarily to make a major life change. Small, desired, slow, planned, confirmed, savored, realistic, free, habitual, fruitful steps are at the heart of these retreats. Only in this way can progress be found, maintained, and kept. The final exercise of each retreat, creating a program for life, will help me to do this (*Spiritual Exercises* 18).

49. Be ready to accept great gifts of God

Ignatius notes that our Creator and Lord desires us to approach and come nearer so that we can be "disposed to receive graces and gifts from his Divine and Supreme Goodness" (*Spiritual Exercises* 20).

50. Seek for inner peace

The First Spiritual Exercises hopes to bring me a certain peace of soul. This deep inner peace is a spiritual consolation and a gift of the Spirit. Over my retreat, the First Spiritual Exercises may stretch me in my desires, take me into new territory, loosen that which binds, and place me, sometimes a little awkwardly, into new relationships with God. This interior growth and renewing change may unsettle me, but in the end God's inner peace will assuredly dwell in me (*Spiritual Exercises* 18).

THE IGNATIAN
GUIDE TO
TWELVE WAYS OF PRAYER

1. Five Ancient Prayers by Word

2. Five Ancient Prayers by Breath

3. Praying the New Commandments

4. Praying the Seven Virtues

5. Praying the Gifts of the Body

6. Praying the Works of Mercy

7. Lectio Divina

8. Meditation

9. Imaginative Contemplation

10. Prayer of the Interior Senses

11. Prayer of Repetition

12. Contemplation

Five Ancient Prayers by Word

Preparation	I will allow my spirit to rest a little and consider where I am going and for what purpose. I make a gesture of reverence and humility. I read the prayer texts.
Opening Prayer	I ask the Father for the grace to direct my whole self toward him.
Desire	I desire to find meaning and delight in the Father.
Prayer	Keeping my eyes closed, or fixed on one spot without wandering, I say the word "Our," staying with this word for as long as I find meanings, comparisons, relish, and consolation in considerations related to it. I do this for each word or sense phrase of the Our Father.
	I spend my whole prayer time on the Our Father. When I am finished I say the Our Father, Hail Mary, Apostles' Creed, Soul of Christ, and Come, Holy Spirit, aloud or silently, in the usual way.
Conversation	I ask the Father for the virtues or graces for which I feel the greatest need.[135]

SPIRITUAL DIRECTION

I need to give myself a minute or so for each of the considerations, "meaning, comparisons, relish, and consolation," that I make of each word. With practice, each one of these considerations will deepen, engaging both my lived experience and my desires.

Ignatius adds the following two notes:

> If I find in one or two words rich matter for reflection, relish, and consolation, I will have no anxiety to go further, even though the whole prayer time is spent on what has been found. When my prayer time is up, I will say the remainder of the Our Father in the usual way. And then the other prayers as named above. (*Spiritual Exercises* 254)

Spiritual consolations are sought in this prayer. Ignatius calls them

> any interior movement produced in the soul which leads her to become inflamed with the love of her Creator and Lord . . . every increase of hope, faith and charity . . . to all interior happiness which calls and attracts to heavenly things . . . leaving the soul quiet and at peace in her Creator and Lord. (*Spiritual Exercises* 316)

In this prayer method, I will pray both word and whole prayer with increasing fertility. But the real power of these exercises comes when the grace of one word in one ancient prayer spills into the other ancient prayers. Then the phrases and delights and meanings begin to sing to each other.

On the second day, I will take the second prayer of the five ancient prayers listed above and pray it, on the third day the third, eventually moving through all five. There is much to be gained by completing this cycle. The words of the five ancient prayers are given below.

SUGGESTED PRAYER TIME: 30 MINUTES

Preparation: 5 minutes. Opening Prayer: 1 minute. Desire: 1 minute. Prayer: 20 minutes. Conversation: 3 minutes. Listening Book after prayer: 10 minutes.

PRAYER TEXTS

Our	Father,	who art in heaven,	hallowed be
your name.	Your	kingdom	come;
your will	be done	on earth	as it is in heaven.
Give us	this day	our	daily bread;
and forgive us	our	sins	as we forgive
those who sin	against us;	and lead us not	into temptation
but deliver	us	from evil.	Amen.

[Jesus] was praying in a certain place, and after he had finished, one of his disciples said to him, "Lord, teach us to pray, as John taught his disciples." He said to them, "When you pray, say:

> Father, hallowed be your name.
> Your kingdom come.
> Give us each day our daily bread.
> And forgive us our sins,
> for we ourselves forgive everyone indebted to us.
> And do not bring us to the time of trial."

I am no longer in the world, but they are in the world, and I am coming to you. Holy Father, protect them in your name that you have given me, so that they may be one, as we are one. I am not asking you to take them out of the world, but I ask you to protect them from the evil one. (Jn 17:11, 15)

FIVE ANCIENT PRAYERS

Our Father

Our Father, who art in heaven,
hallowed be your name.
Your kingdom come;
your will be done on earth as it is in heaven.
Give us this day our daily bread;
and forgive us our sins as we forgive those who sin against us;
and lead us not into temptation but deliver us from evil. Amen. [136]

Hail Mary

Hail Mary, full of grace,
the Lord is with you.
Blessed are you among women,
and blessed is the fruit of your womb, Jesus.
Holy Mary, Mother of God,
pray for us sinners, now,
and at the hour of our death. Amen.[137]

Apostles' Creed

I believe in God, the Father almighty,
Creator of heaven and earth,
and in Jesus Christ, his only Son, our Lord,
who was conceived by the Holy Spirit,
born of the Virgin Mary,
suffered under Pontius Pilate,
was crucified, died, and was buried;
He descended into hell;
on the third day he rose again from the dead;
he ascended into heaven,
and is seated at the right hand of God the Father almighty;
from there he shall come to judge the living and the dead.
I believe in the Holy Spirit,
the holy catholic Church, the communion of saints,
the forgiveness of sins, the resurrection of the body,
and life everlasting. Amen.[138]

Soul of Christ

Soul of Christ, sanctify me.
Body of Christ, save me.
Blood of Christ, inebriate me.
Water from Christ's side, wash me.
Passion of Christ, strengthen me.
O good Jesus, hear me;
within your wounds hide me.
Suffer me not to be separated from thee;
from the malicious enemy defend me.
In the hour of my death call me
and bid me come unto thee that I may praise you
with your saints and with your angels,
forever and ever. Amen.[139]

Come, Holy Spirit—Veni, Sancte Spiritus

Come, Holy Spirit,
fill the hearts of your faithful
and kindle in them the fire of your love.
Send forth your Spirit
and they shall be created.
And you shall renew the face of the earth.
O God, who by the light of the Holy Spirit
did instruct the hearts of the faithful,
grant that by the same Holy Spirit
we may be truly wise
and ever enjoy his consolations,
through Christ our Lord. Amen.[140]

Five Ancient Prayers by Breath

Preparation	I will allow my spirit to rest a little and consider where I am going and for what purpose. I make a gesture of reverence and humility. I read the prayer texts.
Opening Prayer	I ask for the grace to direct my whole self toward the Spirit.
Desire	I desire to breathe in the Spirit.
Prayer	I pray silently on each intake or expulsion of my breath, by saying one word of the Come, Holy Spirit, so that only a single word is pronounced between one breath and the next. I do this with the natural rhythm of my normal breathing.
	Contemplatively, I pay special attention to the meaning of that word or to the Spirit to whom I am praying. In this way I deepen my relationship with the Spirit. I make myself ready for her presence and action in me.
	I spend my whole prayer time on the Come, Holy Spirit. When I am finished I say the Come, Holy Spirit, Our Father, Hail Mary, Apostles' Creed, and Soul of Christ aloud or silently, in the usual way.
Conversation	I ask the Spirit for the virtues or graces for which I feel the greatest need. [141]

SPIRITUAL DIRECTION

The Come, Holy Spirit or *Veni, Sancte Spiritus,* as it is traditionally known, is a prayer asking for the grace of the Holy Spirit. It has been used for centuries in private devotion and appears in the liturgical calendar for the feast of Pentecost.

My breathing in this prayer remains normal, neither too deep nor too shallow, the rhythm unforced. And if it helps, I may pray a sense phrase on a breath or one word on many breaths.

On the second day, I take the second prayer of the five listed above and pray it, on the third day the third, eventually moving through all five to complete the cycle.

The word *ruah* in Aramaic means Spirit, breath, wind, breeze, life, and life of God. The one who hovers over creation is *ruah.* The breath that Jesus breathes into his disciples is *ruah.* The Spirit that the Lord sends forth to renew the earth is *ruah*. This understanding of breath as life-giving, life renewing, and life divine flows through this way of praying.

After this prayer, I can truly say with Job, "I have life within me, the breath of God in my nostrils" (see Jb 27:3).

SUGGESTED PRAYER TIME: 15 MINUTES

Preparation: 3 minutes. Opening Prayer: 1 minute. Desire: 1 minute. Prayer: 10 to 15 minutes or as needed. Conversation: 1 minute. Listening Book after prayer: 5 minutes.

PRAYER TEXTS

Come	Holy	Spirit,	fill
the hearts	of your	faithful	and kindle
in them	the fire	of your	love.
Send	forth	your	Spirit
and they	shall be	created.	
And you	shall renew	the face	of the earth.
O God, who	by the light	of the Holy	Spirit
did instruct	the hearts	of the faithful,	grant
that by the same	Holy	Spirit	we
may be truly	wise	and ever enjoy	his
consolations,	through Christ	our Lord.	Amen.

When the day of Pentecost had come, [the disciples] were all together in one place. And suddenly from heaven there came a sound like the rush of a violent wind, and it filled the entire house where they were sitting. Divided tongues, as of fire, appeared among them, and a tongue rested on each of them. All of them were filled with the Holy Spirit and began to speak in other languages, as the Spirit gave them ability. (Acts 2:1–4)

The Counselor, the Holy Spirit, whom the Father will send in my name, will teach you all things and will remind you of everything I have said to you. Peace I leave with you; my peace I give you. I do not give to you as the world gives. Do not let your hearts be troubled and do not be afraid. (Jn 14:25–27, NIV-G/K)

Praying the New Commandments

Preparation	I will allow my spirit to rest a little and consider where I am going and for what purpose. I make a gesture of reverence and humility. I read the prayer texts.
Opening Prayer	I ask Jesus for understanding of the new commandments that I may live them better for his greater service.
Desire	I desire spiritual progress in the new commandments.
Prayer	1. I consider loving God with all my heart. What is Jesus teaching here?
	2. Where is this heartfelt love present in my life?
	3. Where is it absent in my life?
	4. I reflect on the contrary of this new commandment.
	After 3 minutes, I ask Jesus for what I desire.
	Our Father.
	The same procedure is repeated for each commandment.
Conversation	Now I examine the commandments as a whole. I ask:
	1. Which commandment do I live the best, more than any other?
	2. Which commandment do I desire to live for greater service of God?
	3. Which commandment would give me the greatest inner peace now?
	In conversation with Jesus, I choose one commandment to live well today.[142]

SPIRITUAL DIRECTION

In this prayer, I take each new commandment in turn. I consider its meaning, ponder where it is present or absent in my life, and then reflect on its contrary. It is very important I take about half a minute to consider each question in turn. The same is true of the three questions in the conversation with Jesus.

In practicing a particular commandment today, I can do it when I choose or, with alertness, wait for the Spirit to enact that commandment through me.

SUGGESTED PRAYER TIME: 40 MINUTES

Preparation: 5 minutes. Opening Prayer: 1 minute. Desire: 1 minute. Prayer: 30 minutes. Conversation: 3 minutes. Listening Book after prayer: 10 minutes.

PRAYER TEXTS

The New Commandments

1. To love God with all my heart.
2. To love God with all my soul.
3. To love God with all my mind.
4. To love my neighbor as myself.
5. To love others as Jesus loves me.
6. To surrender my possessions and follow Jesus.
7. To abide in the love and joy of God.

"You shall love the Lord your God with all your heart, and with all your soul, and with all your mind." This is the greatest and first commandment. And a second is like it: "You shall love your neighbor as yourself." On these two commandments hang all the law and the prophets. (Mt 22:37–40)

I give you a new commandment, that you love one another. Just as I have loved you, you also should love one another. By this everyone will know that you are my disciples. (Jn 13:34–35a)

Jesus, looking at him, loved him and said, "You lack one thing; go, sell what you own, and give the money to the poor, and you will have treasure in heaven; then come, follow me." When he heard this, he was shocked and went away grieving, for he had many possessions. (Mk 10:21–22)

As the Father has loved me, so I have loved you; abide in my love. If you keep my commandments, you will abide in my love, just as I have kept my Father's commandments and abide in his love. I have said these things to you so that my joy may be in you, and that your joy may be complete. (Jn 15:9–11)

Praying the Seven Virtues

Preparation	I will allow my spirit to rest a little and consider where I am going and for what purpose. I make a gesture of reverence and humility. I read the prayer texts.
Opening Prayer	I ask God for understanding of the virtues, that I may live them better for his greater service.
Desire	I desire spiritual progress through the virtues.
Prayer	1. I consider faith. What is it?
	2. Where is it present in my life?
	3. Where is it absent in my life?
	4. I reflect on the contrary of faith.
	After 3 minutes, I ask God for what I desire.
	Our Father.
	The same procedure is repeated for each virtue.
Conversation	Now I examine the virtues as a whole. I ask:
	1. Which virtue do I have in the greatest measure, more than any other?
	2. Which virtue do I desire for greater service of God?
	3. Which virtue would give me the greatest inner peace now?
	In conversation with God, I choose one virtue to live well today.[143]

SPIRITUAL DIRECTION

In this prayer, I take each virtue in turn. I consider its meaning, its presence or absence in my life, and I identify its contrary. I need to take about half a minute to answer each in turn. The same is true of the three questions in the conversation with Jesus.

I can practice my chosen virtue throughout the day as I wish, or be ready for the Spirit to enact that virtue through me.

Virtues have been described as the firm and habitual disposition to do the good. Today spiritual guides suggest new virtues like self-esteem, hospitality, gratitude, humility, vigilance, serenity, empathy, humor, restraint, tolerance, generosity, fitness, forgiveness, integrity, and compassion. One of these might be prayed when needed at some time in the future.

SUGGESTED PRAYER TIME: 40 MINUTES

Preparation: 5 minutes. Opening Prayer: 1 minute. Desire: 1 minute. Prayer: 30 minutes. Conversation: 3 minutes or as needed. Listening Book after prayer: 10 minutes.

PRAYER TEXTS
The Virtues
1. Faith
2. Hope
3. Love
4. Self-control
5. Wisdom
6. Justice
7. Courage

Faith, hope, and love abide, these three; and the greatest of these is love. (1 Cor 13:13)

We always give thanks to God for all of you and mention you in our prayers, constantly remembering before our God and Father your work of faith and labor of love and steadfastness of hope in our Lord Jesus Christ. (1 Thes 1:2–3)

[Wisdom] renews all things; in every generation she passes into holy souls and makes them friends of God, and prophets. Her labors are virtues; for she teaches self-control and prudence, justice and courage; nothing in life is more profitable for mortals than these. Therefore I determined to take her to live with me, knowing that she would give me good counsel and encouragement in cares and grief. (Wis 7:27b, 8:7, 9)

Praying the Gifts of the Body

Preparation   I will allow my spirit to rest a little and consider where I am going and for what purpose. I make a gesture of reverence and humility. I read the prayer texts.

Opening Prayer   I ask the Creator for understanding of my senses, that I may use them better for the greater service of God.

Desire   I desire spiritual progress through the gifts of my body.

Prayer   1. I consider my sense of sight. What is the gift?

                     2. Where do I see best in my life?

                     3. Where do I see least in my life?

                     4. I reflect on the contrary of my sight.

                     After 3 minutes, I ask the Lord for what I desire.

                     Our Father.

                     The same procedure is repeated for each.

Conversation   Now I examine senses as a whole. I ask myself:

                     1. Which sense do I excel in, more than any other?

                     2. Which sense do I desire to use for greater service of God?

                     3. Which sense would give me the greatest inner peace now?

                     In conversation with my Creator, I choose one sense to serve with today, or one sense to imitate Jesus with today.[144]

SPIRITUAL DIRECTION

In this prayer, I take each sense in turn. I consider its meaning, see where it is present or absent in my life, and then become aware of its contrary. I need to take about half a minute to answer each of the four questions. This reflective pace is also necessary in the three questions at the end.

In serving with a sense of my body today, I can consciously choose particular times to do so, or I can allow the Spirit to enhance that sense and service through me.

There is a second way to pray the senses of my body. It is to imitate Jesus, Mary, or a living saint. Thus, for a day, I can strive to use my hands in the way Jesus would, or to see with the eyes of Jesus, or hear with the ears of Mary, or taste reality the way the living saint does. I could then move through each sense, imagining how I might imitate these people in each of these senses. I embody their desires.

SUGGESTED PRAYER TIME: 40 MINUTES

Preparation: 5 minutes. Opening Prayer: 1 minute. Desire: 1 minute. Prayer: 30 minutes. Conversation: 3 minutes. Listening Book after prayer: 10 minutes.

PRAYER TEXTS

Five Gifts of the Body

1. Sight
2. Hearing
3. Smell
4. Taste
5. Touch

Sensual God. [In the promised land] you will serve other gods made by human hands, objects of wood and stone that neither see, nor hear, nor eat, nor smell. From there you will seek the Lord your God, and you will find him if you search after him with all your heart and soul. (Dt 4:28–29)

Sensual humanity. God created humankind in his image, in the image of God he created them; God saw everything that he had made, and indeed, it was very good. (Gn 1:27a, 31a)

Sensual witness. We are afflicted in every way, always carrying in the body the death of Jesus, so that the life of Jesus may also be made visible in our bodies. While we live, we are always being given up to death for Jesus' sake, so that the life of Jesus may be made visible in our mortal flesh. (2 Cor 4:8a, 10–11)

Praying the Works of Mercy

Preparation	I will allow my spirit to rest a little and consider where I am going and for what purpose. I make a gesture of reverence and humility. I read the prayer texts.
Opening Prayer	I ask the Lord God for help and understanding of the works of mercy, that I may act for his greater service.
Desire	I desire spiritual progress through the works of mercy.
Prayer	1. I consider feeding the hungry. What is the Lord asking?
	2. Where is this work present in my life?
	3. Where is it absent in my life?
	4. I reflect on the contrary of feeding the hungry.
	After 3 minutes, I ask the Lord for what I desire.
	Our Father.
	The same procedure is repeated for each of the works of mercy.
Conversation	I examine the works as a whole. I ask myself:
	1. Which work do I excel in, more than any other?
	2. Which work do I desire for greater service of God?
	3. Which work would give me the greatest inner peace now?
	In conversation with my Lord, I choose one work of mercy to endeavor today.[145]

SPIRITUAL DIRECTION

I may pray either the bodily or spiritual works of mercy.

The reflections on each work of mercy, considering its meaning, its presence or absence in my life, and its contrary, will break open my personal experience of each work of mercy. So it is vital I take about half a minute with each of the four questions. The same method is followed with the three questions in the conversation with Jesus.

In practicing a work of mercy today, I organize a particular action, or I can open myself to the Spirit to direct that work through me in God's time.

SUGGESTED PRAYER TIME: 40 MINUTES

Preparation: 5 minutes. Opening Prayer: 1 minute. Desire: 1 minute. Prayer: 30 minutes. Conversation: 3 minutes. Listening Book after prayer: 10 minutes.

PRAYER TEXTS

Mercy for the body
1. To feed the hungry
2. To shelter the homeless
3. To clothe the naked
4. To visit the sick
5. To visit the imprisoned
6. To bury the dead
7. To give alms to the poor

Mercy for the spirit
1. To instruct
2. To advise
3. To console
4. To comfort
5. To forgive
6. To bear wrongs patiently
7. To pray for the living and the dead

The king will say to those at his right hand, "Come, you that are blessed by my Father, inherit the kingdom prepared for you from the foundation of the world; for I was hungry and you gave me food, I was thirsty and you gave me something to drink, I was a stranger and you welcomed me, I was naked and you gave me clothing, I was sick and you took care of me, I was in prison and you visited me." (Mt 25:34–36)

Rejoice with those who rejoice, weep with those who weep. Live in harmony with one another; do not be haughty, but associate with the lowly; do not claim to be wiser than you are. Do not repay anyone evil for evil, but take thought for what is noble in the sight of all. If it is possible, so far as it depends on you, live peaceably with all. (Rom 12:9–14)

For we are what he has made us, created in Christ Jesus for good works, which God prepared beforehand to be our way of life. (Eph 2:10)

Lectio Divina

Preparation	Immediately on waking, without allowing my thoughts to stray, I turn my attention to the subject of my sacred reading today. I imagine Jesus himself getting ready to meet me there. I get dressed with thoughts like these.
	At my prayer place, I stand for a minute to consider how Jesus is looking at me with love. In response, I make a gesture of reverence and humility.
	I take time to slowly read the scripture text as a whole.
Opening Prayer	I ask for the grace to direct my whole self toward the service of God.
Desire	I ask for what I desire.
Prayer	In a circular manner, guided by text and Spirit:
	I Read.
	I slowly savor the text—word by word, sentence by sentence.
	I consider the literal meaning—what it is all about.
	I allow it to trigger my feelings, memories, and associations.
	I Meditate.
	I see the subject matter in view of the gift of creation and salvation.
	I enlarge the context. I see how I am given life.
	I Pray.
	I allow the text to nurture my values, to help pattern my life on Jesus.
	As I become aware of my desires and feelings, I address them to God, or to the Father, Son, or Spirit.
	I Contemplate.
	I am lifted up to desire the things of God.
	When so gifted, I rest quietly in God as God rests in me.
Conclusion	I give thanks and enter the graces into my Listening Book.
	Our Father.

SUGGESTED PRAYER TIME: 40 MINUTES
Preparation: 5 minutes. Opening Prayer: 2 minutes. Prayer: 30 minutes. Conclusion: 3 minutes. Listening Book after prayer: 10 minutes.

SPIRITUAL DIRECTION

Sacred reading, or Lectio Divina, is a prayerful reading of scripture leading to communion with God. In the monastic tradition, starting with St.
Benedict's Rule, it distinguishes four moments of sacred reading: reading, meditation, prayer, and contemplation. It provides a way to pray
the gospels. In the classic image of the Carthusian Guido II, reading puts
food whole into the mouth, meditation chews and breaks it up, prayer
extracts its flavor, and contemplation is the sweetness itself, which glad-
dens and refreshes.

The aim of sacred reading is to hear God's call clearly in my daily
life. It begins where study ends and requires commitment. Little will
be gained with occasional reading. A sense of leisure, peacefulness, and
time surrounds sacred reading. I let go of the anxiety of my life proj-
ects and open myself to be challenged, moved, and enlightened. I pray
through one gospel. While there is a certain natural order in sacred reading, the four moments are not independent, and their movement is more
circular than linear. They need not all occur in any one prayer time. Repetition is of the essence.

I begin with a slow, savoring reading and allow this to trigger my
memories and associations. It often helps to verbalize the words or write
them out. Moving between reading and meditation, I explore the different senses of the text: I question the text, and I seek the literal meaning,
the context of my salvation, Christ in all this, and the pattern of my life
now. Revelation and personal experience come together.

Throughout, when moved by the Spirit, I pray spontaneously to God.
At times I may experience the gift of God's presence in a way that quiets
my mind, inflames my desire, and brings me to stillness. Here I leave the
text and embrace God. I rest in contemplation. Later I return to prayer,
meditation, or reading. I allow the text to lead me.

To remember the feelings, inner understanding, desires, or love received, I may write a short prayer around them at the end. Such a prayer
will follow me into the rest of the day.

Meditation

Preparation	Immediately on waking, without allowing my thoughts to stray, I turn my attention to the subject of my meditation. I imagine Jesus at the center of it, and what he desires for me today. I get dressed with thoughts like these.
	At my prayer place, I stand for a minute to consider how Jesus is looking at me with love. In response, I make a gesture of reverence and humility.
	I take time to slowly read the scripture text as a whole.
Opening Prayer	I ask for the grace to direct my whole self toward the service of God.
Desire	I ask for what I desire.
Prayer	I slowly read the text again to feel and taste things interiorly. For each paragraph, sentence, or sense phrase of the text:
	I use my memory to bring the truths of my faith to mind.
	I use my intellect to go over the subject in more detail with greater understanding.
	I use my will to deeply arouse the feelings of my heart.
Conversation	I converse with Jesus, Father, Spirit, or Mary. I speak as one friend speaks to another—at times I may ask for some favor, or express sorrow or reverence, or simply share personal concerns and ask for advice about them.
	Our Father.[146]

SUGGESTED PRAYER TIME: 40 MINUTES

Preparation and reading: 5 minutes. Opening Prayer: 1 minute. Desire: 1 minute. Prayer: 30 minutes. Conversation: 3 minutes. Listening Book after prayer: 10 minutes.

SPIRITUAL DIRECTION

Traditionally, the three powers of the soul are memory, understanding, and will—through them I remember, I see, and I desire God. Just as they are integral to the whole person, I use them in all prayer. As a method for meditation, consciously separated, the memory reminds, the intellect understands, and the will impels.

Memory works with my awareness of two dimensions in each gospel text. The first is the particulars of the gospel event. The second is the truth of it, of what is being revealed by God through Jesus. At this level I bring to mind my faith knowledge. I meditate on both levels, moving from event to truth, Jesus to myself, God to my response.

The intellect meditates on the facts or truths as they apply to me. I discuss and reason within myself to make the event or truth clearer, to feel greater spiritual relish and fruit. I explore and chew over the text. Why did Jesus became human for me? What has he done? What is he doing for me? This thinking stage is not study to gain knowledge. St. Ignatius reminds me that it is not knowledge that fills and satisfies the soul but to feel and to taste things interiorly. Meditation seeks this interior understanding or "felt knowledge."

The will responds to this understanding with natural affections of the heart. It may rouse me to adoration, wonder, sorrow, or thanksgiving. It may move me to hope or love, or urge me to compassion and self-offering. These movements are the impulse of my whole self toward God. They may come in spontaneous prayer, deep emotion, or silent stillness. Here the edges rightly blur between meditation, prayer, and contemplation. The direction a movement takes depends on my desire and God's loving response.

This dance of the three powers is applied to each part of the gospel text in turn. I choose what constitutes a part. The whole meditation culminates in a conversation with the Trinity or Jesus. As with a friend, I listen, and we share our inner feelings, thoughts, desires, and resolutions.

Imaginative Contemplation

Preparation	Immediately on waking, without allowing my thoughts to stray, I turn my attention to the subject of my contemplation. I imagine Jesus at the center of it, and what he desires for me today. I get dressed with thoughts like these.
	At my prayer place, I stand for a minute to consider how Jesus is looking at me with love. In response, I make a gesture of reverence and humility.
	I take time to slowly read the scripture text as a whole.
Opening Prayer	I ask for the grace to direct my whole self toward the service of God.
Desire	I ask for what I desire.
Prayer	Using my natural imagination, I enter the scripture scene.
	First I re-create the place in my mind: the environment, sounds, colors, nature, buildings, weather, smells, etc.
	Then I see the people. How are they dressed? What are they feeling? What do they want? I take the place of the person I wish to be and enter the scene.
	Finally, I allow the action to take place, taking part myself as the scene unfolds. I enter the conversations and allow my feelings to surface. I express my desires to Jesus. The text can guide me here, or, once in relationship with Jesus, I can be guided by my heart. I surrender to the prayer.
	After the above, I may reflect within myself and draw some fruit from it.
Conversation	I converse with Jesus, Father, Spirit, or Mary. I speak as one friend speaks to another—at times I may ask for some favor, or express sorrow or reverence, or simply share personal concerns and ask for advice about them.
	Our Father.[147]

SUGGESTED PRAYER TIME: 40 MINUTES

Preparation and reading: 5 minutes. Opening Prayer: 1 minute. Desire: 1 minute. Prayer: 30 minutes. Conversation: 3 minutes. Listening Book after prayer: 10 minutes.

SPIRITUAL DIRECTION

Imaginative contemplation of the gospels has a rich history. It stresses the humanity of Jesus and the use of imagination and feelings to enter into a relationship with him. It has as its purpose the awakening of self-giving love. Ignatius departs from the monastic traditions in shaping his method to finding God in daily life. His aim is not ascent into union with God but descent into union with Christ working in the world, in our daily life.

I begin with the three introductory steps. First I read the text slowly. As I do, I take the second step: I build up a detailed picture in my imagination. Third, I ask God for what I desire in a simple, concrete way. Thus I compose both the place and myself.

The points help me to structure my prayer. Now I deeply enter the text and, through the imagination, become present to Jesus and to the events of that scene. All the details are important. I can be myself there or be one of the other people. Ignatius divides the points into persons, words, and actions. In practice I imagine these as they happen together. I let the scene unfold, as it will. I stop at those places where I feel engaged. I talk, rest, and interact. Where I find what I desire, I will settle down.

It is not important to "do" the whole text. The aim is to enter into relationship with Jesus, to receive whatever he desires to give. This method encourages me to attend to my feelings and desires, to relish them and deepen them, and to reflect and draw fruit for myself.

I remember the gospels are the Word of God. The events belong to both the past and the present. Mysteriously, in the past events of the gospels I meet the Lord in the present. My prayer culminates in a conversation with God. As with a friend, I share and I listen. I give and I receive. I seek the best way forward.

Prayer of the Interior Senses

Preparation   Immediately on waking, without allowing my thoughts to stray, I turn my attention to how wonderful is the gift of my senses. I will see myself as standing before Jesus who became fully human, who embodies the relationship I desire. I will get dressed with thoughts like these.

At my prayer place, my mind raised up, I consider how Jesus is looking at me with love. I make a gesture of reverence and humility.

I take time to slowly read the scripture text as a whole.

Opening Prayer   I ask for the grace to direct my whole self toward the service of God.

Desire   I ask for what I desire.

Prayer   Using the text, I enter the scene and use my five senses in an interior way, as in the examples below for each sense:

I *see* the persons and the events. I read the language of bodies; I see the light in darkness, the nail-split flesh, the truth beneath, the ready harvest.

I *hear* what they are saying. I hear the healing whisper to arise; the sound of mute grief, joy, or the bound soul; the hidden cry for help; and deep silence.

I *feel* the hearts of the people. I feel the touch of mud in the eye, a father's cloak and ring, a stoning rock, a net too full, a hole in the hand of Jesus.

I *taste* the sweet and bitter things in the relationships. I taste the salt of tears, the wedding wine, the tang of vinegar at spear tip, fresh fish on hot stone, the crust of fear, cool well water, the taste of the Lord's goodness.

I *smell* wild spring flowers, a corpse recently dead, the lake storm coming, the heady aroma of frankincense, or the meaning of sweet-scented nard.

In all this, sense by sense, I become aware of the mystery of divine life in Christ, in myself, and in the whole of creation before me.

Conversation   I converse with Jesus, Father, Spirit, or Mary. I speak as one friend speaks to another—at times I may ask for some favor, or express sorrow or reverence, or simply share personal concerns and ask for advice about them. Our Father.[148]

SUGGESTED PRAYER TIME: 40 MINUTES

Preparation and reading: 5 minutes. Opening Prayer: 1 minute. Desire: 1 minute. Prayer: 30 minutes. Conversation: 3 minutes. Listening Book after prayer: 10 minutes.

SPIRITUAL DIRECTION

When I fall in love with someone, I see them and the world with new eyes. My feelings and relationships taste different. In time, our love and commitment deepen, and we come to share a history. Memories, objects, smell, sounds, and places become special to us because they speak volumes about our love. For the lover, the smallest gesture, touch, look, word, or smile not only communicates a deep love but also holds the whole person within it. Tenderness, spontaneity, and a certain quality of presence are intuitive for lovers. If I were asked to describe my relationship with my loved one, I would use the poetic language of images or the imaginative use of senses. This is the language of the heart and soul.

In description, the five steps of the prayer of the senses struggle for the right language. The prayer separates out that which is of one piece in experience—yet it is intuitive for lovers to pray it. In the Full Spiritual Exercises, this prayer is always prayed after two contemplations and two repetitions on the same gospel scene. So it could be said that the prayer of the senses in depth assumes a sustained prayer experience, a shared history of felt love.

The experience of praying in Lectio Divina, Meditation, or Imaginative Contemplation is my guide for praying with the senses. I already know the taste and touch of God in my soul. It is the word, touch, or look that reached into the marrow of my bones during prayer. It is the moment and place that changed the quality of my relationship with Jesus. This is the felt place I return to in the prayer of senses—to taste and see that the Lord is good, to be fed, nourished, held, and loved.

The soul, for St. Bonaventure, sees, hears, tastes, breathes, and embraces her spouse. There is a sense of wholeness to this prayer—body, mind, and spirit together. It is the simple, loving attention of the whole self to Jesus. In turn, I contemplate the whole person he is.

I will affirm, with the first Christians, that I have seen it, looked upon it, and felt it with my own hands—the Word which gives life.

Prayer of Repetition

Preparation	Immediately on waking, without allowing my thoughts to stray, I turn my attention to the prayer experience I am coming back to today. I imagine Jesus whom I desire to return to and the grace or moment I wish to deepen. I get dressed with thoughts like these.
	At my prayer place, my mind raised up, I consider how Jesus is looking at me with love. I make a gesture of reverence and humility.
	If necessary, I reread the part of the scriptures I am returning to in my prayer.
Opening Prayer	I ask for the grace to direct my whole self toward the service of God.
Desire	I ask for what I desire.
Prayer	I give my attention to the more important places of my past prayer where I experienced greater insight or spiritual delight, healing, forgiveness, mercy, etc.
	Or, I give my attention to that part where I experienced feelings of spiritual consolation or desolation. I seek a greater understanding of these movements in my heart. I seek the way of the good spirit, the path of spiritual consolation.
	Or, I give my attention to that place where I felt closest to my Lord. I return there to deepen my relationship, to receive a gift of greater intimacy.
Conversation	I converse with Jesus, Father, Spirit, or Mary. I speak as one friend speaks to another—at times I may ask for some favor, or express sorrow or reverence, or simply share personal concerns and ask for advice about them.
	Our Father.[149]

SUGGESTED PRAYER TIME: 40 MINUTES

Preparation and reading: 5 minutes. Opening Prayer: 1 minute. Desire: 1 minute. Prayer: 30 minutes. Conversation: 3 minutes. Listening Book after prayer: 10 minutes.

SPIRITUAL DIRECTION

The Prayer of Repetition is a simple way of deepening my prayer experience. This prayer can be done after any kind of prayer. As such, it is part of a natural movement in prayer toward the simple, personal, and contemplative. It is also the way that the word or text is written deep within me until it becomes a very part of myself. Essentially, in the Prayer of Repetition, I return to that place in my previous prayer where I felt most deeply engaged or moved.

I do this, not to repeat the material of my last prayer, but to focus on the more important places. I am selective. I choose that one passage, conversation, strong feeling, response, insight, or interior understanding that moved me most. The chosen experience may be a warm spot or cold spot, a positive or negative experience. It may not always be peaceful, but it will always be fruitful. Then I surrender the whole of my prayer time to this one place.

In praying the gospels, deep interior movements of the heart often signal the moment where meditation becomes contemplation. The Prayer of Repetition has the open quality of a union of hearts or contemplation. The prayer space is large and gentle, without agendas or destinations. I choose to be here because I was invited.

St. Ignatius advises that "where I find what I desire, I will settle down, without any anxiety, until I have satisfied myself" (*Spiritual Exercises* 76). This prayer is a return to that moment of desire found. It is a prayer of interior satisfaction.

In time, the patterns of consolation and desolation in my repetitions will help me to discern the way ahead. They are a sure road to wholeness, union, conversion, and glad offering. I can do many repetitions— as long as there is water for me at the well of this exercise. I can even pray a repetition by contemplating a resonating symbol, for instance, water, light, stone, bread, leaf, or flower.

There is a similar method of Prayer of Repetition given by Ignatius in the Spiritual Exercises called a "resume." He suggests, with the same outline as the Prayer of Repetition, that the central prayer itself be given solely to allowing the understanding to "range over the memory of things contemplated in the previous exercises" (*Spiritual Exercises* 64). This might be a useful alternative, especially to range over more than one prayer time.

Contemplation

Preparation	Immediately on waking, without allowing my thoughts to stray, I will turn my attention to the Trinity. I imagine Jesus settling any anxieties I have and inviting me to dwell in the Father and the Spirit with him. I get dressed with thoughts like these.
	At my prayer place, my mind raised up, I consider how the Trinity look at me with love. I make a gesture of reverence and humility.
Opening Prayer	I ask for the grace to direct my whole self toward the service of God.
Desire	I desire to enter the mystery of divine relationship.
Body	I sit alert and relaxed with a straight back.
	I breathe calmly and regularly. I close my eyes. I relax.
Prayer	I gently pray a prayer word—heart spoken, gathering all.
	I rest in the presence of God, utterly personal, yet boundlessly mysterious.
	I am open, in surrender, silent, wordless, imageless, still, and desiring.
	When distracted, I simply and gently return to God by using my prayer word.
Conclusion	I let my prayer word go. I allow the Our Father to pray itself quietly within me.

SUGGESTED PRAYER TIME: AS NEEDED.

SPIRITUAL DIRECTION

Contemplative prayer is silent love. It is the gift of union in God. It is possible for anyone—for such is the generosity of God's love. It is a journey home. Many traditions encourage, teach, and provide maps for this enlightening journey.

Here two of these maps are offered. The first is a natural movement in sacred reading that leads to Contemplation. It moves from my head to my heart, from recollection to quiet, from desire to gift. Following this way, the door to God's heart will be a word, image, or event from my prayerful reading, Meditation, or Imaginative Contemplation.

The second map uses a word or verse from scripture. Jesus prayed with "Abba" or "Father." I could use "Jesus Christ," "Lord Jesus," or "Jesus." The author of *The Cloud of Unknowing,* an English mystic, suggests a sharp, one-syllable word like "God" or "Love." The traditional Jesus Prayer, of eastern and western Christianity, uses "Lord Jesus Christ, Son of God, have mercy on me" or part of the same phrase.

This way of contemplative prayer through the use of a prayer word is simple. The World Christian Meditation Movement uses the word "Maranatha," which means "Come, Lord Jesus." The prayer method outlined here uses a similar method, called "Centering Prayer." It uses a single word that holds many words of desire, one word to say, "I am all yours, Lord."

The World Christian Meditation Movement repeats the prayer word interiorly, in a slow and rhythmical manner, with the syllables equally stressed. Centering Prayer just allows the prayer word to be present. In both, all thoughts and images that arise are distractions. I let them pass and use the prayer word to gently return to silence. Following this way, the door to God's heart is the attentive stillness created by the prayer word.

Contemplation will involve a radical detachment from material anxieties and my ego. Time for solitude and mindfulness is needed—a willingness to remain in the peace of now. It leads to a poverty of self and an absolute dependence on God. Ultimately, the Father desires me, Jesus is my companion, and the Spirit guides me home.

THE IGNATIAN GUIDE
TO CHRISTIAN BELIEF

Someone who gives to another a way and a plan for meditating or contemplating must provide a faithful account of the history to be meditated or contemplated, but in such a way as to run over the salient points with only brief or summary explanations. If one begins contemplating with a true historical foundation, and then goes over this history and reflects on it personally, he or she may come upon things which throw further light on it or which more fully bring home its meaning.

Whether this arises out of the person's own reasoning or from the enlightenment of divine grace, more gratification and spiritual fruit is to be found than if the giver of the Exercises had explained and developed the meaning of the history at length. For it is not great knowledge but the inner feeling and relish of things that fills and satisfies the soul. (*Spiritual Exercises* 2)

One of the important ways Christian belief is named, held, protected, and shared is with a creed. A creed is a response to Jesus asking, "Who do you say I am?" The question is not abstract; it is addressed to me. It implies a relationship to God and community. Peter learned this the hard way in his betrayal of both the man he loved and his fellow disciples. Afterward, Jesus questioned his love and belief three times, then forgave and missioned him. Peter is evidence that creeds can cry.

Do I have a creed I can live by? Am I credible as a Christian? With my lifestyle, would my fellow workers give credence to my beliefs? Am I a credit to my community or church? All these questions hold the root word "credo"—"I believe." I am not a child anymore. The authority of the Church cannot make me believe. A creed is a matter of my belief—my choice. It is a set of beliefs I live by, the same beliefs Christians still die by. Creeds give life to communities. Creeds can bleed.

Prayer can break open the shell of a creed to reveal the sweet flesh and seeds inside. If I eat, a heartfelt knowledge, an inner feeling and relish, will begin to grow in me. Creeds can nourish me.

Gospel Creeds: I Believe

Instead of learning a creed, Ignatius suggests I pray it. First I read the gospel creeds below and choose one to which I am attracted. Then, with imagination, I enter into the scene. I fill in the details of place, sounds, and people. Becoming the one talking to Jesus, I slowly pray the words in *italic* found in each scripture text. If it is a statement by Jesus, then I pray his words. Either way, I slowly repeat the words, in phrase or sentence, savoring both feelings and meanings for myself. After a while, I allow Jesus to respond. What might he say to me? What might I reply?

GOD THE FATHER TO HIS SON

When Jesus had been baptized, just as he came up from the water, suddenly the heavens were opened to him and he saw the Spirit of God descending like a dove and alighting on him. And a voice from heaven said, *"This is my Son, the Beloved, with whom I am well pleased."* (Mt 3:15–17)

JESUS TO A SCRIBE

[The scribe] asked [Jesus], "Which commandment is the first of all?" Jesus answered, "The first is, *'Hear, O Israel: the Lord our God, the Lord is one; you shall love the Lord your God with all your heart, and with all your soul, and with all your mind, and with all your strength.'* The second is this, 'You shall love your neighbor as yourself.' There is no other commandment greater than these." (Mk 12:28b–31)

PETER TO JESUS

[After feeding the five thousand, Jesus] asked his disciples, "Who do people say the Son of Man is?" And they said, "Some say John the Baptist, but others Elijah, and still others Jeremiah or one of the prophets." He said to them, "But who do you say that I am?" Simon Peter answered, *"You are the Christ, the Son of the living God."* (Mt 16:16)

BARTIMAEUS TO JESUS

Bartimaeus son of Timaeus, a blind beggar, was sitting by the roadside. When he heard that it was Jesus of Nazareth, he began to shout out and say, *"Jesus, Son of David, have mercy on me!"* Many sternly ordered him to be quiet, but he cried out even more loudly, "Son of David, have mercy on me!" Jesus stood still and said, "Call him here." And they called the blind man, saying to him, "Take heart; get up, he is calling you." So throwing off his cloak, he sprang up and came to Jesus. Then Jesus said to him, "What do you want me to do for you?" The blind man said to him, "My teacher, let me see again." Jesus said to him, "Go; your faith has made you well." Immediately he regained his sight and followed him on the way. (Mk 10:46b–52)

DISCIPLES TO JESUS

[Jesus] said, "Come." So Peter got out of the boat, started walking on the water, and came toward Jesus. But when he noticed the strong wind, he became frightened, and beginning to sink, he cried out, *"Lord, save me!"* Jesus immediately reached out his hand and caught him, saying to him, "You of little faith, why did you doubt?" When they got into the boat, the wind ceased. And those in the boat worshiped him, saying, *"Truly you are the Son of God."* (Mt 14:29–33)

MARTHA TO JESUS

Martha said to Jesus, "Lord, if you had been here, my brother would not have died. But even now I know that God will give you whatever you ask of him." Jesus said, "Your brother will rise again." Martha said to him, "I know that he will rise again in the resurrection on the last day." Jesus said to her, *"I am the resurrection and the life.* Those who believe in me, even though they die, will live, and everyone who lives and believes in me will never die. Do you believe this?" She said to him, *"Yes, Lord, I believe that you are the Messiah, the Son of God, the one coming into the world."* (Jn 11:21–27)

CENTURION TO THE CRUCIFIED JESUS

The chief priests, along with the scribes, were also mocking him among themselves and saying, *"He saved others; he cannot save himself. Let the Messiah, the King of Israel, come down from the cross now, so that we may see and believe."* . . . When it was noon, darkness came over the whole land until three in the afternoon. At three o'clock Jesus cried out with a loud voice, "Eloi, Eloi, lema sabachthani?" which means, "My God, my God, why have you forsaken me?" Then Jesus gave a loud cry and breathed his last. Now when the centurion, who stood facing him, saw that in this way he breathed his last, he said, *"Truly this man was God's Son!"* (Mk 15:31–34, 37, 39)

THOMAS TO THE RISEN JESUS

[Thomas] said to [the disciples], "Unless I see the mark of the nails in his hands, and put my finger in the mark of the nails and my hand in his side, I will not believe."

Although the doors were shut, Jesus came and stood among them and said, "Peace be with you." Then he said to Thomas, "Put your finger here and see my hands. Reach out your hand and put it in my side. Do not doubt but believe." Thomas answered him, *"My Lord and my God!"* (Jn 20:25b, 26b–28)

MARY MAGDALENE TO THE RISEN JESUS

Jesus said to [Mary], "Woman, why are you weeping? Whom are you looking for?" Supposing him to be the gardener, she said to him, "Sir, if you have carried him away, tell me where you have laid him, and I will take him away." Jesus said to her, "Mary!" She turned and said to him in Hebrew, *"Rabbouni!" (which means Teacher)*. Jesus said to her, "Do not hold on to me, because I have not yet ascended to the Father. But go to my brothers and say to them, *'I am ascending to my Father and your Father, to my God and your God.'"* (Jn 20:13–17)

RISEN JESUS TO HIS DISCIPLES

[Jesus] opened their minds to understand the scriptures, and he said to them, "Thus it is written, that *the Messiah is to suffer and to rise from the dead on the third day, and that repentance and forgiveness of sins is to be proclaimed in his name to all nations, beginning from Jerusalem.* You are witnesses of these things. And see, I am sending upon you what my Father promised; so stay here in the city until you have been clothed with power from on high." (Lk 24:45–49)

Community Creeds: We Believe

In this exercise I read through the Christian community's and Church's creeds below to appreciate the great unfolding story of divine love. I see how a creed progresses from a personal relationship of faith in the gospels to the great symbol of communal faith in the Nicene Creed.

In the way of Lectio Divina, the prayer of sacred reading that moves through the steps of reading, meditation, prayer, and contemplation, I trace the work of each person in the Trinity. I slowly savor the text and chew over the inner meaning of these early Christian creeds. I seek relish and consolation in the faith that I share with my sisters and brothers throughout the world.[150]

ONE GOD THROUGH WHOM ALL THINGS EXIST

There is one God, the Father, from whom are all things and for whom we exist, and one Lord, Jesus Christ, through whom are all things and through whom we exist. (1 Cor 8:6)

CHRIST JESUS EMPTIED HIMSELF UNTO DEATH

Let the same mind be in you that was in Christ Jesus, who, though he was in the form of God, did not regard equality with God as something to be exploited, but emptied himself, taking the form of a slave, being born in human likeness. And being found in human form, he humbled himself and became obedient to the point of death—even death on a cross. Therefore God also highly exalted him and gave him the name that is above every name, so that at the name of Jesus every knee should bend, in heaven and on earth and under the earth, and every tongue should confess that Jesus Christ is Lord, to the glory of God the Father. (Phil 2:5–11)

THE GOSPEL OF GOD

Paul . . . set apart for the gospel of God, the gospel concerning his Son, who was descended from David according to the flesh and was declared to be Son of God with power according to the spirit of holiness by resurrection from the dead, Jesus Christ our Lord, through whom we have received grace and apostleship to bring about the obedience of faith among all the Gentiles for the sake of his name, including yourselves who are called to belong to Jesus Christ. (Rom 1:1, 3–6)

A PLAN FOR THE FULLNESS OF TIME

Blessed be the God and Father of our Lord Jesus Christ, who has blessed us in Christ with every spiritual blessing in the heavenly places, just as he chose us in Christ before the foundation of the world to be holy and blameless before him in love. He destined us for adoption as his children through Jesus Christ, according to the good pleasure of his will, to the praise of his glorious grace that he freely bestowed on us in the Beloved.

In him we have redemption through his blood, the forgiveness of our trespasses, according to the riches of his grace that he lavished on us. With all wisdom and insight he has made known to us the mystery of his will, according to his good pleasure that he set forth in Christ, as a plan for the fullness of time, to gather up all things in him, things in heaven and things on earth. (Eph 1:3–10)

IN THE BEGINNING WAS THE WORD—THEN GRACE UPON GRACE

In the beginning was the Word, and the Word was with God, and the Word was God. He was in the beginning with God. All things came into being through him, and without him not one thing came into being. What has come into being in him was life, and the life was the light of all people. The light shines in the darkness, and the darkness did not overcome it. He was in the world, and the world came into being through him, yet the world did not know him. He came to what was his own, and his own people did not accept him. But to all who received him, who believed in his name, he gave power to become children of God, who were born, not of blood or of the will of the flesh or of the will of man, but of God.

And the Word became flesh and lived among us, and we have seen his glory, the glory as of a father's only son, full of grace and truth. From his fullness we have all received, grace upon grace. The law indeed was given through Moses; grace and truth came through Jesus Christ. No one has ever seen God. It is God the only Son, who is close to the Father's heart, who has made him known. (Jn 1:1–5, 10–14, 16–18)

THE NICENE CREED

I believe in one God, the Father almighty,
maker of heaven and earth, of all things visible and invisible.
I believe in one Lord, Jesus Christ,
the Only Begotten Son of God, born of the Father before all ages.
God from God, Light from Light, true God from true God,
begotten, not made, consubstantial with the Father;
through him all things were made.
For us men and for our salvation he came down from heaven,
and by the Holy Spirit was incarnate
of the Virgin Mary, and became man.
For our sake he was crucified under Pontius Pilate;
he suffered death and was buried,
and rose again on the third day in accordance with the Scriptures.
He ascended into heaven and is seated at the right hand of the Father.
He will come again in glory to judge the living and the dead
and his kingdom will have no end.

I believe in the Holy Spirit,
the Lord, the giver of life,
who proceeds from the Father and the Son,
who with the Father and the Son is adored and glorified,
who has spoken though the prophets.
I believe in one, holy, catholic, and apostolic Church.
I acknowledge one Baptism for the forgiveness of sins,
and I look forward to the resurrection of the dead
and the life of the world to come. Amen.

Spiritual Conversation

THE IGNATIAN GUIDE
TO SPIRITUAL JOURNALING

With no worry at all, I persevered in my reading and my good resolutions; and all my time of conversation with members of the household I spent on the things of God; thus I benefited their souls. As I very much liked those books, the idea came to me to note down briefly some of the more essential things from the life of Christ and the saints, so I set myself very diligently to write a book . . . part of the time I spent in writing and part in prayer.[151]

Yet there was this difference. When I was thinking of those things of the world, I took much delight in them, but afterwards, when I was tired and put them aside, I found myself dry and dissatisfied. But when I thought of going to Jerusalem barefoot, and of eating nothing but plain vegetables and of practicing all the other rigors that I saw in the saints, not only was I consoled but even after putting them aside I remained satisfied and joyful. I did not notice this, however; nor did I stop to ponder the distinction until the time when my eyes were opened a little, and I began to marvel at the difference and to reflect upon it, realizing from experience that some thoughts left me sad and others joyful. Little by little I came to recognize the difference between the spirits that were stirring, one from the devil, the other from God.[152]

In the two texts above, Ignatius describes how he used his spiritual journal. It helped him to discern the different spirits stirring in his prayer, reflections, spiritual conversations, and daily life. Those walking in the Ignatian tradition know this prayer-reflection-action-prayer cycle as the way of "contemplatives in action."

This repeated rhythm of prayer, reflection, and action is how my sacred desires break into happy and graced action. Nothing is immediate, and change is realistically slow, but, like a flower opening, I move with the light and in the due season become who I truly am. This frees great energies in me. Soon enough, my spiritual journal will speak in the clear and extraordinary voice of the Holy Spirit.

Sometimes I forget the great number of good things in my life but remember the few bad things. This can be a disheartening pattern. But reading my spiritual journal will unmask such a pattern. The good running through my life will shine through, even in times of suffering. In this way, spiritual journals are the keepers of consolations and truth. They are source springs for gratitude.

A tighter focus and process has been given to the spiritual journal for those making the First Spiritual Exercises in the creation of the Listening Book.

INTRODUCING THE LISTENING BOOK

What is a Listening Book? A Listening Book is a book I listen to after giving it my reflections. It is a bit like a good friend. So after a spiritual exercise, I consider the questions listed below in the first use of the Listening Book. I note my responses in the Listening Book. Then I close it.

After some time, an hour, two hours, a day or week, I open it and read what I have written. I "listen" to my Listening Book as it reveals new meanings, understanding, and fresh feelings. The original prayer experience in a spiritual exercise virtually always has much more in it than I might realize at first. Indeed most graces birth over time. So I listen with great care as I reread these words.

Using the Listening Book also gives my inner self, and my unconscious self, both time to absorb my prayer experience and a way to tell me what they have discovered. Even the Holy Spirit will speak to me through my Listening Book.

In the First Spiritual Exercises, my Listening Book will accumulate wisdom as I enter into the full dynamic of a retreat, becoming a familiar and potent voice in my life. Practically, I will need to buy a nice book to have as my Listening Book. Then I should title it beautifully and bless it before use.

Ignatius promotes reflection after prayer: "After finishing the exercise I will either sit down or walk around for a quarter of an hour while I see how things have gone for me during the contemplation or meditation."[153] He says that "every day I used to write down what passed through my soul, and so could now find these things in writing."[154]

Apart from the first use after a spiritual exercise or other prayer, the Listening Book has three other direct uses. The second use is after a spiritual conversation, the third is after praying the Awareness Examen, and the fourth is during an important life event. Three of the four uses are outlined below with their own reflection questions. The fourth can take the same reflection questions as those for the Awareness Examen.

Luis Gonçalves De Câmara writes of Ignatius, "He said to me that as for the Exercises he had not produced them all at one time, rather that some things which he used to observe in his soul and find useful for himself it seemed to him could also be useful for others, and so he used to put them in writing."[155] My Listening Book will also help me when I teach others a spiritual exercise or find myself in a spiritual conversation.

The Practice of the Listening Book

1. AFTER A SPIRITUAL EXERCISE

Preparation   After my spiritual exercise I will reflect on how things have gone in my prayer.

Reflection   What were the more important things in my prayer?

What were my stronger feelings? What detail gave rise to them?

Has my relationship with the Lord grown? How? Why?

Have I received the grace I asked for? Other insights? Delights?

Have I felt spiritual consolation or desolation since my prayer time?

Is there an action I wish to take?

Listening Book   I note my responses to the above in my Listening Book.

I return, when I desire, to listen to new revelations from my prayer.

2. AFTER A SPIRITUAL CONVERSATION

Preparation   After the spiritual conversation I reflect on how it has gone.

Reflection   What were the more important things I heard in the spiritual conversation?

Where was I most engaged? What did I learn?

What were my stronger feelings? Insights?

Did any of my desires sharpen or deepen?

Have I felt consolation or desolation since my conversation?

Is there action I wish to take?

Listening Book   I note my responses to the above in my Listening Book.

I return, when I desire, to hear new wisdom from this conversation.

3. AFTER AN AWARENESS EXAMEN

Preparation	After my awareness examen, I note the following:
Reflection	For what did I feel gratitude today?
	How did God act in my life today?
	What life-giving patterns are revealed in the past week?
	In what direction is the good spirit leading me? The bad spirit?
	Have I felt consolation or desolation since my examen?
	Is there action I wish to take?
Listening Book	I note my responses to the above in my Listening Book.
	I return, when I desire, to receive new insights from my examen. [156]

THE
IGNATIAN GUIDE
TO SPIRITUAL CONVERSATION

Jesus entered a certain village, where a woman named Martha welcomed him into her home. She had a sister named Mary, who sat at the Lord's feet and listened to what he was saying. But Martha was distracted by her many tasks; so she came to him and asked, "Lord, do you not care that my sister has left me to do all the work by myself? Tell her then to help me." But the Lord answered her, "Martha, Martha, you are worried and distracted by many things; there is need of only one thing. Mary has chosen the better part, which will not be taken away from her. (Lk 10:38–42)

Endeavor to be profitable to individuals by spiritual conversations, by counseling and exhorting to good works, and by conducting Spiritual Exercises.[157]

The good angel touches the soul gently, lightly, and sweetly, like a drop of water going into a sponge.[158]

The three texts above introduce sacred listening, spiritual conversation, and discernment of spirits. These lie at the heart of spiritual conversation. Both speakers and listeners seek to understand how God is at work in their daily life. It is not about teaching, proselytizing, or counseling. For Ignatius, the spirit of such conversation is clear: be slow to speak, listen quietly, treat others as equals, be humble and sincere, speak with kindness and love, and see the Trinity at work in all.

During the First Spiritual Exercises, the content of spiritual conversation will be on what happened in a spiritual exercise, or some days of exercises, what was noted in Listening Books after prayer, and what was just heard in listening to others. (Listening Books are introduced in The Ignatian Guide to Spiritual Journaling.) A plan for spiritual conversation in a group is set out below:

SPIRITUAL CONVERSATION PLAN		MINUTES
Time of Silence	Contemplative silence in the loving Trinity	5
Listening	Sharing one new thing from my prayer	15
Conversation	Reflecting on my prayer experience	20
Discernment	Sharing mini-discernments of spirits	15
Time of Silence	Contemplative silence in the active Trinity	5

Spiritual conversation begins and ends with silence. Silence creates the space for listening. Silence also allows one to simply be, simply be in the now, simply be in the presence of the other. Contemplative silence is simply being in the presence of God. This is the "better part" that Mary chose over Martha's activity.

To begin spiritual conversation, I imagine the Trinity, God the Father, Son and Spirit, surrounding me. I imagine them loving me unconditionally, then I remain silently in this loving presence for five minutes. When I am distracted, I return to the presence of the Trinity by simply praying, "I receive your love."

After silent prayer together, there are three phases. The first phase is sacred listening. Here each shares something of their prayer experience if they wish. Everyone listens in the manner set out below in "The Practice of Sacred Listening." (Each phase has its own "practice of" list.)

The second phase is spiritual conversation itself. Here the group has the opportunity for dialogue on the graces experienced in prayer, those just heard or those noted in Listening Books. Ignatius sets out below the quality of such conversation in "The Practice of Spiritual Conversation." These instructions come verbatim from two letters he wrote, to men he sent out on mission, on how to deal with people in conversations.

The third phase is discernment of spirits. Here the group may share, if desired, the results any mini-discernment described in The Practice of Discerning the Spirits (found in The Ignatian Guide to the Discernment of Spirits). It is very important that the group returns to only listening in this phase; there is no discussion on another's experience of the spirits. Rather, listening here is to appreciate, with some awe, just how the good spirit works in everyone.

Silence ends the session as it began. The only difference this time is that I imagine the active Trinity surrounding me, each person desiring to work in and through me. If distracted I return to the presence of the

Trinity by praying "work through me." I remain in this contemplative presence for five minutes and the session is ended.

To conclude, each person I am listening to, or conversing with, should be afforded the same loving reverence I would give if Jesus himself were the one before me. So Ignatius writes, "Let no one seek to be considered a wit, or to affect elegance or prudence or eloquence, but look upon Christ, who made nothing at all of these things and chose to be humbled and despised by men for our sake rather than to be honored and respected."[159]

Litany for Listeners

Dearest Lord, companion on the road,
voice in the night, here we are, gathered to listen.
Open our ears, our whole being,
that we may become a listening presence to each other,
that we may enjoy the gift of our spiritual conversation.

Give us the generosity to listen with openness	Listen to us
the wisdom to understand what is heard	Listen to us
the strength to be changed by what is shared	Listen to us
the listening that never judges	Listen to us
the curiosity of a child.	Listen to us
Increase in us the peace to forgive and be forgiven	Listen to us
the reverence to honor both gift and loss	Listen to us
the acceptance that allows failure to be shared	Listen to us
the prudence to know when not to speak	Listen to us
the surrender that treasures silence after word.	Listen to us
Enliven in us the freedom to let mystery be	Listen to us
the joy to celebrate new discovery	Listen to us
the readiness for laughter when it rises	Listen to us
the grace to listen with humble love	Listen to us
the awe to hear you speaking in us.	Thank you.

THE PRACTICE OF SACRED LISTENING

1. Listen before speaking.
Allow the person who is speaking time to complete their thought; wait a few seconds before responding. Ask "Is there anything else?"

2. Listen to yourself.
Be in touch with your inner voice. Ask "What wants to be said next?"

3. Listen with an open mind.
Be curious and appreciative of what you are listening to. Listen for new ideas instead of judging and evaluating.

4. Listen for understanding.
You do not have to agree with what you hear, or even believe it, to listen to understand the other person.

5. Listen with empathy and compassion.
Put your agenda aside for the moment. Put yourself in their shoes.

6. Listen with patience and presence.
Listening well takes time and your full "listening presence."

7. Listen in relationship. Let the speaker know that you have heard them.
Use body language: nodding, facial expressions.[160]

8. Listen with reverence to the Divine in the other.
Every person is created in the image of God. Listen with humility.

9. Listen for the Spirit at work in the other.
Listen for the Spirit who touches the soul of the other "gently, lightly, and sweetly, like a drop of water going into a sponge."[161]

10. Listen for Jesus who may seek me through the other.
The friendship Jesus offers is communal—one vine but many branches. Jesus may speak to me through the graces of another.

THE PRACTICE OF SPIRITUAL CONVERSATION

1. Spiritual conversation is a great opportunity. Be prepared.
Associating and dealing with many people for the salvation and spiritual progress of souls can be very profitable with God's help. In the following notes, which may be modified or amplified according to need, we may be able to offer some assistance.

2. Be slow to speak. Be considerate and kind on matters discussed.
Be slow to speak. Be considerate and kind, especially when it comes to deciding on matters under discussion, or about to be discussed.

3. Listen quietly, to understand. Learn when to speak or be silent.
Be slow to speak, and only after having first listened quietly, so that you may understand the meaning, leanings, and wishes of those who do speak. Thus you will better know when to speak and when to be silent.

4. Be free of attachment to your own opinion.
When matters are under discussion, I should consider the reasons on both sides without showing any attachment to my own opinion, and try to avoid bringing dissatisfaction to anyone.

5. Do not cite authorities. Deal with everyone equally.
I should not cite anyone as supporting my opinion . . . and I would deal with everyone on an equal basis, never taking sides with anyone.

6. In giving your opinion, speak with humility and sincerity.
If you ought not to be silent, then give your opinion with the greatest possible humility and sincerity, and always end with the words "with due respect for a better opinion."

7. Accommodate yourself to the convenience of the other.
If I have something to say, it will be of great help to forget about my own leisure or lack of time—that is, my own convenience. I should rather accommodate myself to the convenience of him (or her) with whom I am to deal so that I may influence him (or her) to God's greater glory.

8. Ask the Spirit to descend with abundant gifts.
Pray and lead others to pray particularly to God our Lord . . . to send forth his Holy Spirit on all who take part in the discussions . . . so that the

Holy Spirit may descend in greater abundance with his grace and gifts upon the (conversations).

9. Awaken knowledge and love in souls.
Awaken in souls a thorough knowledge of themselves and a love of their Creator and Lord.

10. Adapt yourself to others.
First consider their temperaments and adapt yourselves to them. If they are of a lively temper, quick and cheerful in speech, follow their lead while speaking to them of good and holy things, and do not be serious, glum, and reserved. If they are shy and retiring, slow to speak, serious, and weighty in their words, use the same manner with them, because such ways will be pleasing to them.[162]

Prayer Before a Spiritual Conversation
Lord of Emmaus, give me the time I need for this conversation.

Help me to let go of my own convenience and work,
to be fully present to each person here.

May I be slow to speak. Give me the wisdom to listen quietly,
to sense the meaning, positions, and desires of each speaker,
to know whether to be silent or speak.

Free me to listen without prejudice, to treat each speaker equally.

Keep me considerate and kind with matters that arise,
sincere in my opinion, respecting better opinions.

Help me to hold each speaker's prayer experience reverently,
their talents and faith gently,
and to enkindle in them love of our Creator and Lord,
and to serve them in body as well as in word.

Let the Spirit descend upon this circle with an abundance of her gifts.

Above all, give me the greatest possible humility,
to be simple rather than eloquent, as you are to us all. Amen.

THE IGNATIAN GUIDE TO
THE DISCERNMENT OF SPIRITS

The kingdom of heaven may be compared to someone who sowed good seed in his field; but while everybody was asleep, an enemy came and sowed weeds among the wheat, and then went away. So when the plants came up and bore grain, then the weeds appeared as well. The slaves of the householder came and said to him, "Master, did you not sow good seed in your field? Where, then, did these weeds come from?" He answered, "An enemy has done this." The slaves said to him, "Then do you want us to go and gather them?" But he replied, "No; for in gathering the weeds you would uproot the wheat along with them. Let both of them grow together until the harvest; and at harvest time I will tell the reapers, Collect the weeds first and bind them in bundles to be burned, but gather the wheat into my barn." (Mt 13:24–30)

In Ignatian discernment, I accept the movement or action of the good spirit and reject the same of the enemy or bad spirit. As invited by Jesus, I identify the weeds in the wheat but focus on bringing in the harvest.

Ignatius defined his guidelines for discernment as "the rules by which to perceive and understand to some extent the various movements produced in the soul: the good that they may be accepted, and the bad, that they may be rejected" (*Spiritual Exercises* 313).

St. Paul spoke about two spirits, one of life and peace, and one of death. Like Paul, Ignatius understood that the Spirit of God already dwells in me, guiding me.

The law of the Spirit of life in Christ Jesus has set you free from the law of sin and of death. For those who live according to the flesh set their minds on the things of the flesh, but those who live according to the Spirit set their minds on the things of the Spirit. To set the mind on the flesh is death, but to set the mind on the Spirit is life and peace. But you are not in the flesh; you are in the Spirit, since the Spirit of God dwells in you. (Rom 8:2, 5–6, 9a)

The first four guidelines of Ignatius will help me to "test everything, hold fast to what is good" (1 Thes 5:16–22). This life for good is the great treasure buried in my retreat. Indeed, guideline three defines the very purpose of the First Spiritual Exercises. After the guidelines, instructions are provided in four simple mini-discernments.

FOUR GUIDELINES TO DISCERN THE SPIRITS

Guideline 1   Moving from bad to worse. With people who go from one deadly sin to another, it is the usual practice of the enemy to hold out apparent pleasures, so that he makes them imagine sensual delights and satisfactions in order to maintain and reinforce them in their vices and sins.

With people of this kind, the good spirit uses the opposite procedure, causing pricks of conscience and feelings of remorse by means of the natural power of rational moral judgment.

Guideline 2   Moving from good to better. In the case of people who are making serious progress in the purification of their sins, and who advance from good to better in the service of God our Lord, the procedure is the contrary to that described in guideline one. For then *it is characteristic of the bad spirit to harass, sadden, and obstruct, and to disturb with false reasoning, so as to impede progress;* while the *characteristic of the good spirit is to give courage and strength, consolations, tears, inspirations, and quiet, making things easy and removing all obstacles so that the person may move forward in doing good.*

Guideline 3	On spiritual consolation. I use the word *"consolation"* when any interior movement is produced in the soul which leads her to become *inflamed with the love of her Creator and Lord,* and when as a consequence there is no creature on the face of the earth that the person can love in itself, but they love it in the Creator and Lord of all things.

Similarly, I use the word "consolation" when a person sheds tears which lead to the love of our Lord, whether these arise from grief over sins, or over the passion of Christ our Lord, or because of other reasons immediately directed toward his service and praise.

Lastly, I give the name *"consolation" to every increase of hope, faith and charity, to all interior happiness which calls and attracts to heavenly things and to the salvation of one's soul, leaving the soul quiet and at peace in her Creator and Lord.*

Guideline 4	On spiritual desolation. *"Desolation"* is the name I give to everything contrary to what is described in guideline three, for example, *darkness and disturbance in the soul, attraction to what is low and of the earth, disquiet arising from various agitations and temptations.*

All this leads to a lack of confidence in which one feels oneself to be without hope and without love. One finds oneself thoroughly lazy, lukewarm, sad, and as though cut off from one's Creator and Lord.

For just as consolation is contrary to desolation, in the same way, the thoughts that spring from consolation are contrary to the thoughts that spring from desolation.[163]

THE PRACTICE OF DISCERNING THE SPIRITS

In the beginning it will be enough to just try the first mini-discernment below, identifying and accepting the feelings characteristic of the good spirit, and in later days or weeks of the retreat, to try the others, one by one, until I am confident enough to identify the discernments that matter the most after any particular exercise.

These discernments are called mini-discernments because I can make them simply and shortly in three to ten minutes after a spiritual exercise, after a spiritual conversation, or at the end of a day. I need not be too concerned about catching everything at first, because my discerning will become better and finer with practice. Furthermore, good discernment is made with a progression of mini-discernments over time rather than in any one day.

The first two mini-discernments are made referring to the feelings and descriptions that are italicized in the four guidelines above. I may experience additional feelings, not listed in the italicized, that are also filled with the good spirit. All in all, I seek to recognize the good spirit who is calling me forward in the life direction I desire, increasing my happiness, and bringing me into a quiet peace with my Creator.

Mini-Discernment 1	**Feelings and spirits**
	What feelings in my prayer are characteristic of the good spirit? These I accept. Characteristic of the bad spirit? These I reject.
Mini-Discernment 2	**Consolations and desolations**
	Did I experience interior happiness, quiet, love, or another spiritual consolation? Contrary disturbances in desolation?
Mini-Discernment 3	**Good spirit over time**
	Can I see the movement of the good spirit over several exercises or some longer time? In what direction am I drawn? Contrary movement of the bad spirit?
Mini-Discernment 4	**Good spirit through others**
	Has my spiritual journal, the Listening Book, revealed the desires of the good spirit for me?
	In my sacred listening to others, did I also hear the voice of the good spirit speaking to me? Saying what?
	After my spiritual conversations, do I understand better the life-giving patterns of the good spirit in my life?

Prayer to the Good Spirit

Good Spirit, inflame me with love of my Creator and Lord.
Help me to recognize you at work in my day,
to find you in the flowing of my courage and strength,
to source you in my consolations, in my tears,
and join you when you offer inspirations and quiet.
Open my eyes to the disturbance of the bad spirit,
    to the sadness and disquiet.
Reveal the darkness of desolation for what it is,
    and turn me in the contrary direction.
Please, make all things easy for me,
    remove the obstacles in my life
so that I may move forward in doing good.
Direct me toward your service and praise,
increase in me your gifts of hope, faith, and love,
fill me with that interior happiness
    which calls and attracts to spiritual things,
and leaves my soul quiet
    and at peace in her Creator and Lord. Amen.

A NOTE ON THE TEXTS

The official text of *The Spiritual Exercises* is annotated with paragraph numbers. All modern translations use this reference numbering. The text of this book follows the official text closely and provides these numbers in parentheses and in the endnotes.

This book uses the original Spanish text of the Exercises, one of the three approved texts, called the *Autograph Spiritual Exercises*. The translator, Michael Ivens, S.J., was an authority on the text and a very experienced Giver of the Exercises. His translation is published as *The Spiritual Exercises of Saint Ignatius Loyola*, Iñigo Texts Series 8 (New Malden, England: Gracewing, 2004).

Excerpts from the autobiography and letters of Ignatius are taken from *Personal Writings: Reminiscences, Spiritual Diary, Select Letters including the Text of the Spiritual Exercises*, trans. J. Munitiz, S.J., and P. Endean, S.J. Penguin Books, London; New York, 1996. (The excerpts from the autobiography have be reframed into the first person.)

Excerpts from letters of Ignatius are taken from *Ignatius of Loyola Letters and Instructions*, M. Palmer, S.J., J. Padberg, S.J., J. McCarthy, Institute of Jesuit Sources, St. Louis, 2006.

Excerpts from the Constitutions are taken from *The Constitutions of the Society of Jesus: Translated with an Introduction and a Commentary*, G. Gnass, S.J., Institute of Jesuit Sources, St. Louis, 1970.

Excepts from the General Congregations are taken from *For Matters of Greater Moment*, J. Padberg, S.J., M. O'Keefe, S.J., M. McCarthy, S.J., Institute of Jesuit Sources, St. Louis, 1994.

The scripture texts are from the *New Revised Standard Bible*.

The Ignatian Guide to Twelve Ways of Prayer builds on the guides in *The Gospels for Prayer* by Michael Hansen, S.J. (Melbourne, Australia: John Garrett Publishing, 2009).

NOTES

1. *Spiritual Exercises* [313–36].
2. Letter of Ignatius, Ep 1:162.
3. *Spiritual Exercises* [314–15] [327].
4. *Spiritual Exercises* [23] [315-16] [329].
5. *Spiritual Exercises* [315–16] [329].
6. *Spiritual Exercises* [230–37].
7. *Spiritual Exercises* [45–81] [23].
8. *Spiritual Exercises* [18].
9. S. Bermudez-Goldman, S.J., trans. Unpublished translation, Judicial Processes of Yñigo Loyola, Alcalá, 1526–27. Archivum historicum Societatis Iesu. Romae: Institutum Scriptorum de Historia S. I.,1932- . MI Fontes Docum, 334.
10. Ibid.
11. General Congregations C24/D.20; C27/D.221; C35/D2.27. For Matters of Great Moment, J. Padberg, S.J., M. O'Keefe, S.J., M. McCarthy, S.J., Institute of Jesuit Sources, Saint Louis 1994.
12. Letter of Ignatius, to Rev. M. Miona, 1536, [EP. 10:].
13. Saying of Ignatius, [Bartoli, D., Histoire de Saint Ignace et de l'origine de la Compagnie de Jésus, 2:255].
14. *Spiritual Exercises* [5].
15. *Spiritual Exercises* [6] [12–13].
16. *Spiritual Exercises* [352–70].
17. *Spiritual Exercises* [21].
18. *Spiritual Exercises* [1–2] [4] [18].
19. *Spiritual Exercises* [6–10] [17] [313–19] [329] [335].
20. *Spiritual Exercises* [18].
21. *Spiritual Exercises* [46–48] [54] [75–76].
22. *Spiritual Exercises* [46–48] [54] [75–76].
23. *Spiritual Exercises* [46–48] [54] [75–76].
24. *Spiritual Exercises* [46–48] [54] [75–76].
25. Liturgy of the Eucharist, Eucharistic Prayer II, Institution narrative.
26. *Spiritual Exercises* [2] [46–48] [54] [75–76] [231] [234–35].
27. *Spiritual Exercises* [2] [46–48] [54] [75–76] [231] [234–35].
28. *Spiritual Exercises* [2] [46–48] [54] [75–76] [231] [234–35].
29. *Spiritual Exercises* [2] [46–48] [54] [75–76] [231] [234–35].
30. Liturgy of the Eucharist, Doxology.
31. *Spiritual Exercises* [32–42] [44] [71].
32. Autobiography of Ignatius [96].
33. Liturgy of the Eucharist, Eucharistic Prayer II, Preface.
34. *Spiritual Exercises* [43].
35. *Spiritual Exercises* [189].
36. Spiritual Exercises of Master John, First Principle and Foundation.
37. Letter of Ignatius [Ep 6:524].
38. *Spiritual Exercises* [46–48] [54] [76] [230–31].
39. Sacrament of the Eucharist, Final Blessing and Sending.
40. *Spiritual Exercises* [46–48] [54] [74–75] [111–17].
41. *Spiritual Exercises* [46–48] [54] [74–75] [111–17].
42. *Spiritual Exercises* [46–48] [54] [74–75] [111–17].
43. *Spiritual Exercises* [46–48] [54] [74–75] [111–17].
44. *Spiritual Exercises* [24–31].
45. The Liturgy of Baptism.

46. *Spiritual Exercises* [46–54] [74–75].
47. *Spiritual Exercises* [46] [55–61] [74–75].
48. *Spiritual Exercises* [46] [65–71] [74–75].
49. *Spiritual Exercises* [46] [62–63] [74–75].
50. *Spiritual Exercises* [32–42] [44] [71].
51. Autobiography of Ignatius [96].
52. *Spiritual Exercises* [46–48] [71] [74–75] [111–17].
53. *Spiritual Exercises* [46–48] [71] [74–75] [111–17].
54. *Spiritual Exercises* [46–48] [71] [74–75] [111–17].
55. The Liturgy of the Sacrament of the Anointing of the Sick.
56. *Spiritual Exercises* [23].
57. *Spiritual Exercises* [23].
58. *Spiritual Exercises* [23].
59. *Spiritual Exercises* [23], trans. Michael Ivens, S.J., *The Spiritual Exercises of Saint Ignatius Loyola*, Iñigo Texts Series 8, New Malden, England: Gracewing, 2004.
60. *Spiritual Exercises* [23], paraphrased by Gerald M. Hughes, S.J., *God of Surprises*, Darton, Longman and Todd, Cambridge, 1985.
61. *Spiritual Exercises* [23], paraphrased by J.S. Bergan and M. Schwan, C.S.J., *Praying with Ignatius of Loyola*, Word Among Us Press, Ijamsville, MD, 2004.
62. *Spiritual Exercises* [23], paraphrased by Sr. K. Doyle, cited in T. Ryan, *Four Steps to Spiritual Freedom*, Paulist Press, New York, 2003, 192.
63. *Spiritual Exercises* [189].
64. Spiritual Exercises of Master John, First Principle and Foundation, Rogelio García Mateo, trans., *The Way*, 44/1 (January 2005), 111.
65. Letter of Ignatius, [Ep 6:524].
66. *Spiritual Exercises* [43].
67. *Spiritual Exercises* [46–48] [54] [74–75] [104] [110–17] [234] [257].
68. Blessing and invocation of God over the baptismal water, Liturgy of Baptism.
69. *Spiritual Exercises* [46–48] [54] [74–75] [104] [110–17] [257] [235–36].
70. *Spiritual Exercises* [46–48] [54] [74–75] [101–9].
71. *Spiritual Exercises* [46–48] [54] [74–75] [104] [110–17] [257].
72. *Spiritual Exercises* [43].
73. *Spiritual Exercises* [46–48] [54] [74–75] [104] [110–17] [257].
74. *Spiritual Exercises* [46–48] [54] [74–75] [104] [110–17] [257].
75. *Spiritual Exercises* [46–48] [54] [74–75] [104] [110–17] [257].
76. *Spiritual Exercises* [46–48] [54] [74–75] [104] [110–17] [257].
77. The Liturgy of the Sacrament of Healing.
78. *Spiritual Exercises* [46–48] [54] [74–75] [104] [110–17] [257].
79. *Spiritual Exercises* [46–48] [54] [74–75] [104] [110–17] [257].
80. *Spiritual Exercises* [46–48] [54] [74–75] [104] [110–17] [257].
81. *Spiritual Exercises* [46–48] [54] [74–75] [104] [110–17] [257].
82. *Spiritual Exercises* [32–42] [44] [71].
83. Autobiography of Ignatius [96].
84. *Spiritual Exercises* [46–48] [54] [74–75] [104] [110–17] [257] [218–26].
85. *Spiritual Exercises* [46–48] [54] [74–75] [104] [110–17] [257].
86. *Spiritual Exercises* [46–48] [54] [74–75] [104] [110–17] [257].
87. *Spiritual Exercises* [189].
88. Spiritual Exercises of Master John, First Principle and Foundation.
89. Letter of Ignatius, Ep 6:524.
90. *Spiritual Exercises* [24–31].
91. *Spiritual Exercises* [239] [250–57] [316].
92. *Spiritual Exercises* [43].
93. *Spiritual Exercises* [75–76] [239] [250–53] [256–57].
94. see Lk 11:1–13; Jn 16:23–24; 17:11–26
95. see Lk 1:26–42
96. see Jn 6:65–69; 11:17–27; Mt 3:11; Rom 8:15–17
97. see Jn 19:17, 32–34; 20:19–29; Rom 8:35, 37–39
98. see Acts 2:1–4; Jn 14:15–27; Mt 3:11

99. *Spiritual Exercises* [75–76] [239] [250–53] [256–57].
100. *Spiritual Exercises* [75–76] [239] [250–53] [256–57].
101. Liturgy of the Eucharist, Eucharistic Prayer II, Institution Narrative.
102. *Spiritual Exercises* [75–76] [239] [250–51] [258–60].
103. Liturgy of the Eucharist, Eucharistic Prayer II, Our Father.
104. *Spiritual Exercises* [75–76] [239] [250–51] [258–60].
105. *Spiritual Exercises* [75–76] [239] [250–51] [258–60].
106. *Spiritual Exercises* [75–76] [239] [250–51] [258–60].
107. *Spiritual Exercises* [24–31].
108. *Spiritual Exercises* [18] [239–45].
109. *Spiritual Exercises* [18] [239–45].
110. *Spiritual Exercises* [18] [239–45].
111. Autobiography of Ignatius [35].
112. *Spiritual Exercises* [32–42] [44] [71].
113. Autobiography of Ignatius [96].
114. *Spiritual Exercises* [18] [239–43].
115. *Spiritual Exercises* [18] [239–43] [247–48].
116. *Spiritual Exercises* [18] [239–43].
117. *Spiritual Exercises* [189].
118. Spiritual Exercises of Master John, First Principle and Foundation.
119. Letter of Ignatius, Ep 6:524.
120. Letter of Ignatius, to young Jesuit students, 1547, Ep. 169:495–510.
121. Letter of Ignatius, to young Jesuit students, 1547, Ep. 169:495–510.
122. *Spiritual Exercises* [18] [44].
123. Letter of Ignatius, to young Jesuit students, 1547, Ep. 169:495–510.
124. *Spiritual Exercises* [230–37].
125. Letter of Ignatius, Ep Ign, 1:71–72.
126. *Spiritual Exercises* [62–63] [76] [118].
127. Letter of Ignatius, to Rev. M. Miona, November 16, 1536.
128. MonFabri, 32–35, Ep 17.
129. *Spiritual Exercises* [43].
130. *Spiritual Exercises* [24–31].
131. *Spiritual Exercises* [32–42] [44] [71].
132. Autobiography of Ignatius [96].
133. The Liturgy of the Sacrament of Healing.
134. *Spiritual Exercises* [1–20] [73–81].
135. *Spiritual Exercises* [75–76] [239] [250–53] [256–57].
136. See Lk 11:1–13; Jn 16:23–24; 17:11–26.
137. See Lk 1:26–42.
138. See Jn 6:65–69; 11:17–27; Mt 3:11; Rom 8:15–17.
139. See Jn 19:17, 32–34; 20:19–29; Rom 8:35, 37–39.
140. See Acts 2:1–4; Jn 14:15–27; Mt 3:11.
141. *Spiritual Exercises* [75–76] [239] [250–51] [258–60].
142. *Spiritual Exercises* [18] [239–45].
143. *Spiritual Exercises* [18] [239–45].
144. *Spiritual Exercises* [18] [239–43] [247–48].
145. *Spiritual Exercises* [18] [239–43] [247–48].
146. *Spiritual Exercises* [45–54] [74–76].
147. *Spiritual Exercises* [45–54] [74–76].
148. *Spiritual Exercises* [45–54] [74–76].
149. *Spiritual Exercises* [45–54] [74–76].
150. *Spiritual Exercises* [250–53].
151. Autobiography of Ignatius [11].
152. Autobiography of Ignatius [8].
153. *Spiritual Exercises* [77].
154. Ignatius Autobiography [99].
155. Ibid.
156. *Spiritual Exercises* [43].

157. The Constitutions of the Society of Jesus [684]. Institute of Jesuit Sources, St. Louis, 1996.
158. *Spiritual Exercises* [335].
159. Letter of Ignatius to the scholastics at Alcalá. [Unpublished Historia de la Assistencia de España, Book 1, ch. 6], 1543.
160. Practices 1–7 from Top Ten Powerful Listening Practices. Kay Lindahl, www.sacredlistening.com, 2003.
161. *Spiritual Exercises* [236, 335].
162. Pts. 1–9, Letter Ignatius to Laínez, Salmerón, Favre. [Ep. 123], 1546; Pt. 10, Letter Ignatius to Broët, Salmerón. [Ep.18], 1549.
163. *Spiritual Exercises* [314–17].

Michael Hansen, S.J., is a retreat leader, speaker, and spiritual director on the retreat team at the Campion Centre of Ignatian Spirituality in Kew, Victoria, Australia. He has worked in schools and parishes and produced radio and television programs. He is the author of four other books.

Founded in 1865, Ave Maria Press,
a ministry of the Congregation of
Holy Cross, is a Catholic publishing
company that serves the spiritual and
formative needs of the Church and its
schools, institutions, and ministers;
Christian individuals and families; and
others seeking spiritual nourishment.

———※———

For a complete listing of titles from

Ave Maria Press

Sorin Books

Forest of Peace

Christian Classics

visit www.avemariapress.com

ave maria press® / Notre Dame, IN 46556
A Ministry of the United States Province of Holy Cross